D E L

Merchant Kings

When Companies Ruled the World,
1600-1900

Stephen R. Bown

MERCHANT
KINGS

DOUGLAS & MCINTYRE
D&M PUBLISHERS INC.
Vancouver/Toronto

Douglas & McIntyre
A division of D&M Publishers Inc.
2323 Quebec Street, Suite 201
Vancouver BC Canada V5T 4S7
www.dmpibooks.com

Library and Archives Canada Cataloguing in Publication
Bown, Stephen R
Merchant kings : when companies ruled the world, 1600-1900 /Stephen R. Bown.
Includes bibliographical references and indexes.

ISBN 978-1-55365-342-4

1. Colonial companies—History. 2. Merchants—Europe—Biography.
3. Europe—Commerce—History. 4. Monopolies—Europe—History.
5. Monopolies—History. 6. International business enterprises—History.
7. International trade—History. I. Title.

HF481.B72 2009   382.09   C2009-902939-1

Editing by John Eerkes-Medrano
Copy editing by Michael Mundhenk
Jacket and text design by Naomi MacDougall
Maps by Eric Leinberger
Jacket illustration © Mary Evans Picture Library
All other illustrations public domain, courtesy of the author

Printed and bound in Canada by Friesens
Printed on acid-free paper that is forest friendly (100% post-consumer
recycled paper) and has been processed chlorine free or printed on paper that
comes from sustainable forests managed under the Forest Stewardship Council
Distributed in the U.S. by Publishers Group West.

We gratefully acknowledge the financial support of the Canada Council for the
Arts, the British Columbia Arts Council, the Province of British Columbia through
the Book Publishing Tax Credit, and the Government of Canada through the Book
Publishing Industry Development Program (BPIDP) for our publishing activities.

Contents

· · ·

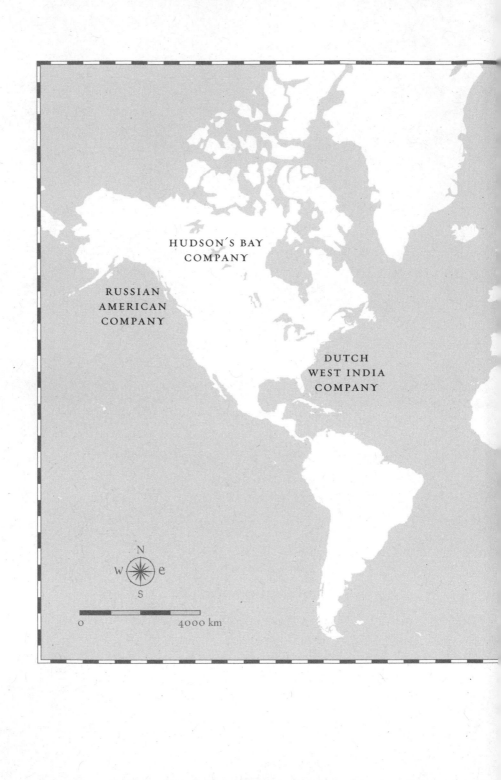

HUDSON'S BAY
COMPANY

RUSSIAN
AMERICAN
COMPANY

DUTCH
WEST INDIA
COMPANY

N
W   e
S

0   4000 km

GLOBAL MONOPOLIES OF THE AGE
OF HEROIC COMMERCE, 1600–1900

ENGLISH
EAST INDIA
COMPANY

DUTCH
EAST INDIA
COMPANY

BRITISH
SOUTH AFRICA
COMPANY

ALASKA

Cook Inlet

KODIAK ISLAND

Sitka

ALEUTIAN ISLANDS

Fort Victoria

Fort Vancouver

OLD OREGON

Pacific Ocean

Fort Ross

CALIFORNIA

HAWAII

0   1000 km

TERRITORY OF
THE DUTCH WEST INDIA COMPANY,
THE HUDSON'S BAY COMPANY
AND THE RUSSIAN AMERICAN COMPANY

Hudson Bay

• York
Factory

RUPERT'S LAND

Red River

*Lake
Superior*   NEW   FRANCE   *Gulf of St. Lawrence*

Montreal •

Fort Orange (Albany)
•
NEW ENGLAND
•
NEW   Manhattan (New Amsterdam)
NETHERLAND

MARYLAND
AND VIRGINA

Atlantic Ocean

CUBA

Caribbean Sea

Introduction

"Whosoever commands the trade of the world, commands
the riches of the world and consequently the world itself."

SIR WALTER RALEIGH, C. 1600

FROM THE EARLY 1600S TO THE LATE 1800S, MONOP-
oly trading companies were the unofficial agents of European
colonial expansion. They seized control of vast territories and
many peoples, acquiring a variety of governmental and military functions in the wake of their commercial success. For
European nations, granting monopoly trading rights to these
companies was a convenient way of bankrolling the astronomical cost of colonial expansion. This tapping of private capital
spurred what became known as the Age of Heroic Commerce.
As each of these privileged enterprises grew, it first assumed civil
authority over all Europeans in its employment overseas and
then expanded this authority by subjugating local peoples. In
working towards their political objectives, the merchant trading
companies maintained their own police forces and, sometimes,
standing armies, and either controlled the local governments

or became the sole government of their territories. These territories were managed as business interests, in which people were considered as either employees, customers or competitors. Beginning as traders, the leaders of these companies, "the merchant kings," ended up with dictatorial political power over millions of people. This book is an account of six of these merchant kings and their impact.

Jan Pieterszoon Coen was the ruthless pioneer of the Dutch East India Company, a trading enterprise that within its first two decades was in conflict with nearly every maritime nation in the world. During his "reign," the company became the foundation for the wealth of the Netherlands' golden age by supplying most of Europe with exotic spices. "Despair not," he proclaimed in a letter to his subordinates in 1618. "Spare your enemies not, for God is with us." Sometimes his enemies were his customers—when they did not want to trade with his agents or preferred the wares of his rivals, the English or the Portuguese, Coen ordered his company's troops to attack. He tolerated neither competitors nor challenges to his authority.

The one-legged *Pieter Stuyvesant* was the autocratic governor of the Dutch West India Company's colony at Manhattan. For decades he resisted all attempts by the increasing numbers of non-employee citizens of the expanding colony to provide responsible government. Stuyvesant ultimately placed his company's interests ahead of those of his country, an approach that resulted in the loss of the entire territory of New Netherland to a foreign power. When during the third Anglo-Dutch war British war ships anchored off Manhattan offered the people of New Netherland civil government if they surrendered, the entire militia laid down their arms without firing a shot.

The English trader *Robert Clive* rose from his position as a lowly company clerk to head the military arm of the neophyte English East India Company in the mid-eighteenth century.

Despite having no formal training, Clive was a military genius who transformed the company's fortunes with a series of astonishing military victories, using company troops, over the French East India Company and various local rulers in India during the dying days of the Mughal Empire. He created the foundation for the English East India Company's wealth and political power—after Clive's work, the company was both a monopoly trading enterprise and a civil and taxation authority ruling over thirty million people. Clive later was made a baron and became one of the wealthiest men in Britain. When, in 1772, he was questioned by Parliament about his possible corruption and the sources of his wealth, he indignantly proclaimed: "I stand astonished at my own moderation."

Aggressive and efficient, *Aleksandr Andreyevich Baranov* was an itinerant Russian merchant and trader who first migrated east to Siberia, then to Alaska. In 1799 he assumed command of the Russian American Company, a semi-official monopoly colonial trading company chartered by Czar Paul I. Baranov pushed Russian enterprise and colonization further south along the Alaskan coast, warring both with First Nations and with competing Russian businesses in the name of his company. In 1804, firing from a Russian warship, he bombarded a Tlingit village for days, forcing the Tlingit to accept the authority of the Russian American Company. He died after twenty-seven years of solidifying his country's territorial claims on the frontier and extracting vast quantities of sea otter furs for the company's shareholders and directors in St. Petersburg.

George Simpson, haughty and impatient, was the financial and structural genius who steered the Hudson's Bay Company to its greatest financial success and territorial dominion in the early nineteenth century. "The Little Emperor," as he was known, was the virtual dictator of a good chunk of North America. Responsible for shipping hundreds of thousands of beaver furs to London every year, he was chauffeured about in his vast fur domain perched in the back of a giant canoe, from where he exhorted his exhausted voyageurs to paddle harder so that he could set speed records—and claim all the credit for himself. Soon after he died in 1860, most of Simpson's domain passed from the Hudson's Bay Company's power and became part of the new nation of Canada.

Cecil John Rhodes, the British-born South African mining magnate, politician, businessman and racist promoter of British colonialism, was the founder of the diamond company De Beers. In 1889 he secured British government support for the creation of the British South Africa Company to operate in Rhodesia, a territory he created and "allowed" to be named after himself. The company was a monopoly trading enterprise that had been granted the right to raise its own private army, regulate banking and govern while theoretically respecting the rights of native Africans. In reality it used its power to enrich its shareholders through violent land seizures until 1923, when Britain revoked the company's charter. Rhodes and the British South Africa Company became fabulously rich exploiting southern Africa's mineral resources under the pretext of governance. Given the opportunity, Rhodes would have gone further. "All of these stars," he lamented, "these vast worlds that remain out of reach. If I could, I would annex other planets." Whether he wanted to annex them to his country or to his company is not known.

From their inconspicuous and unlikely beginnings, these eventual merchant kings faced similar dilemmas after rising to positions of authority in their companies. They were vested with enormous powers by both their companies and their countries, yet there was a clear conflict of interest between advancing the business interests of companies and acting as civil authorities. The merchant kings were monopolists, not capitalists. Their enterprises—occupying that grey zone between political and mercantile power, combining the ruthless tactics of despots with the legal structure of a profit-seeking, shareholder-driven joint stock corporation—were abhorrent to free-market thinkers like Adam Smith. It was a difficult job being both monopoly trader and the civil government, and the temptation to subsume one of these roles under the other is obvious. By making far-reaching decisions according to their conflicted consciences, the merchant kings had a profound influence. Companies are not generally known for having sweeping political control, but in trying to balance the interests of their companies with the interests of their countries, the merchant kings changed history as significantly as the most celebrated military generals, political leaders and technological innovators did.

The seven deadly sins: Pride, Greed, Sloth, Lust, Envy, Wrath and Gluttony. Each of us is overly familiar with one or more of them at some time in our lives. But for most people, these sins are balanced by the seven virtues: Humility, Charity, Diligence, Chastity, Kindness, Patience and Temperance. Among the merchant kings in the Age of Heroic Commerce, the seven deadly sins might seem overrepresented—the absolute, unaccountable power they wielded magnified their more unsavoury characteristics—but there was goodness in most of them too. Complex and intriguing characters, they were neither heroes nor angels. As with military and political leaders, they had their character traits amplified by power and success, making them seem larger than life. Placed in the unique historical setting of societies on the cusp of great upheaval, they seized the opportunities they were given and had an impact on the world as great as that of the most famous monarchs, despots and generals. By transforming commercial trading entities into political entities, and with their feet firmly anchored in both worlds, these men truly fought for their markets.

Chapter 1

"Your Honours should know by experience
that trade in Asia must be driven and maintained
under the protection and favour of Your Honours'
own weapons, and that the weapons must be
paid for by the profits from the trade; so that we cannot
carry on trade without war, nor war without trade."

JAN PIETERSZOON COEN, C. 1614

THE DUTCH EAST INDIA COMPANY
IN THE SPICE ISLANDS

Pacific Ocean

*South
China
Sea*

PHILIPPINES

Strait of Malacca

TERNATE AND
TIDORE

SUMATRA

BORNEO

SULAWESI

Ambon
(Amboyna)

BANDA
ISLANDS

Batavia JAVA

Indian Ocean

N
W e
S

AUSTRALIA

0   400 km

First among Equals

JAN PIETERSZOON COEN AND THE

DUTCH EAST INDIA COMPANY

· 1 ·

THE THIRTEEN HEAVILY ARMED SHIPS SAILED TOWARDS
the East Indies' remote Banda Islands in the spring of 1609,
after nearly a year's voyage from Amsterdam. The heady, sweet
scent of flowering nutmeg trees filled the humid air. The commander of the squadron, one of the largest corporate fleets yet to
depart the Netherlands for "the spiceries," was Admiral Pieter
Verhoeven (Peter Verhoef), a veteran not of trade and exploration but of combat at sea. He was now employed by the Dutch
East India Company, the VOC (Vereenigde Oost-Indische
Compagnie), with the objective of securing for his employers the
exotic cloves and nutmeg of the Moluccas, as the "Spice Islands"
of Indonesia were then known. The admiral commanded more
than a thousand fighting men, including a contingent of Japanese mercenaries, and his orders from the "Heeren XVII" (the
Lords Seventeen), his powerful corporate directors in the Netherlands, were direct and clear: "We draw your special attention

to the islands in which grow the cloves and nutmeg, and we instruct you to strive after winning them for the company either by treaty or by force." Force was something Verhoef understood well, having earned distinction at the Battle of Gibraltar two years earlier, when Dutch ships virtually wiped out a mighty fleet of Holland's bitter enemy, Imperial Spain.

As Verhoef and his fleet neared the principal harbour of Great Banda, the admiral was astonished and annoyed to spy an English ship in the sheltered port. For several years now, the Dutch East India Company had been engaged in a simmering conflict with the traders and merchants of the English East India Company. The two companies, vying for control of the lucrative spice trade in Indonesia, each sought to oust the Portuguese and dominate the trade. Captain William Keeling and his ship, *Hector,* had been cruising the Banda Islands, the world's sole source of nutmeg and mace, trying to secure a cargo of spices for the past month. He had struck up a cordial relationship with Dutch traders stationed on the remote and tiny islands, enjoying dinners ashore and tours of the plantations. All the friendliness dissipated, however, with the arrival of Verhoef's fleet. One of Verhoef's first actions to frustrate Keeling's business was to pay the Bandanese headmen, the *orang kaya,* to stop trading with the English. Keeling complained that Verhoef treated him and his men "most unkindlye, searching his boate disgracefullye and not suffering him to have any further trade, not to gather in his debts, but with a peremptory command, to be gone." More ominously, an English sailor employed in the Dutch fleet deserted and informed his countrymen that Verhoef was planning a secret attack on them within weeks.

Keeling pondered his predicament. "Sixty-two men against a thousand or more could not perform much," he wrote despondently. Weighing anchor, he took the *Hector* off to one of the more distant islands, Ai, and began to purchase and load his ship with nutmeg far from the interference of the Dutch. The largest island of the tiny archipelago was called Lonthor, or Great Banda, where several thousand Bandanese tended the largest and most valuable nutmeg plantations. The islands of Neira and Gunung Api were clustered within gunshot of Great Banda. Ai was a little distance to the west, and the smallest of the islands, Run, was farther west. On Great Banda, Verhoef wasted no time in menacing and overawing the islanders, and in enforcing a Dutch company monopoly that excluded all English, Portuguese, Malay and Chinese traders from acquiring a cargo of nutmeg.

On April 19, Verhoef ordered 250 heavily armed company troops to disembark from the ships and form up on the beach. He then summoned the *orang kaya* to hear his speech and petition. When they had gathered, under the shade of a great tree, he distributed gifts and ceremoniously unfurled a parchment. He proceeded to read his pronouncement, first in Portuguese and then in Malay. The islanders had broken their promise, Verhoef intoned, "to have trade only with them, who had now traded there six years." Verhoef pointed across the narrow waterway that separated Lonthor from Neira, and informed them that "to defend themselves and the whole country from the Portugals," his men would soon begin building a fort and permanent factory on Neira. The *orang kaya* were as dismayed as Verhoef was determined.

The trouble stemmed from an incident that had occurred several years earlier. On May 23, 1602, Dutch captain Wolfert Harmenszoon persuaded some of Neira's chiefs to sign a contract, in Dutch—a language they couldn't read—granting the Dutch East India Company a monopoly in the nutmeg trade. Some, but not all, of the *orang kaya* had signed the agreement, fearing to offend the merchants and invite violent reprisals if they refused. But since there was no real benefit in reserving all their spice for the Dutch, they had not abided by the agreement—if, indeed, they had ever considered doing so. Now it appeared that the Dutch were taking this document seriously and intending to apply it to all of the nutmeg trade on all the Banda Islands, not just to the region controlled by the signatories.

The Bandanese lived in a series of interrelated coastal villages on the islands but, unlike others in the Moluccas, had no overall king or chief. Verhoef did not understand the islands' loose governing structure, nor did he know with whom to deal; he simply wanted to secure a veneer of legality for his conquest. The several hundred *orang kaya* of Great Banda were stunned and perplexed by Verhoef's demands, and their response was evasive and guarded—Neira was a separate island with its own *orang kaya*. They delayed, requesting more time to deliberate the issue: the fact that they had little control over what Verhoef did across the waterway. But the prospect of a permanent stone fort within gunshot distance of their own harbour boded ill.

The Bandanese were reminded of a prophecy made a few years earlier by a Muslim holy man that foretold of white strangers from afar who would one day conquer their islands. English traders had mirthfully associated this prophecy with the Dutch. The islanders, however, did not want to be locked into dealing with the Dutch. They much preferred Chinese, Arab and Javanese traders, who were frequently in port, bringing goods the Bandanese valued, such as batiks, calicoes, rice, sago palm, porcelain and medicines. They shared cultures with these peoples, and sometimes religion. The Dutch traders, on the other hand, did not impress with their often useless trade goods, such as woollen and velvet cloth, their strange religion, their irregular visits, ignorance of local customs and inflexible prices. Particularly annoying was Verhoef's demand that the islanders stop selling nutmeg and mace to anyone but the Dutch traders. Further unsettling the Bandanese was the eruption of a volcano on nearby Gunung Api. Ominously, the volcano belched a cloud of cinders and ashes onto Neira just as Verhoef's fleet arrived.

As the days and weeks passed in stalled negotiations, Verhoef became agitated and uneasy. He had other business to attend to, particularly his similar mission of securing the Dutch East India Company monopoly over cloves at the islands of Tidore and Ternate, farther north. On April 25, 1609, he ordered about 750 of his soldiers ashore on Neira and set them to work clearing the foundations of an abandoned Portuguese fort. The people of the nearby villages fled to the hills or other islands, and Dutch troops and workers soon occupied their dwellings. Lacking the military power to dislodge the Dutch, and with the walls of the fort creeping ominously higher, the islanders on May 22 sought a meeting with Verhoef to discuss the details of the monopoly he demanded. They selected a remote site on the east of the island for the meeting, and Verhoef set off with a coterie of compatriots, including his most trusted captains, senior merchants and a contingent of heavily armed soldiers. He also dragged along, according to a biased English account, a string of English captives chained together to demonstrate his dominance over that upstart nation.

The clearing, however, was deserted. No one was waiting for Verhoef at the appointed meeting place, underneath a giant tree on the beach. Curious rather than afraid, he ordered his interpreter, Adriaan Ilsevier, to scout the surrounding woods, where Ilsevier stumbled upon a group of *orang kaya* suspiciously concealed in the brush. They informed him that they had become frightened at the sight of so many armed Dutchmen. Would Verhoef please leave his soldiers, arms and guns under the tree, bringing only his senior negotiators to them so that they could talk safely, without the soldiers shadowing the talks?

Secure in his assumed superiority, Verhoef consented. He and dozens of his staff marched unarmed into the brush, "and being entered among them he found the woods replenished with armed blackamoores, Bandanese, and *orang kaya* who instantly encircled them and without much conference between them . . . , were by them treacherously and villainously massacred." They screamed out "To arms!" and "Admiral, we are betrayed!" but to no avail. Unarmed, they were quickly killed and none escaped. It happened so fast and unexpectedly that the armed guards who rushed the short distance to defend their commander and comrades arrived to find them all slaughtered. Verhoef had been decapitated, and his head was placed on a spiked stick. Over the next few weeks, there was a general uprising of the Bandanese against the Dutch, who scarcely left their ships or the fort. Their work on the half-completed castle, Fort Nassau, continued at an accelerated pace.

The new leader of the Dutch company's forces, Simon Hoen, began to "execute and practise all revenge possible" by attacking islanders, burning villages, burning and destroying boats and plundering anything of value. After some of his troops suffered a defeat by Bandanese forces on July 26, Hoen retreated and ordered a naval blockade of the islands to stop the food imports vital to the survival of the people and to bring commerce to a halt. Soon many of the *orang kaya* were willing to accede to the company's demands, and they sat down to negotiate with the Dutch invaders. On August 13 they grudgingly agreed to the Dutch monopoly over the nutmeg trade; all incoming ships now had to present themselves at Fort Nassau for inspection and to obtain a pass. And, furthermore, no one could settle on the islands without the permission of the company commander. The entire island of Neira was to become a dominion of the Dutch East India Company, "to be kept by us forever"—the first territorial acquisition by the company.

Hoen then sailed north, with the bulk of his fleet, to do business with Ternate and Tidore. But even after this first conquest the Bandanese showed no compunction about working around the Dutch monopoly, secretly shipping their nutmeg to English merchants who had established factories on the outlying islands of Ai and Run. Securing a trade monopoly was simple in theory but difficult to enforce, even on the remote and tiny Banda Islands.

IN THE seventeenth and early eighteenth centuries, the Netherlands was arguably the wealthiest and most scientifically advanced of the European nations. This period, known as the Dutch Golden Age, brought a flourishing of the arts and sciences that reflected the period's unbounded optimism and affluence. Prosperous burghers and merchants became patrons of the arts, including sculpture, poetry and drama, and of public debates. They commissioned architects to design beautiful houses. Paintings and sculptures adorned the interior walls of these impressive homes. Rembrandt van Rijn, Johannes Vermeer, Jacob van Ruisdael and many others revolutionized painting, infusing new life into landscapes, portraiture and still life, as well as portraying contemporary life and society in the flourishing cities that were the most cosmopolitan in Europe. In science, the list of internationally prominent luminaries included the philosopher René Descartes; acclaimed jurist and theorist of international law Hugo Grotius; mathematician, astronomer and inventor of the pendulum clock Christiaan Huygens; and Anton van Leeuwenhoek, inventor of the microscope and founder of the study of microbiology. Book publishing flourished in the climate of tolerance and intellectual curiosity; ideas concerning religion, philosophy and science that were considered too controversial in other nations found their way into print in the Netherlands, and the books were secretly shipped abroad.

The Dutch Republic, newly freed from Spanish domination and relishing its freedom, was admirably situated to dominate

European trade by providing an artery into the interior. Thousands of ships crowded its many harbours. The great city of Amsterdam was the centre of the international trade in the exotic luxuries of the Americas, India and the "Spice Islands." The Amsterdam stock exchange, founded in 1602, was the world's first, created by the Dutch East India Company (VOC) for dealing in its own stocks and bonds. The VOC was the first-ever trading company with a permanent share capital. This joint stock company attracted huge wealth in initial capitalization from over 1,800 investors, most of whom were merchants and other wealthy middle-class citizens, and the speculation on the fluctuating value of these shares relied on the success or failure of the company's ships in bringing spices back to Europe from the Far East.

The first great global corporation, the VOC, was by the late seventeenth century the most powerful and richest company in the world. Its private fleet boasted nearly 150 merchant ships and 40 giant warships. At the height of its power, it employed nearly 50,000 people worldwide—seamen, artisans, stevedores, labourers, clerks and builders. The company was involved in a multitude of commercial activities, such as construction, sugar refining, cloth manufacturing, tobacco curing, weaving, glass making, distilling, brewing and other industries related to its global business enterprises. The payroll also included a 10,000-man private army.

The VOC, one of the foundations of Dutch prosperity and with its mighty fleet a key force propelling the young republic to look to the world for commerce, held a virtual monopoly over the global spice supply. It achieved this in a bloody struggle at the dawn of the Age of Heroic Commerce. Ironically, the company's wealth was founded on a system and on values imposed in Indonesia that ran counter to the liberal and tolerant culture of many of its shareholders. Furthermore, its rise to global supremacy as a state monopoly, and its contribution to the artistic and cultural flourishing of the Dutch Republic, was founded on the ruthless strategy of a man whose character was entirely at odds with the character of his nation.

Sailing as part of Peter Verhoef's expedition, and witness to what he termed the "Vile Bandanese Treachery of 1609," was a junior trader named Jan Pieterszoon Coen. The Bandanese uprising and resistance to the VOC, he believed, had been sponsored by perfidious English agents and furthered by the untrustworthy nature of the Bandanese. Coen was destined for historical greatness and, some would argue, infamy. More than a decade later, as the governor general of the VOC's enterprise in the East Indies, Coen would see to it that such disrespect for his company did not go unpunished.

· 2 ·

THE SPICES OF THE EAST INDIES COME FROM A VARIETY of sources. Nutmeg and mace grow together on the same tree, a shiny-leaved evergreen that can reach a height of nearly twenty metres. The fruit is yellow and peach-like and bursts open when fully ripe, exposing a small brown nut encased in a red membrane. The meat of the nut is the nutmeg, and the red membrane, after being dried in the sun until brown, is the mace. Cloves are the unopened flowers of the clove trees which blanket hillsides with their reddish new-growth leaves. The pink buds are harvested by hand and dried in the sun. A mature tree yields upwards of fifteen kilograms of dried buds per year. Pepper comes from a dark-leaved climbing vine, whose berries grow in clusters of as many as fifty. Picked unripe and green, the berries dry black in the sun. White pepper is derived from fully ripened red berries. The aromatic inner bark of the cinnamon and cassia trees is cut off the branches and dried in the sun until it rolls up. The bulbous root of a narrow perennial with leaves like grass yields ginger, historically eaten fresh in the East but dried and ground for shipment to Western markets. Bright yellow turmeric is likewise derived from a rhizome of a plant in the ginger family, and other exotic spices also have their prosaic origin in plants that grew historically in Indonesia.

These well-known spices were used as primary ingredients in medicines, perfumes and food flavourings, as an aid to digestion and as a preservative of meat. Their aromatic properties were so powerful that minute amounts masked foul odours and enlivened otherwise monotonous cuisine. Their odour disguised the stench of crowded cities and the reek of slightly rotten salted meats. These spices were so valuable that they doubled as currency, and people killed for them. A single pouch of some spices could be exchanged for a small herd of cattle or sheep, or offered as a fabulous wedding dowry. Spices were presented as gifts to kings, demanded as tribute by conquering generals and graciously received by popes as their due. The Roman Emperor Tiberius complained of the drain on the empire's resources that resulted from paying for "exotic Asian products." In AD 408 King Alaric of the invading Goths demanded three thousand pounds of pepper as payment for not plundering Rome. Nutmeg and ginger were even believed to ward off the plague. For centuries, gold and silver flowed east while dried and powdered plant matter flowed west.

In seventeenth-century Europe fashionable and well-off households possessed ornate spice graters and storage canisters, as well as small silver plates specially designed to serve spice cake and candied spiced fruit. Gentlemen and ladies wore pomanders loaded with spices and perfume blends to ward off infectious diseases and disguise body odours. An orange or apple might be punctured with dozens of cloves and left to scent a room of hanging clothes. Cloves were especially popular as breath fresheners; in ancient Han China a rule of the imperial court dictated that supplicants and courtiers must chew cloves to sweeten their breath before speaking to the emperor.

Apothecaries and physicians prescribed a melange of spices to ward off a variety of both minor and serious ailments. Nutmeg was reputed to stifle coughs and improve memory; pepper cured common colds, improved eyesight and reduced liver pains; cloves were a remedy against earache; tamarind was efficacious against the plague. Last, but certainly not least, it was widely rumoured that many spices, including nutmeg, mace and ginger, were aphrodisiacs. Not surprisingly, demand for these spices had long outstripped supply, and their prices frequently put them out of reach of all but the wealthy, except on special occasions. "The art of their various uses was common among civilized peoples," writes historian J. Innes Miller in *The Spice Trade of the Roman Empire,* "in their homes, their temples, their public ceremonial, and in the seasoning of their food and wine. A peculiar attribute was their medicinal power. That they were dried and of small bulk made them easy of transport, and their rarity a form of royal treasure."

For centuries, most people who used cloves, cinnamon, pepper, nutmeg and ginger, and even most of those who trafficked in them, had no idea where these spices originated or how they grew. Most of what the purchasers and users "knew" about these aromatic and astringent seeds, berries, roots and barks was myth and fantasy. The famous Roman natural philosopher Pliny the Elder described the adventurous methods by which spices were believed to be transported from distant lands—lands that he himself had never visited: "They bring spices over vast seas on rafts which have no rudders to steer them or oars to push . . . or sails or other aids to navigation but instead only the spirit of man and human courage . . . These winds drive them on a straight course, and from gulf to gulf. Now cinnamon is the chief object of their journey, and they say that these merchant sailors take almost five years before they return, and that many perish."

Marco Polo falsely boasted that he had seen clove trees growing on islands in the China Sea, describing them in his *Travels* as little trees "with leaves like a laurel." Arab middlemen, who profited immensely from their coveted role, discouraged inquiry into their sources by spinning blood-curdling tales: that "the spiceries," the region where spices originated, were guarded by ferocious beasts, that the seas were perpetually storm-plagued and that fearsome pirates lurked along the route to sally forth and plunder unsuspecting ships and enslave their crews. Giant birds known as rocs dwelt in rock-bound aeries, went one common tale, and made their nests with cinnamon branches. Only the intrepid dared to climb the steep cliffs and claim the coveted bark, risking death from the razor-sharp beaks of the rocs. The route to the spiceries was also populated with giant crocodiles, went another tale. These monsters had an inordinate fondness for human flesh. Alternatively, the route was infested with prodigious swamp snakes that would devour unwary travellers. The tales of many other fanciful beasts were likewise deterrents to the curious—and certainly justified the exorbitant price demanded for spices in the marketplace.

Although no mythical beasts guarded the trade routes running east and west from the spiceries, the journey was long and arduous. The most desirable spices originated in two of the remotest island clusters of the Far East. The Indonesian archipelago, which ranges southeast from mainland Asia, is the largest archipelago in the world and comprises thirteen thousand islands, spattered like stars in the night sky, over roughly five thousand square kilometres of water. Bordering the equator, the archipelago has a climate that is hot and humid, and its soil is fertile due to frequent volcanic activity. The islands of Java and Sumatra, in the west of the archipelago, produced pepper (of all spices the greatest in demand), ginger, cinnamon and resinous camphor and were well positioned to dominate the spice trade through control over both the Malacca and Sunda straits. The second spice region in the archipelago was the famed Moluccas. Only five of these small islands had the soil and climatic conditions required to grow cloves. All were clustered together west of the giant island Halmahera and were dominated by sultanates on two islands, Ternate and Tidore. Hundreds of kilometres to the south, in the lonely expanse of the Banda Sea, were the tiny Banda Islands, the sole home of the elusive nutmeg tree.

The commerce in spices dates back to before the recorded history of the area, preceding the arrival of the first European ships by two thousand years. Javanese, Malay and Chinese ships were frequent visitors to the early, remote marketplaces where local spices were exchanged for rice, cotton, silk, coins, porcelain or beads in an ancient and intricate web of commerce. The demand inspired merchants to create elaborate trade routes that wound their way through these mostly tiny islands by sea and over land. Spices found their way to the great trading centres of Sumatra and Java, changed hands and then wended their way to India, where they were passed on to Hindu merchants who resold them to Arab merchants, who in turn took them west across the Indian Ocean to Egypt and the Middle East, and eventually north to the rim of the Mediterranean. There, Alexandria was the first great trading emporium for this lucrative commerce; centuries later, commercial power in the region shifted to Constantinople. And, of course, each time the goods traded hands, the prices increased as successive merchants took their profits and successive governments took their taxes and tariffs. By the time the spices reached Europe, what could be had for a basket of rice or a few pieces of cloth on the Banda Islands might be worth a small fortune in silver.

For hundreds of years during the Middle Ages, the spice trade in the West was dominated by the city state of Venice. Venetian merchants shut out all others from the marketplaces in Alexandria, and then Constantinople, where the Arab merchants offered their exotic wares for sale while concealing what they knew of their origin. In 1453, however, in a devastating siege, Constantinople fell to the Ottoman Turks and was sacked by the invading army, ending what remained of the Byzantine Empire. The fall of Constantinople placed the spice trade entirely in the hands of the Ottomans, who soon raised taxes and increased tariffs to virtually shut off the spice supply to "infidel" Europe.

During the late fifteenth century, however, the Portuguese discovered a sea route to the East by pushing south along the coast of Africa and around the Cape of Good Hope, conquering numerous east African cities and founding the colony of Goa on the western coast of India in 1510. A few years later Portuguese adventurers seized cities in Indonesia, where they constructed fortified settlements to dominate and control the local spice trade. Soon Portugal was one of the richest nations in Europe, boasting a complex trade network that extended around the world. But in its very success was the kernel of Portugal's downfall: the nation had a population of only two million, and the Eastern spice trade, with its continuous wars, shipwrecks and deaths from disease, took a heavy toll on Portugal's small population of males. To keep the enterprise running, Portugal hired foreign sailors, who soon shared the knowledge of this astonishing wealth. Others also wanted a share of the spice trade.

Beginning in 1519, in one of the greatest voyages of all time, a Spanish expedition led by the disaffected Portuguese nobleman Ferdinand Magellan circumnavigated the world by sailing around South America, crossing the Pacific Ocean and establishing a Spanish presence in the Spice Islands. Despite their quarrelling, the Spanish and Portuguese reaped great profits by monopoliz-ing the spice trade in Europe for decades. In the mid-sixteenth century, dynastic politics in Europe resulted in Charles V, the ruler of the Holy Roman Empire, inheriting the throne of Spain as well as the dukedom of Burgundy and the provinces in the north, roughly in the region of today's Belgium, the Neth-erlands and Luxembourg. In 1549 these provinces became an independent state under the emperer's rule. When he abdicated the throne in 1555 to devote his life to the church, he divided this vast and unwieldy empire between his brother, Ferdinand, and his son, Philip. While Ferdinand retained control of the old Holy Roman Empire, Philip became king of Spain and the newly created Spanish Netherlands. The powerful chartered cities of this region were vital to the prosperity of the Spanish Crown. In 1580 Philip annexed Portugal, uniting the competing nations under one monarchy and one spice monopoly.

The Protestant reformation interrupted this cozy arrange-ment. In 1567 King Philip sent the ruthless Duke of Alva and an army of Spanish soldiers to the Netherlands to put down a revolt and collect a new series of taxes on the cities of the Low-lands. On February 16, 1568, the Inquisition declared that all three million citizens of the Netherlands, apart from a few exceptions, were heretics and were therefore condemned to death. Now Philip ordered Alva to carry out the Inquisi-tion's sentence. The cities of the Lowlands, chafing under their financial burden, Alva's brutal massacre and the execution of thousands of citizens by rope, fire and sword, rose in revolt. Declaring the Spanish to be "cruel, bloodthirsty, foreign oppres-sors," they coalesced around the leadership of William III of Orange. Since Spanish rule was strongest in the southern Neth-erlands, most leading merchants and capital fled north during the conflict, as economic and religious refugees from Spanish and Catholic rule.

The prime beneficiary of this movement of wealth and knowledge was the city of Amsterdam. For decades in the late sixteenth century, Spanish and rebel armies clashed inconclusively, effectively shutting down the port of Antwerp, and with it Portuguese commercial access to northern Europe. Amsterdam merchants began sailing to Lisbon to acquire spices until 1595, when King Philip shut down Lisbon, and thus closed Europe's spice centre, to merchants from the Netherlands. This closure gave the merchants of what was becoming one of the greatest trading centres of northern Europe the incentive to launch their own voyages to the East.

· 3 ·

IN 1592 A DUTCH TRAVELLER NAMED JAN HUYGHEN van Linschoten returned from an eleven-year journey throughout the East Indies in the service of Portuguese merchants. "My heart," he mused, "is longing day and night for voyages to far away lands." In 1596 he had completed and published his travelogue *Itinerario,* a detailed guide to the peoples and products of India and Indonesia. *Itinerario* was a route map to the wealth of the Portuguese trading network, the native kingdoms, their customs and interests, the goods they desired and the goods they traded—a sort of commercial *Lonely Planet* guidebook for merchants new to the region. In it van Linschoten described for the first time the original locations of cloves, nutmeg, mace, cinnamon and other spices, blending his account with quaint observations of their daily uses. "The Indian women," he recorded, "use much to chawe Cloves, thereby to have sweete breath, which the Portugales wives that dwell there, doe now begin to use." Regarding nutmeg and mace, he related that "the fruite is altogether like great round Peaches, the inward part whereof is the Nutmegge...This fruite of Apples are many times conserved in Sugar being whole, and in that sort carried throughout India, and much esteemed." The wandering Dutchman described the great benefits of all the spices, in case anyone still doubted that these were amazing substances.

The historian Bernard Vlekke writes in his *Nusantara: A History of Indonesia* that "Linschoten also avowed, and again probably many others brought the same information, that the Portuguese empire in the East was decayed, rotten and tottering, a structure which would collapse if given even a moderate blow, or to change the metaphor, it was a plum ripe for the picking." To Dutch merchants, flushed with idle capital and waging war against Spain for their independence, this was good news. They recognized a good opportunity: Portuguese power was waning.

Thus Dutch merchants began to organize local expeditions to get to the spiceries themselves. Unlike the Portuguese ventures, which were directed and sponsored by the Crown, these were independent enterprises funded by private investors. Nine of them schemed in 1594 to form a "Company for Far Places" in defiance of the Portuguese monopoly and the papal decree that underpinned the Treaty of Tordesillas, which divided the world into two spheres of sovereignty, one belonging to Spain and the other to Portugal. The first voyage of four ships was led by Cornelis de Houtman, a merchant who had lived for a time in Portugal and was related to one of the key investors. De Houtman proved an unpredictable and dangerously erratic leader: one of his ships sank, 145 sailors out of 249 died and de Houtman insulted local traders wherever he landed. Since he had no maps and carried with him a poor choice of trade goods, including heavy woollen cloth and blankets, the enthusiastic reception he was given was due more to Malay traders being pleased with the competition he offered to the Portuguese and Spanish, who had earned a reputation for heavy-handed brutality and were openly hostile to local religions. De Houtman's

officers forced him to return to Holland without even attempt-
ing to reach the Moluccas, but he did manage to secure a small
cargo of spices, and the expedition was hailed a success in
Amsterdam.

The investors quickly grasped the great potential of securing a full cargo of spices. Aided by the wealth of practical advice
on navigation and local customs that had been detailed in Linschoten's newly published *Itinerario* and the experience of de
Houtman's surviving crew, they formed a new company. The
new commander would be Jacob Corneliszoon van Neck, and
the seven ships in the expedition would be armed—they did not
expect to be welcomed by the Portuguese. Van Neck, a level-
headed, diplomatic trader, formed friendly relations wherever
his ships stopped throughout the Spice Islands. He returned
with a full cargo of spices, particularly pepper, that brought a
staggering 400 per cent return on invested capital, and the race
was on. By 1598 five separate trading companies had launched
twenty-two ships to the spiceries. Wherever they sailed in the
Indies, they announced themselves as enemies of the Portuguese and as a result were warmly welcomed by the islanders.
Within a few years, the mariners and merchants of the numerous Dutch trading companies had explored nearly every coast
and visited every port in the region. In 1601 alone, sixty-five
Dutch ships left for the Spice Islands.

The Dutch merchants were so successful, swarming and
overwhelming the Portuguese traders, that they started to com-
pete with each other, lowering the price of spices in Europe
and raising them in the East Indies. The investors, now worried, came upon a simple yet effective solution: they would form
a single company to limit competition among themselves and
combine their efforts against the Portuguese and Spanish. The
merchants of Amsterdam approached the States General, the

governing body representing all the provinces of the United
Netherlands, requesting a monopoly for themselves only and
excluding merchants from other Dutch cities and provinces. For
years the States General had been admonishing merchants from
the various provinces to cease their cutthroat competition and
join in common cause against their enemies. Their warning met
with bitter opposition, however: each region feared losing its
independence. Yet, after much negotiating, on March 20, 1602,
the Dutch East India Company, the VOC, was formed under
the auspices, direction and coercion of the States General. The
company was to have a twenty-one-year monopoly on all trade
with the East Indies.

The new company's governing "Council of Seventeen"
gentleman merchants met periodically in their offices in
Amsterdam. Eight were representatives from the Amsterdam
city government, four hailed from Middelburg, and one each
came from the cities of Enkhuizen, Hoorn, Delft and Rotter-
dam. The final director was elected in rotation from cities other
than Amsterdam, so that Amsterdam itself, the Netherlands'
largest commercial centre, could never hold a majority of the
votes and decision-making power. Theoretically, any Dutch cit-
izen could become a shareholder, but soon the entire enterprise
was governed by a small number of powerful merchants, with
capital invested for a ten-year period rather than in each voyage. This venture, the world's first "joint stock company," was
set to become the world's largest single business enterprise of
the seventeenth century. Mere days after the initial public offering, and before the first shareholders had even paid for their
shares, those shares were being traded on the Amsterdam stock
exchange for a 17 per cent premium.

More significantly, the new monopoly was granted powers
over the Eastern trade, not normally the province of merchants.

It would be a private commercial corporation operating free from the direct control of the government of the United Netherlands, yet it would have the authority to make decisions in the name of that government. The VOC could make treaties and declare war or peace in the name of the States General, construct forts and arm them with cannons, hire troops, establish colonies, dispense justice and enact laws, even issue its own currency—its coins were not stamped with the symbol of a nation or head of state, but with the company insignia. The VOC would essentially operate as a state within a state. In the ensuing years, it forged its way around Africa in the wake of the Portuguese and proceeded to battle them for control of the spice trade, rapidly displacing its erstwhile enemy. The historian Philip D. Curtin has commented wryly, "The VOC began with its military force more important than its trade goods. It was less a capitalist trading firm than it was a syndicate for piracy, aimed at the Portuguese power in Asia, dominated by government interests, but drawing funding from investors rather than taxpayers."

The first VOC fleet sailed from Amsterdam on December 18, 1603, with orders not only to trade but to attack Portuguese ships and forts wherever possible. The VOC's relentless assault on the Portuguese progressed relatively smoothly and rapidly, the company pursuing trade and war with equal vigour. In the first years of its existence, cargoes on VOC ships sent out by the Council of Seventeen were weighted as heavily with guns and ammunition as they were with trade goods and silver bullion. When VOC ships clashed with Portuguese galleons, the Dutch almost always won. In 1605 the VOC captured the Portuguese fort on the island of Ambon, its first territorial acquisition, and continued its conquest rapidly. Within a few years the Dutch company spread across the East from Arabia to Japan, with a vast network of trade depots, forts and factories, many of them seized from the Portuguese, who retreated from this violent onslaught. But soon the VOC faced competition from a source closer to home, from an erstwhile ally in the struggle against Imperial Spain: England.

Although English merchants had formed their East India Company, with royal assent, in December 1600, two years earlier than the VOC had been set up, they pursued the spiceries at a more stately pace and with less capital. Having fewer ships and men and meagre financing, they had no choice, and in their absence the Dutch traders of the VOC swarmed the entire region with cannons blazing. The objective: to eliminate not only the Portuguese but also to redirect local trade networks into the fold of their monopoly. They had no interest in tolerating yet other competitors, such as the English. Edmund Scott, an English merchant at Bantan, wrote in February 1604 that "blowe which way the winde would, they had shipping to come thither, eyther from the East or from the West; insomuch that one woulde have thought they want to carry away the pepper growing on the trees." English traders had difficulty obtaining spices because the Dutch company collected them first, so the English began shadowing Dutch company ships and erecting factories alongside VOC posts. Regarding the English merchants as interlopers and violators of their monopoly, the Dutch viewed them with hostility right from the start. Soon, even while peace reigned in Europe, the servants of the two nations' companies were shooting at each other. Long before the VOC's first twenty-one-year monopoly ended, its ships had engaged in naval battles with every major maritime nation in the world.

After several setbacks—enduring the huge expenses of the ongoing military campaign while failing to completely oust either the Spanish or the Portuguese, and witnessing the increasing presence of English traders—the Council of Seventeen realized the need for more coordinated activity in the region if its traders were ever to secure their monopoly—and the enormous profits that would then be forthcoming. It restructured the governing council at Bantam, now called the Council of the Indies, as a central authority over the VOC's affairs in the spiceries and created a new position, that of the governor general, who would have unchallenged authority over all the company's activities in the East Indies. Pieter Both, a trader of many years' experience in the East, was the first man chosen for this lofty position. He arrived at Bantam in December 1610 with a group of colonists, including craftsmen, clerks, traders, artisans and thirty-six women. Both also brought with him Jan Pieterszoon Coen, now on his second voyage to the East Indies, as a senior trader and as Both's assistant. Observing the terrible conflict descending on the merchant world of the Indies, Coen foresaw great opportunities opening up—opportunities both for revenge and for profit.

· 4 ·

THE MAN STARES FROM HIS PORTRAIT WITH RIGID, self-righteous indignation. Sleek and manicured, Jan Pieterszoon Coen was a man of impeccable grooming, from his slicked hair to his neatly trimmed Vandyke beard, from his coiled moustache to his expensive clothes. His embroidered doublet is patterned with paisley that has detailed trim around the seams. His neck ruff is starched and perky, and he stands erect and stiff, almost regal, while his left hand grips the handle of a sword. His lean and hungry face is dominated by a large hooked nose and eyes that do not betray a shred of humour or liveliness. His eyes are his most distinguishing characteristic—they do not hint at warmth, forgiveness, humanity or empathy. They are hard and shiny like little pebbles. Overall, the painting conveys an impression of humourless arrogance. Coen was a harsh man, living in a harsh era, and the events of his life and his overriding competitiveness conspired to suppress his more empathetic characteristics.

On one occasion, when he discovered his twelve-year-old foster daughter, Saartje Specx, who had been left in his care when her father returned briefly to the Netherlands, in the arms of a fifteen-year-old soldier in his home, Coen displayed his characteristic, stunning inhumanity: the soldier was publicly beheaded and Saartje was publicly whipped. This was a reprieve from Coen's first inclination, which was to have Saartje placed in a tub and drowned. Historian Holden Furber notes in his book *Rival Empires of Trade in the Orient, 1600–1800* that "in single-mindedness of purpose, in ambition for personal wealth, in callous disregard for human suffering, Coen much resembles many empire builders in Africa in the later nineteenth century."

Those who associated with him learned to fear Coen's grim pronouncements. He was disliked even by his own men. Having little tolerance for anything other than work and defeating his enemies, Coen saw the lack of these essential characteristics in others as a failing. He despised the local peoples, considering them dishonourable, corrupt and untrustworthy, but he also was repulsed by his own countrymen, disdaining their love of alcoholic drink and the less-than-strict morality of some of the female colonists. Coen was ambitious and never shy to denigrate the soft-hearted opinions and actions of others if it made for the greatest profit. With everyone, he seemed to be locked in a death struggle from which only one would emerge victorious. All challengers had to be crushed, and all contracts enforced to the letter—with force, if necessary. Coen certainly believed that the use of violent force was the only path to prosperity for the voc. An accountant by training, he proved to be a master tactician and ruthless strongman.

Born on January 8, 1587, in the village of Twisk, near Hoorn, a small seafaring community on the Zuider Zee, Coen was well educated. When he was thirteen his parents sent him to Rome, where they had secured for him a position with a Dutch merchant, Joost de Visscher (or Justus Pescatore), possibly a distant relative who lived and ran a trading enterprise there. Here he learned bookkeeping and general accounting, as well as some Italian, Spanish, Portuguese, French and Latin. He sailed with the VOC's Fourth Fleet in 1607 as a junior merchant. The fleet, under Verhoef, had orders to use force and coercion to secure the monopoly of cloves and nutmeg in the Spice Islands, particularly in the Moluccas. Coen witnessed the failure of those ambitious goals, the killing of Verhoef and what he believed to be the culpability of the English in aiding the Bandanese in their attack on the Dutch. After his youthful experience with Verhoef's disastrous expedition in 1609, his opinions hardened, and his distrust and hatred solidified. He never forgot these events, and they influenced much of his future behaviour.

After that calamitous voyage, Coen returned home to the Netherlands in 1610. He gained the confidence of his superiors with his forthright manner and shrewd analysis of the company's operations. In 1612 he accepted a promotion to senior merchant, in charge of two ships, and sailed in the entourage of the new governor general, Pieter Both. After a grand tour of the VOC's holdings in the Spice Islands, Both was impressed with Coen's fervour, dedication and clear understanding of the company's operations. Both appointed him chief bookkeeper and director of commerce at Bantam. Here the twenty-eight-year-old Coen produced his famous treatise—the "Discourse on the State of India," a report on the company's affairs that singled him out for further promotion—which he submitted to the Council of Seventeen in 1614. That same year, the Seventeen promoted him to the position of director general, the second-highest rank in the spiceries.

Coen's analysis of the issues facing the VOC was clear and cogent, with a logical, if brutal, conclusion: the spice trade was vital to the economic prosperity of the Netherlands. Not only did profits accrue to the company's benefit and the benefit of the United Netherlands, but their gain at the same time damaged the prosperity of their enemy Spain, and therefore weakened Spain's military capacity to dominate the Low Countries. The VOC, Coen argued, had a legitimate right to be in the Spice Islands: it had acquired much of its territory by conquest, defending itself against Portuguese and Spanish aggression. Furthermore, the VOC's claims of monopoly were not based on ancient papal proclamations but on formal legal treaties with various Indonesian nations, particularly in Ternate, the Banda Islands and on Ambon. Spices grew in such abundance in these regions that there was no shortage of supply. Hence competition from the English could not be tolerated, because this would lower prices in Europe and make the business unprofitable.

The spice supply had to be restricted to make the whole enterprise viable. Coen advocated a vast expansion of the company's operations throughout the region, as well as insisting that the VOC's monopoly over cloves, mace and nutmeg (these being the only spices that could be monopolized, because of their isolated region of origin) be ruthlessly enforced to artificially restrict supply and keep prices high. A powerful corporate fleet should be mustered to complete the assault on the remaining Portuguese and Spanish holdings, attacking them in the Philippines at Manila and in China at Macao. Finally, Dutch colonists, as well as slave labour, should be transported to the company's distant commercial outposts. When the VOC was entrenched and its competitors had been eliminated, local rulers would have no alternative but to respect their contracts and deal only with the VOC under that company's terms. Only then, Coen asserted, would the VOC become stable and secure in accruing vast and ongoing profits.

It was an absurdly ambitious vision, beguilingly wide in scope. The Council of Seventeen bought into this intoxicating scheme, overlooking the unsavoury, though unspecified, violence needed to secure it. They now dreamed of dominating not only the Europe-Asia trade, but Asian inter-island shipping as well. It was here that the greatest profits could be made, "as these countries of Asia exceed those of Europe in population, consumption of goods, and industry." Coen argued that the only route for profit and stability lay in the conquest of the company's enemies, a restriction on the production of spices and a monopoly on their sale not just in Europe, but throughout the world. Coen's breathtaking vision called for the VOC to control and dominate the commerce of millions of people with ancient traditions and economies far greater than those of the Netherlands, or even of Europe. "Under this system," writes Bernard Vlekke in *Nusantara: A History of Indonesia,* "the silk from Persia, the cloth from India, the cinnamon from Ceylon, the porcelain from China, and the copper from Japan would be exchanged for the spices from the Moluccas and the sandalwood from Timor, all under the supervision of the officials of the Company." The VOC would be like a spider astride its giant web, strands stretching to the shores of distant lands none had yet visited, controlling all commercial activity throughout the vast, heavily populated region. The profits, of course, would slide back to investors in the tiny Netherlands, on the other side of the world.

But there was much work to be done before Coen's landmark proposals could be implemented. In the meantime, Coen strove to rationalize and professionalize the company's business activities from his base in Bantam and from the island of Ambon, a major administrative centre. During this time he also prosecuted his personal war against anyone who dared to challenge the voc's monopoly as best he could, given that he was still in a subservient position. Coen was furious to see profits slipping through his fingers, but he was not yet in a position to enforce all the voc's contracts. The governors general under whom he served during these years, Gerard Reynst and Pieter Both until December 1615 and then Laurens Reael, were far too lenient and genial, in Coen's opinion, in their co-operation with the English and their respect for the rights and traditions of the local rulers and inhabitants.

In particular, Coen despised the traders of the English East India Company and did all he could to frustrate their efforts to secure spices. In one instance in 1613, when an English East India Company expedition led by John Jourdain cruised to Ambon to trade in cloves, Jourdain was shocked to hear Coen's response to his proposal to buy his stock from the Dutch at slightly above their cost, rather than purchasing cloves from the locals: Coen flatly refused him and ordered him to abandon the island because the voc had already secured contracts for all the cloves "growinge upon the iland." Coen told Jourdain in a letter "nott to deal with the contrye people for any cloves." He then sent notice to the local villages that he would attack and burn their dwellings if they traded with the English. When Jourdain, unable to convince the locals, went to meet Coen in person, the youthful-looking Dutchman strode out to meet the English captain. Not surprisingly, the two arrogant men took an immediate dislike to each other. They insulted each other "in a chollericke manner"—Jourdain mocked the younger Coen's scanty beard and, according to an English account, "did everything to frustrate his endeavours, for it would have been all up with us there had he succeeded." Admitting defeat, however, Jourdain sailed off without a cargo of cloves. Coen knew that depriving the English company of revenue was as important as gaining it for the VOC.

Coen's particular interest was in securing the nutmeg monopoly in the Banda Islands, a task he knew to be possible because of the islands' remote location and tiny size and because they were the only source in the world of the valuable spice. But the English company also had plans for the Bandas: two of the outlying islands, Ai and Run, had not signed monopoly agreements with the VOC and traded freely with English merchants. In 1615 the governor general, Gerard Reynst, led more than a thousand company troops to Ai but was repulsed by the Bandanese, who had received guns and training from English company troops. This resulted in a great defeat for the VOC, which was driven off the island. Reynst died a few months later, never having recovered from the humiliation. Coen dispatched letters to the Council of Seventeen, fuming that the English "want to reap what we have sowed, and they brag that they are free to do so because their king has authority over the Netherlands nation." He also reported that "you can be assured that if you do not send a large capital at the earliest opportunity . . . the whole Indies trade is liable to come to nothing." The following year the VOC sent out another, even larger, fleet to capture the island. Coen sent a letter to the English company troops, who were helping the islanders defend themselves, claiming that "if any slaughter of men happened . . . they would not be culpable." The English company, cowed, abandoned the island and its people to the brutal, smothering embrace of Coen and the VOC.

With the VOC's conquest of Ai, there remained only a single nutmeg-producing island, Run, free from the company's control. That island became a focal point for Coen's wrath. Even though the Netherlands and England were at peace in Europe, their two

East Indies companies were at war in Asia, and Coen began laying plans for a final conquest. He wrote a condescending note to
his superiors in Amsterdam: "If by night and day proud thieves
broke into your house, who were not ashamed of any robbery or
other offence, how would you defend your property against them
without having recourse to 'maltreatment'? This is what the English are doing against you in the Moluccas. Consequently, we are
surprised to receive instructions not to do them bodily harm. If
the English have this privilege above all other nations, it must be
nice to be an Englishman."

There were those on the Council of Seventeen who were sympathetic to Coen's vision and dismissive of the price to be paid;
after all, it was a price to be paid by others. Until Coen coolly laid
out his grand scheme, the directors of the VOC had been content to make money in the usual manner: by commerce and trade.
Coen's proposal, argued logically and passionately, changed the
paradigm for viewing the company's distant activities—activities
which were far from the scrutinizing view of citizens and government in the Netherlands. Who was there to hold the company
accountable to the customs and laws that restricted behaviour in
Europe? Coen's strict Calvinist morality and conservative temperament urged him to take a greater interest in the affairs of
others than a business entity should under healthy circumstances.
Coen wanted to rule people and get rich as a bonus. Through
force of will, single-mindedness of purpose, narrowness of
thought, righteousness of conviction and the persuasiveness of
greed, he was able to make the VOC's business activities conform
to his hatreds and his need for revenge.

In October 1617 Coen got a chance to implement some of
his schemes. Although the Council of Seventeen was reluctant
to embrace his bloody vision, his reports and actions hinted at
an unusual talent and force of will, of decisiveness. When the
temporary governor general, Laurens Reael, a dandy who had

taken over from Gerard Reynst, resigned in protest over his low pay, Coen was the natural choice as the new head of Eastern operations, especially by those who were in favour of a more aggressive policy to secure and stabilize the VOC's profitability. Coen assumed command on April 30, 1618, when he was only thirty-one years old. His initial orders from Amsterdam called for action: "Something on a large scale must be done against the enemies; the inhabitants of Banda must be killed or driven out of the land, and if necessary the country must be turned into a desert by uprooting the trees and shrubs." Four years after he had conceived his vision for expanding the VOC's trade and securing the spice monopoly, Coen could put his scheme into action. Finally he had a free hand to indulge his long-held conviction that violent force was necessary for profitability. "Your Honours should know by experience," he wrote to the Council of Seventeen, "that trade in Asia must be driven and maintained under the protection and favour of Your Honours' own weapons, and that the weapons must be paid for by the profits from the trade; so that we cannot carry on trade without war, nor war without trade."

· 5 ·

WHEN THE COUNCIL OF SEVENTEEN APPOINTED COEN as the new governor general of its operations in the East Indies, the VOC was still on a shaky foundation. In more than a decade of warring, and after numerous agreements attesting to their monopoly trading rights, many of the Dutch traders had pushed their hosts too far. They had refused to acknowledge their hosts' cultural and religious traditions and had annoyed others with their rudeness and constant quarrelling, including bickering with other foreigners, such as the English and the Chinese. There were attacks on VOC merchants and ships. Other peoples, at Ambon and the Banda Islands, continued to flout signed monopoly agreements and secretly traded with English, Chinese and Malay merchants. When Spanish and Portuguese prisoners escaped from a VOC ship and sought protection in the English company's fort at Bantam in 1618, this caused an open rift in the fragile peace between the Dutch and English companies, and they began to skirmish with each other in the streets. Coen recounted with pride the chaos he had sowed: "One day they threaten to sail to Banda in force and take revenge, and the next they say they will attack our ships at sea. They expect to get even by reprisals in the Channel at home and they are going to break our heads. Daily they come up with new threats which clearly shows that they are quite confused." The pretence of peaceful business was shed.

Coen had always hated Bantam for its cloying, fetid airs, so when the Sultan of Bantam commanded him to stop fighting with the English there, Coen ordered the removal of his headquarters from Bantam eighty kilometres east along the same coast to the little town of Jakarta, where he was welcomed by the prince. Coen had not been in Jakarta long, however, when he ordered a small English factory in the city burned and destroyed. Unexpectedly, an English East India Company fleet then arrived, led by Sir Thomas Dale. He ordered eleven of his ships to blockade Coen's seven ships in the port and demanded Coen's surrender. Although he was outmanned, Coen refused. After several days of stalling, naval warfare began between the two companies' ships on January 2, 1619. They lined up in battle formation in front of Jakarta and slid past each other in "a cruel bloody fight." All shipping in the Indonesian port stopped as thousands of cannons roared, acrid smoke clouded the air and hundreds of men were torn open by shards of splintered wood, mangled by flying grapeshot and picked off by sharpshooters in the rigging. As the fleets disengaged for the night, it was obvious that the English company's fleet was trouncing the VOC's ships. That night, Coen called his captains together for a council of war to discuss their weak position, a result of their battered ships, numerous wounded and depleted stocks of ammunition. When three more English company ships arrived the next morning, Coen, gritting his teeth in humiliation, ordered the men in his Jakarta factory to defend the depot to the death and then gave the signal for his ships to turn and flee before the superior forces of his hated enemy. It was something he had never done before.

As his battered fleet hoisted its sails and headed to the Moluccas, where he planned to regroup and reassemble a stronger fleet from the vessels stationed at his many trading entrepôts throughout the region, Coen, glowering with frustration, retreated to his cabin. His bony hand clutching a quill, he dashed off a letter to the Council of Seventeen castigating them for not providing him with enough men, ships and weapons. It is not difficult to discern the arrogance behind his caustic missive: "And now see what has happened . . . I swear that no enemies do our cause more harm than the ignorance and stupidity existing among you, gentlemen!" he wrote to his superiors.

But then things went from bad to good for Coen. Sir Thomas Dale, feckless, unfocused and unable to unify the independent captains of his fleet, allowed Coen to escape and then bungled the assault on the fort. Dale directed his ships not to hunt down the remnants of Coen's shattered fleet. Instead, he headed to the coast of India, where he died of disease a few months later. The once-formidable English East India Company fleet scattered, partly because of the awkward governing structure of the English company. Dale's fleet was not truly under his command: he relied on persuasion, since each captain was responsible for the profit or loss of his own expedition, with no overarching or coordinated corporate directive and no long-term financing.

After successfully holding off their English attackers, on March 2, the men of the VOC garrison decided to name their little fortress Batavia, "as Holland used to be called in days of antiquity." In May, Coen returned in triumph to Jakarta, victorious in the face of the English company's awkward, decentralized governing structure. He marched a thousand fresh troops into the fortress and on May 28 ordered them to attack. The local prince, stunned at the unexpected treachery, was unable to fend off Coen's troops. Coen conquered the town of three thousand, burned down most of its buildings and seized the land for the VOC. He then drew up plans for a new settlement on the traditional Dutch model with which he was familiar.

Coen kept the name Batavia for the new settlement, a solid stone fortress surrounded by angled streets, canals and bridges. "All the kings of these lands know full well what the planting of our colony at Jakarta signifies, and what may follow from it, as well as the cleverest and most far-seeing politician in Europe might do," he boasted. He then pressed his attack against the English company ships, which were now dispersed into smaller groups, and defeated them, capturing seven for his own use, effectively ending the English company's challenge to the VOC in Indonesia. "It is certain that this victory and the fleeing of the English will create quite a furor throughout the Indies," he admitted. "This will enhance the honour and the reputation of the Dutch nation. Now everyone will want to be our friend."

On the verge of achieving his grand objective, the culmination of nearly a decade of dreaming, Coen received the worst news of his career. On July 17, 1619, he opened a letter from the Council of Seventeen: he must desist in his attack on the English company's shipping. The letter was a truce, signed by representatives of both companies as part of an agreement between the two national governments to "forgive and forget" past hostilities. They would each return captured ships and prisoners and "henceforth live and converse as trusted friends." The two companies agreed to work jointly to expel the Portuguese and Spanish from the Moluccas and to maintain their forts and factories. But the monopoly would no longer be exclusive to either company; it was to be shared, one third to the English company and two thirds to the Dutch company, with each supplying its share of ships and men and receiving its portion of the spices to sell as it wished.

Sensible though the partnership was, it infuriated Coen. He was either unaware of or uncaring about the European repercussions of the hostilities between the two companies in the East Indies, nearly sparking a costly war that would consume all the profits from the spice trade and then some. He knew only that the price of the spices in Europe would plummet and that the cost to purchase them in Indonesia would rise if there was competition. He fired off an impetuous letter to the Council of Seventeen, a letter dripping with sarcasm: "The English owe you a debt of gratitude," he sneered, "because after they have worked themselves out of the Indies, your Lordships put them right back again . . . It is incomprehensible that the English should be allowed one third of the cloves, nutmegs and mace since they cannot lay claim to a single grain of sand in the Moluccas, Amboyna, or Banda."

Coen had no intention of abiding by the treaty. In any case the VOC was too powerful to be compelled to listen to the dictates of the Dutch government. So far from Europe—with communication taking up to a year to get a reply—Coen knew he had a certain latitude in his interpretation of orders. He went about organizing a joint "fleet of defence" that would congregate in the bustling new capital of Batavia, where he now grudgingly permitted English agents to operate. Getting wind of the English company's lack of capital, men and ships, he proposed a succession of grandiose plans to oust the Spanish and

Portuguese by attacking their remaining bases. Not surprisingly it was not long before the English company was unable to meet its commitment to pay one third of the costs. At one convening of the joint council, on January 1, 1621, Coen proposed his long-delayed plan to invade the Banda Islands and seek revenge for the failed 1609 mission. He laid out his plans for a mighty invasion force and called upon his English allies to ante up a third of the men and ships—something they were unable to do, since most of their ships were already at sea, as Coen knew, having sent them all off on joint missions. He would proceed without them, he announced, under his own authority.

In February 1621 Coen arrived at Fort Nassau on Great Banda Island with a fleet of thirteen ships, dozens of smaller craft and nearly two thousand troops, including a small contingent of Japanese mercenaries trained as executioners, as well as Javanese rowers and labourers. Fort Nassau itself had a garrison of around 250, making Coen's private army the greatest military force ever to assemble in the Banda Islands. Despite the apparent joint operation of the companies, Coen suspected, correctly, that many disaffected English were secreted on the mountainous islands helping the Bandanese to prepare for the impending invasion by training them in the use of guns and the construction of fortifications. One English merchant, at the request of some village elders, delivered a letter to Coen urging him to forestall violence. Coen reputedly swore at the messenger, pushed him out the door of his office and announced that "whomsoever he should find he would take them for his utter enemies, and they should fare no better than the inhabitants."

With little fanfare, Coen launched his attack by ordering a small ship to circle the island in order to draw fire so that he could determine the location of gun emplacements. He secured this information with two men killed and ten injured. A few days later, after he had harangued his men about their indifferent morale and urged them on with appeals to their courage (and the suggestion of cash rewards for victory), the VOC troops began the assault. It was not easy, as Great Banda consisted of densely forested, inaccessible mountains and had become the focal point for Bandanese resistance to the VOC's hegemony, drawing fighters from the other islands. After two days of fierce fighting along the crags and ridges, Coen bribed several turncoats with bags of thirty gold coins each to betray their comrades and undermine the defences of the island. His company troops then quickly seized control of most of the island's defences and settlements. Suffering only six dead and twenty-seven wounded, Coen took over the entire island, with enormous casualties to the defenders.

A small group of *orang kaya* slunk down from the mountains and filed into a clearing to request a meeting with Coen, who awaited their surrender aboard his ship. They bowed low and offered him a golden chain and a copper kettle as a sign of their sincerity. In victory, Coen was not magnanimous: he demanded they surrender all their weapons, help destroy all remaining defensive forts and give to him all their sons, to be held as hostages aboard his ships. His economic terms were no less harsh: they would agree to cede sovereignty over all the islands, donate a tenth of all the nutmeg they produced each year to the governor general (that is, himself) and sell the remaining 90 per cent to the VOC at prearranged low prices. In return, Coen promised to protect them from their enemies—presumably meaning not himself but the Portuguese. Coen also promised them that they would not be enslaved or forced into labour or military service outside the Banda Islands.

Since the *orang kaya* had seen their mosques desecrated, their houses burned and commandeered for troops and their people terrorized, there was slim chance they would believe Coen's promise of humane treatment. By his own admission, Coen did not expect the Bandanese to abide by these terms, though they had technically agreed to them. The *orang kaya* obliged him by remaining hidden in the mountains and delivering neither additional hostages nor weapons. "They are an indolent people," he wrote, "of which little good can be expected." Indeed, after a few weeks and on several occasions, armed groups of Bandanese ambushed and killed voc patrols. Coen was waiting for just such an event for a pretext to completely crush them. Giles Milton, in his book *Nathaniel's Nutmeg*, notes that Coen's demand for the Bandanese to cede their sovereignty was "significant for any future uprising would not be considered as an act of war but an act of treason, and treason in Holland was punishable by death."

Coen now brought from the hold of his ship the forty-five *orang kaya* whom he had seized earlier, when they originally came to treat with him. He ordered them to be tortured. Coen's judicial process consisted of the rack and burning irons, and soon the *orang kaya* either died or confessed to a secret plan to attack the voc. This treason, Coen concluded, was to be punishable by death. Coen's Japanese mercenaries herded the terrified elders, bound in tight cords, into a bamboo enclosure. There they were convicted of treason and sentenced without a proper trial.

voc lieutenant Nicolas van Waert—whose own men could not fight the order and some of whom were killed when refusing to comply—expressed the general revulsion towards Coen's methods: "Six Japanese soldiers were also ordered inside, and with their sharp swords they beheaded and quartered the eight chief *orang kaya* and then beheaded and quartered the thirty-six others. This execution was awful to see. The *orang kaya* died silently without uttering any sound except that one of them, speaking in the Dutch tongue, said, 'Sirs, have you no mercy?' But indeed nothing availed." Van Waert continued: "All that happened was so dreadful as to leave us stunned. The heads and quarters of those who had been executed were impaled upon bamboos and so displayed. Thus did it happen: God knows who is right. All of us, as professing Christians, were filled with dismay at the way this affair was brought to a conclusion, and we took no pleasure in such dealings." Another VOC officer wrote that "things are carried on in such a criminal and murderous way that the blood of the poor people cries to heaven for revenge."

Coen, however, was not finished. His plan had been brewing since 1609: he wanted to depopulate the islands to replace their inhabitants with imported slave and indentured labour under VOC control. He proceeded with the ethnic cleansing of the Banda Islands. Over the next several months VOC troops burned and destroyed dwellings, rounding up entire villages and herding the captives onto ships, so that they could be transported to Batavia and sold as slaves. Thousands of men, women and children died of disease and starvation during the voyage. Out of a total population of perhaps 13,000 to 15,000, barely 1,000 of the original residents remained in the Banda Islands. Several hundred others were later returned as slaves to work the plantations.

Coen also defied the agreement between the VOC and the English East India Company by capturing all the English on the islands, torturing some of them, manacling them, placing them in the holds of ships as prisoners, seizing their goods and destroying their factories and dwellings. For Coen it was total war—winner take all—and he expected no less from the English. He then began to ship in slaves and colonists to work the plantations. For his actions Coen earned a mild rebuke from the Council of Seventeen, but received a bonus of three thousand guilders for securing Banda nutmeg and mace—the entire world supply—to the VOC's monopoly.

· 6 ·

HIS PRIMARY BUSINESS COMPLETED AND HIS HUNGER for revenge sated—the Bandanese punished for their defiance, the English company effectively defeated, the VOC monopoly on a sound footing and his plan to replace local peoples with imported slave labour well underway—Coen decided to take a rest, return to the Netherlands and enjoy the wealth he had accumulated. In 1623 he set sail for Batavia and Amsterdam, deciding on one final bit of business before he left the Indies. He had his ship put into Fort Victoria on Ambon, where he made a special effort to warn Herman van Speult, the governor of the VOC post there, to be wary of suspicious English activity. Coen was certain there would be retaliation for his actions on the Banda Islands. Ambon, a strategically important island on several major trade routes, was a major producer of cloves.

Coen then sailed to Batavia to tidy up his affairs and arrange for the settlement of the now depopulated Banda Islands. His plan for Banda was to exterminate all the nutmeg trees on the farthest-outlying islands and then to divide the remaining plantations into sixty-eight 1.2-hectare *perken,* which would be leased by the company to Dutch planters, who were to be paid $^1/_{122}$ of the selling price of nutmeg in Amsterdam. This was apparently enough, particularly given the low wages and slave labour, for enormous profits to be made not only for the company but also for the *perkeniers,* who in the following decades commissioned opulent estate mansions to highlight their wealth and status as landowners.

While Coen sailed triumphantly to his homeland, his parting words to van Speult on Ambon were propelling events down a horrifying—though, to Coen, not unexpected—path. The seeds he planted were about to bear sickening fruit. Fort Victoria was manned by two hundred company soldiers, who controlled dozens of great guns mounted on tall stone towers. It was separated from the town by a deep moat and was bounded on one side by the sea. Armed VOC ships lay at anchor in the harbour—it would take a mighty force to challenge the power of the VOC fortress at Ambon. Nevertheless, from the battlements of his strong castle, van Speult cast a suspicious glance about the island and narrowed in on the small English East India Company factory, a dilapidated compound of about a dozen men that reflected the company's fortunes. Van Speult's network of spies and paid informants soon turned up the expected suspicious activity: a sentry spotted a Japanese mercenary employed by the English merchants skulking about the battlements of the VOC fortress. The next day, rumours that the man was a spy awakened van Speult's fears, and he ordered the hapless man to be brought in for questioning. After a judicious application of torture, the man agreed that he and his thirty or so compatriots had a plan to seize the castle. All the other Japanese in the area were quickly rounded up and tortured until they were broken—after which they also "revealed" the complicity of the English chief factor, Gabriel Towerson. That Towerson routinely dined with van Speult and his men and had regular access to the fortress does not seem to have allayed van Speult's suspicions.

Van Speult invited his erstwhile dinner companions to meet him in his castle. When they walked in unarmed, the VOC men-at-arms seized them. Some were manacled and tossed into the dungeons, others were locked below water level aboard a Dutch ship. The screams started soon afterward. In the atmosphere of fear and intimidation, many of the Dutch traders seemed to lose their humanity. While being questioned about their role in the alleged secret attack, the English merchants endured the fate of the Japanese mercenaries who had been compelled to betray them: they were burned, stabbed, stretched on the rack and partially drowned. Several of them, while chained to a stone wall, had their limbs blown off with gunpowder. A pamphlet published after the event, titled *A True Relation of the Unjust, Cruel and Barbarous Proceedings Against the English at Amboyna,* written by a conscience-stricken VOC employee, related how the English company employees had been forced to confess to the preposterous scheme of planning an attack against the heavily fortified VOC post and ordered to sign documents attesting to their villainy before they died. Ten Englishmen, nine Japanese and a resident Portuguese native were beheaded on March 9, 1623. Towerson, the alleged ringleader, was cut into quarters and then beheaded. His head was stuck on a pole and displayed for public viewing. In *Nusantara: A History of Indonesia* Bernard Vlekke writes that "for two hundred and fifty years the 'massacre' of Amboina retained its propaganda value in Europe. In Indonesia it was only one of many bloody episodes in the history of ruthless commercial competition." The English company, now effectively eliminated from the Indonesian spice race, was never to regain a toehold in the Indies, and not surprisingly the massacre ended the joint agreement between the two companies. Coen had won. He had maintained all along that the enterprise would only be profitable if prices could be controlled, and after 1623 he set the VOC on the path to achieving this objective.

Back in the Netherlands, Coen settled into the comfortable life of a gentleman. He assumed the headship of the VOC chamber in Hoorn and settled himself in a stately house befitting a man of his wealth. He acquired a suitable wife, the daughter of one of the VOC's leading directors, and had his and his wife's portraits painted by a prominent artist. The Dutch historian Jurrien van Goor has called them "a testament to Coen's ambition, pride and self-esteem . . . His robe and pose are almost regal." But as news of his business methods trickled back to Europe, many of his countrymen were appalled by Coen's actions and feared the horrible reputation the VOC was giving the entire Dutch nation. Coen's plans for the Indies also raised

eyebrows: if native Indonesians were replaced with Dutch colonists—working under the auspices of the VOC, with a monopoly
on all trade and using slave labour to grow their food—how
would the local people live? The VOC was a trading company,
was it not? "There is no profit at all in an empty sea, empty
countries, and dead people," claimed one of the directors. But
the immediate profits appeared to be enormous, and no one
seriously challenged the VOC's monopoly; its overseas activities
were not governed, after all, by the laws of the United Netherlands. Outside of Europe, the only external laws they obeyed
came from opponents with bigger guns. So, after much debate
within the VOC, Coen sought and was appointed to a second
term as governor general in 1624. His departure for Batavia
was, however, delayed because of diplomatic fallout from the
massacre at Ambon. By 1627 things had settled down enough
for him to board a ship in Amsterdam incognito, along with
his wife and her brother and sister, for his final voyage to the
spiceries.

Coen did not arrive in Batavia until September 1627. Once
there, he lost little time in continuing to consolidate the VOC
monopoly. The local people did not, however, easily give up
their livelihoods and ancient traditions and freedoms. In
December, a few months after Coen arrived, Sultan Agung,
who ruled Mataram, an expanding central Javanese empire
that potentially threatened the VOC's headquarters in Batavia,
launched two deadly sieges against Coen at the headquarters.
Once again, Coen proved that he was a master tactician. After
a month-long failed attack, Agung's army disbanded, and as
punishment to his forces for their defeat, the humiliated sultan ordered 750 executions within view of the VOC castle walls.
Before the end of 1628 Sultan Agung returned with an even
greater force, numbering in the tens of thousands. The entire
military strength of his empire, it was sure to crush the VOC's

private army and conquer Batavia. But during the months of the siege, Coen again proved a sly and dangerous adversary. Sensing a weakness in the seemingly overwhelming military forces arrayed against him, Coen narrowed in and devised an attack. At sea, the VOC was by far the most powerful force in the region, and Coen used its naval superiority to destroy all of Agung's grain barges, which were slowly lumbering along the coast. By the time the remnants of Agung's supply fleet arrived at Batavia, thousands of his troops were on the verge of starvation. Heartened by Coen's early victory, the defenders of the VOC's fort held out until Agung's fleet fled, leaving a trail of dead bodies.

The VOC's predominance was now recognized throughout the region. Unfortunately for Coen, the siege of Batavia was accompanied by a number of ailments that were common among crowds of humanity locked in a confined space for prolonged periods of time. Chief among these ailments were dysentery and cholera, and Coen himself died in his castle of one of these diseases on September 20, 1629. He was forty-two years old. Some claimed that his death was hastened by the fear of meeting his successor, Jacques Specx, whose daughter, Saartje, Coen had ordered publicly whipped years earlier.

After Coen's death, Batavia and the Dutch were established as masters of the Indonesian trade and the most powerful military force in the region. A true merchant king, Coen had built the foundation of the Dutch company's empire—without him and his bloody vision the VOC would have remained a trading company, content to let the symbiotic daily commercial activity of others flourish alongside its own. After he died, the VOC kept to Coen's chosen path, becoming more entrenched, consolidating power, continuing to conquer and seizing as much autonomy from local peoples as military might permitted. In 1641 the company finally conquered Portuguese Malacca after a six-year naval blockade of the strait. The city and sultanate of

Bantam capitulated in 1684, and the sultan agreed to expel all non-Dutch or non-VOC foreigners. The VOC continued its corporate war with the English East India Company, which mostly focused on the west coast of India. However, the war between the two companies significantly contributed to the three seventeenth-century Anglo-Dutch wars that were mostly fought in European waters, although they spilled over to North America and involved the corporate holdings of the Dutch West India Company as well. By virtue of its size, the VOC dominated much of the trade in Europe, controlling half of Europe's foreign trade by mid-century.

To control production and keep prices high, VOC troops uprooted nutmeg and clove trees that were growing outside VOC-approved plantations. Islanders in Tidore and Ternate were forbidden to grow any clove, previously their sole source of income, and planting a clove tree became an offence punishable by death. The VOC depopulated entire islands and relocated the peoples to places where they could be controlled on plantations. There were, understandably, revolts by local peoples, but these outbursts were easily crushed. In the process of securing enormous profits, the VOC impoverished entire societies. By deciding where and in what quantity spices could be grown, by relocating peoples, by reordering whole societies and ancient cultural practices to ensure the highest possible return for distant shareholders, the VOC evolved from being just a company to becoming a quasi-colonial entity that intruded into the lives of Indonesians and determined all aspects of their lives—their commercial patterns, relationships, religious practices, food, clothing and freedoms.

By the late seventeenth century the VOC was the largest, richest and most powerful multinational company in the world. It traded from the Red Sea to Japan and had sent over a million Europeans to Asia, not incidentally contributing to a widespread exchange of ideas and culture. It directly employed tens of thousands of people at a time when the Dutch population was barely two million. Its navy dwarfed that of many nations; its private army approached ten thousand. Its shareholders and investors prospered. Yet, there were troubles. The company made dividend payments in most years, yet it was also servicing an increasing debt load. The government of much of the Dutch East Indies, responsible only to the Seventeen in Holland, the company grew fat, corrupt and inefficient.

The following century of the VOC's history included many adventures—both advances and setbacks—that were tied into global political events. But, ultimately, maintaining the monopoly cost more than the spices were worth, particularly when the value of nutmeg and cloves declined in the mid-eighteenth century with a change in consumer tastes. The VOC's policy of restricting local trade, including the trade in necessary food supplies, resulted in smuggling and piracy. Suppressing these infractions required troops, ships and constant inspection and vigilance. The battle for monopoly could never be won: the VOC would never be free of conflict, and maintaining fleets, forts and garrisons consumed its profits, as did the considerable corruption of its officials in Asia.

Although the VOC declared great dividends for over a century and a half and possessed enormously valuable stock, when the once-mighty company went bankrupt in 1799, during the Napoleonic Wars, it was twelve million guilders in debt. Despite paying huge dividends, it had been steadily losing money for over a century—the years it made profits decreased in number while losses grew as the decades passed. The VOC's enormous income stream allowed it to incrementally increase its debt, to raise capital by issuing bonds. The historian Willard Hanna writes in his book *Indonesian Banda* that "Retroactive bookkeeping traced the troubles right back to the days of the

VOC's greatest glory . . . So the enormously wealthy and powerful VOC may have been a losing proposition all along." Most
historians, however, point to the company's vitality during the
eighteenth century, and its inability to adapt to changing consumer demands in Europe and the financial repercussions of
the Fourth Anglo-Dutch War, between 1782 and 1784. "After
the war," writes Jurrien van Goor, "the VOC's directors in the
Republic spent vain efforts trying to revive the Company in
its former state rather than looking for new ways of operating,
with the result that, like a rudderless ship, the VOC sailed onto
the financial rocks." The Fourth Anglo-Dutch War was the
final blow, revealing staggering debt that the company had been
supporting for over a century. The debt was assumed by the
government and taxpayers of the Netherlands when the nation
took over the VOC's former empire as a colonial holding. The
new colony, known as the Dutch East Indies, continued under
Dutch national rule until 1949. For over 150 years the VOC
had been the effective government in much of Indonesia, governing not in the interests of local peoples or to maintain local
traditions and culture, but simply to enrich shareholders and
directors who lived tens of thousands of kilometres away and
had in all likelihood never left Europe at any time in their lives.

The company's success and ultimate failure, the cycle of
its life, was based on the logical but somewhat warped dream
of its greatest merchant king. Coen strove to reduce all commercial activity in the East Indies to a few transactions over
which he could exercise total control—reducing the collective
decisions of thousands and bending them to his will, reordering them for the maximum profit. He was a brilliant strategist
and logistician, but either through hyper-competitiveness or a
sickness of the mind, he tended to view the world much like a
game board, with pieces to move about, gambles and sacrifices
to be made, without regard for the value of human life. For

Coen, winning was everything; the lives of other people—even his own countrymen—were mere externalities to be dealt with quickly and efficiently. One tends to believe, or hope, that there must have been more to his character than what has survived in the historical record. Perhaps, if he had lived longer, this would have become apparent, or perhaps he would have mellowed as he aged. But although he was long considered to be a Dutch national hero for putting the VOC on solid footing—he provided the gilded age of the Netherlands with not only a prime source of its wealth but also its worldly identity—his cruelty and violence, the corporate culture of the VOC that he created, overshadow his reputation now.

Coen's vision for the VOC coaxed great things from the company and from his little nation, but like an addict on a high, they eventually burned out from exhaustion. Despite the company's monopoly status, the costs of controlling and governing the spiceries eventually outweighed the benefits. And, along with the company, the brief flash of the Dutch Golden Age petered out. Many generations enjoyed the VOC's profits until the final accounting revealed the company's decayed inner workings. The rot had begun with its inception, along with Coen's grand plan to use a private army to conquer and dominate the world's most valuable commodities in the seventeenth century. The kingdom of the world's first great merchant king eventually crumbled on its own faulty foundation.

· *Chapter 2* ·

"We derive our authority from God
and the West India Company, not from
the pleasure of a few ignorant subjects."

PIETER STUYVESANT, C. 1647

Divided Loyalties

PIETER STUYVESANT AND

THE DUTCH WEST INDIA COMPANY

· 1 ·

ON MARCH 22, 1664, THE FLAMBOYANT KING CHARLES II of England, recently restored to the English throne after living in exile during a decade of parliamentary rule following the Civil War, made an epochal decision. To his ambitious brother James, Duke of York and Albany, he granted control over a vast tract of land in eastern North America: "all of Maine between the Croix and Kennebec rivers and from the coast to the Saint Lawrence, all islands between Cape Cod and the Narrows, and all land from the western boundary of Connecticut to the eastern shore of Delaware Bay." The charter, which included the right to govern under the English Crown, specifically mentioned the "River called Hudsons River," and it was this north-flowing river and the valuable entrepôt that had grown at its confluence—the only significant settlement south of Boston and north of the Caribbean—that was the central point of interest.

In return for this magnanimous gift, James was to dutifully forward to the king an annual stipend of forty prime beaver skins. Perfectly normal sibling generosity, perhaps, apart from the fact that the land the king was graciously giving to his brother consisted essentially of the quasi-colonial holdings of the Dutch West India Company, all of the Dutch colony of New Netherland, including, presumably, all the native peoples as well. But giving this kingly gift was not a flippant or whimsical decision; it was a carefully calculated policy organized at the highest levels of the English government and undertaken with the full knowledge that force would be required to wrest control of New Netherland from the Dutch West India Company.

If English troops could lay siege to and take the Dutch quasi-colony run by the West India Company, it would give England control over the entire eastern coast of North America and link the New England colonies in the north with the British settlements in the Chesapeake. Not only was New Amsterdam, on Manhattan Island, the centre of Dutch commercial activity in the western Atlantic, it had also emerged as the centre of trade for much of the commerce of the English colonies. As the critical port in eastern North America, New Netherland, particularly the Dutch settlement of New Amsterdam, had become a pawn in the epic commercial struggle between Holland and England. James and some of his cronies had incorporated several other companies aimed at challenging the Dutch commercially, such as the Royal African Company, with the objective of destroying the Dutch-controlled West African slave trade and taking over the transport of slaves to the plantation colonies of the Caribbean. In 1663 this company, headed by the duke, seized all the Dutch slave-trading posts in West Africa. Ousted from the Spice Islands and the East Indies, the English were not prepared to be dominated closer to home in the Atlantic, and as a result to have their expansionist ambitions thwarted. New Amsterdam, and all of New Netherland, had to be taken—and reports indicated that, against all probability, the Dutch company trusted with managing it had devoted little to the town's defence.

James moved swiftly. In 1665 four frigates under the command of Colonel Richard Nicolls left England on a secret mission to assault New Netherland. Nearly two thousand troops were prepared for the invasion. Separated on the voyage across the Atlantic, the small squadron regrouped and anchored in Gravesend Bay on August 26. It unloaded the infantry: 450 troops marched to commandeer the ferry at Breukelen (present-day Brooklyn), and others marched along the coast to drum up support from the many English settlers and towns in the Dutch colony. About 1,500 people lived in New Amsterdam, and about 10,000 populated the entire colony, in towns and on farms throughout the territory centred on the Hudson River. Despite entreaties from the citizens and from its governor, however, the West India Company had refused all requests for additional ammunition and soldiers, not wanting to shoulder the expense. The board of directors suggested optimistically in a letter to Pieter Stuyvesant, the governor of the colony, that he need not worry about an English invasion because "we are in hopes that as the English at the north have removed mostly from old England for the causes aforesaid [religious freedom], they will not give us henceforth so much trouble, but prefer to live free under us at peace with their consciences than to risk getting rid of our authority and then falling again under a government from which they had formerly fled." The directors hoped that the company's policy of religious toleration would galvanize its citizens to fight any invasion.

The four English frigates cruised into the harbour of New Amsterdam and disembarked hundreds of troops. Although Fort Amsterdam was poorly manned for defence against such a strong force, Stuyvesant had received advance warning of the invasion fleet and had shored up the fort's defences, organizing guard watches, digging defensive ditches and repairing the dilapidated walls. He dashed off a letter to the captain of the small English fleet. What was the reason for the ships, he inquired, stating that he hoped that since their nations were at peace, the commander was not "apt to entertain any thing of prejudice intended against us."

A courier delivered Colonel Nicolls's response to Stuyvesant in his office in Fort Amsterdam on September 4: "In his Majesties Name," it read, "I do demand the towne, Scituate upon the Island commonly knowne by the Name of Manhatoes with all the Forts there unto belonging, to be rendered unto his Majesties obedience, and Protection into my hands." Neither he nor the king wanted bloodshed or violence, the note calmly proclaimed, but if the terms were not met by the West India Company, Stuyvesant would bring on "the miserys of a War."

Courtly civility was the order of the day. When presented with the letter, Stuyvesant sniffed and declined to reply because the missive was not properly signed. He sent it back, and Nicolls, rising to the occasion, wrote a new note addressed to "the Honorable, the Governor of the Manhatoes," wherein he reiterated his demands and beseeched Stuyvesant not to delay: "Your speedy Answer is necessary to prevent future inconveniences, and will very much oblige." Nicolls signed it "Your affectionate humble Servant."

Stuyvesant considered the company's position: Nicolls had nearly a thousand fighting men ready to attack, whereas the company had left New Amsterdam garrisoned with merely five hundred; Nicolls also had nearly a thousand more soldiers scattered throughout Long Island, in addition to having dozens of cannons on his ships. Stuyvesant had possession of the fort and its handful of cannons, and an intimate knowledge of the surrounding lands. He could hold out for a while but would lose eventually if reinforcements did not arrive. To surrender without a fight, however, was dishonourable, perhaps even cowardly to a man like Stuyvesant, and would likely end his career with the company. He loudly proclaimed that he "would rather be carried to my grave" than give up without a fight. Yet he stalled, suggesting to Nicolls that he was awaiting orders from his directors in Amsterdam.

Stuyvesant then met with an English representative at a popular local tavern and, after quietly reading the terms of surrender presented to him, tore the paper to shreds. This outraged the gathered crowd—onlookers who demanded that Stuyvesant relay the English offer to them. But that would have been too undignified for the man who had been in a struggle with these very people for years over the government of the settlements and colony. He refused to show the generous terms of surrender either to his subordinates or to the leading citizens of the settlement, knowing they would argue for surrender if he did—many of the terms on offer were the very things the people of New Netherland had been seeking for years: freedom of religion, property rights, inheritance laws, continued trade with Holland, "every man in his Estate, life, and liberty."

Stuyvesant slowly collected the ripped pieces of the letter and offered the crumpled pieces to the mob. Many hands grabbed the pieces and glued them back together. Many eyes then squinted at the damaged handwriting, and some people read the words aloud. Stuyvesant stalked away on his stump leg, mounted the battlements of his fort and stared across the water at the ships that were waiting with their guns trained on the settlement. He let the wind ruffle his long hair and contemplated ordering one of his cannons to fire. The long-standing and accepted rules of war allowed that if a stronghold surrendered when presented with a formal demand, the civilians would be spared and the town too;

but, if even a single shot were fired in aggression, the community would be open for plunder and destruction. One shot from Stuyvesant's cannon, and the people would have to defend themselves—he could unleash a great torrent of violence that would surely result in the destruction of the town and the death of many people. Only a clergyman with the impressive name of Domine Megapolensis joined him and a gunner at the battlements. They talked. Time passed. Finally reaching an agreement, Stuyvesant descended from the battlements. The next morning, on September 5, 1664, ninety-three of the leading citizens of New Amsterdam presented Stuyvesant with a petition, signed by his own son, demanding that he surrender to prevent the inevitable "misery, sorrow, conflagration, the dishonour of women, murder of children in their cradles, and, in a word, the absolute ruin and destruction of about fifteen hundred innocent souls." Stuyvesant knew he had lost their loyalty.

The terms of surrender that Nicolls offered were shrewdly calculated to deflate any opposition to the foreign power. They were something the citizens had lacked under the West India Company's administration and feared they would never gain. The hated foreigners—enemies of Holland through several recent wars—offered the people of New Amsterdam if not a better life, at least a life of greater freedom. Why the citizens of Holland's premiere North American colony preferred conquest by a foreign nation, a nation with which they had been at war for decades, to fighting for their own country is an intriguing question. Answering that question requires some familiarity with the legacy of Pieter Stuyvesant and the Dutch West India Company.

· 2 ·

HENRY HUDSON IS NOW REMEMBERED, WHEN HE IS remembered at all, for his tragic death at the hands of his mutinous crew in 1610 in the bay that bears his name. The famous portrayal of the event, painted several centuries later, depicts the forlorn mariner—bearded, dressed in rags with sad, soulful eyes—staring morosely from the seat of a small, crowded boat. Forbidding, snowy mountains dominate the background, and great icebergs loom ominously. The wizened mariner clutches the hand of his teenaged son, John, who stares beseechingly at his father. A vast expanse of inhospitable, frozen wilderness is apparent in all directions. Hudson, along with a handful of loyalists and all the sick and dying members of his ill-fated expedition, was cast adrift in the ice-choked waters and left to perish when he, tenaciously and with a deranged optimism, announced his intention to continue his quest for a west-leading waterway from the bay to the clove- and nutmeg-scented climes of the Moluccas in the spring. All this despite a horrifying winter spent in a miserable, scurvy-ridden encampment on a nearby frozen island. The mutiny was a melancholy and dramatic event that for decades put a stop to English attempts to locate the elusive northern route to the spiceries.

Many people lost a lot of money with Henry Hudson's failure; Hudson was not commissioned or employed by the English government, but rather by a handful of merchants under the auspices of the Virginia Company, the Muscovy Company and the English East India Company. It was a private venture that did not pay off, just like Hudson's three other voyages in search of the elusive waterway. While most Dutch and English merchant adventurers struggled to establish routes to the Moluccas around the Cape of Good Hope, battling Spaniards, Portuguese and Malaysians for a share of the spice trade, others sought an alternate northern route. It was potentially shorter, less infested with the agents of enemy nations and populated by northern people who were more likely to be interested in one of England's chief exports: wool.

Maps from the early seventeenth century show the frag-
mented vision of the world's geography available to mariners. A
vast, blank expanse filled these maps, a frightening *terra incognita*
concealing unknown possibilities for commerce or plunder. The
only viable trade route to the silks, spices and gems of the mysterious Eastern lands was precarious and long, circumnavigating
the globe and passing through uncharted waters teeming with
the ships of hostile Spanish and Portuguese competitors. One
of the routes with the greatest potential ran through the frigid
waters of northern Canada; another followed the northern
coastline of Europe eastward. Whichever way it lay, the discovery of a navigable sea route was believed to be only a matter of
time and persistence. English merchants, shut out of the spice
trade after the English East India Company was founded in
1600, were in search of new markets. In 1607 a group of leading merchants in the city of London decided to take matters
into their own hands. They would outfit and promote a voyage
to discover a fabulous new route to the Orient.

Hudson, at the time an experienced and skilled mariner in
his mid-forties, married with three children, set off to sail over
the top of the world via the northeast passage in a tiny seventy-
foot ship with a crew of twelve. He returned after a horrifying
ordeal, encountering an endless morass of ice, the only consola-
tion of the voyage being its discovery of an abundance of whales.
The next year, 1608, he set out a second time for the northeast
passage but was again turned back by ice. When he followed
his cherished idea of heading to the northwest by crossing the
Atlantic, his crew rebelled and forced him to return to London.
Confident of sailing off on a third voyage the next spring, Hudson was stunned and demoralized when the directors of the
Muscovy Company turned him down. Fuming as he left their
offices, he hardly had time to ponder his next move before being
accosted by the illustrious Emanuel van Meteren, a foreigner

who represented equally his country and its greatest corporation. Van Meteren, the urbane and highly educated Dutch consul in London, presented Hudson with a tantalizing prospect that would allow the mariner to pursue his dream of exploration. He lured Hudson to Amsterdam at the behest of leading Dutch merchants who shared his vision for a northwest passage through North America to the Orient. These merchants were inspired by the start of a twelve-year truce with Spain, a pause in the Dutch Republic's struggle for independence from a weary and near-bankrupt Spanish Empire.

England's main trading rival offered Hudson good terms. Not content with their existing trade routes to the East Indies, which were long and fraught with danger, the VOC's Council of Seventeen wanted to ensure that a potentially easier, shorter rival route, traversing regions not dominated by entrenched fortifications, was not pioneered by yet another competitor: the English. Hudson convinced the Seventeen of the viability of his northern route by claiming that as he sailed north past the Arctic Circle, the climate became warmer and he had seen grass-covered land that supported wild, roaming animals. Hudson's claims, which then as now seemed counter to common sense, were nevertheless supported by the Dutch geographer and promoter Petrus Plancius, who claimed that "near the pole the sun shines for five months continually; and although his rays are weak, yet on account of the long time they continue, they have sufficient strength to warm the ground, to render it temperate, to accommodate it for the habitation of men, and to produce grass for the nourishment of animals." So, in 1609, the year before his fateful and dramatic death and the same year that Coen first sailed to Indonesia, Hudson was employed by the Dutch East India Company to undertake a voyage to a wholly unlikely location for a passage to the spiceries.

Hudson set off from Amsterdam in early April on the *Halve*

Maen (*Half Moon*) under orders to retrace his earlier voyage to the
north and east. His crew of about twenty were half Dutch and
half English, neither group speaking the other's language. Not
surprisingly, Hudson soon encountered the same impassable ice
that had thwarted his earlier voyages. Ignoring the terms of his
contract, which specifically warned him "to think of discovering no other routes or passages, except the route around by the
North and North-East above Nova Zembla," he turned the ship
around and rushed south and west across the Atlantic to follow up on a rumour he had heard from his friend Captain John
Smith, from Jamestown in the colony of Virginia, who informed
him that reports from several natives told of a great river or
waterway that led to the west. By early July, the *Half Moon* sighted
the coast of Newfoundland or Cape Breton and cruised south
past Cape Cod, en route to Chesapeake Bay before turning north
and slowly retracing the coastline to search for the secret opening that would guarantee Hudson's historical immortality and,
more importantly, wealth. Eventually, in September 1609, the
Half Moon dropped her anchor in "a very good harbour, and four
or five fathoms, two cables length from the shore," at the mouth
of a wide river that would soon bear Hudson's name.

The *Half Moon* had anchored off what is now known as
Coney Island, and a shore party rowed a small boat ashore to
explore. They were astonished at the size of the "very goodly
oaks... of a height and thickness that one seldom beholds" and
encountered curious and friendly people who proffered tobacco
and furs and wanted knives and coloured beads in exchange.
Hudson and his men marvelled at the luxuriant vegetation,
especially at the fruits dangling from trees and bushes, and at
the wildflowers with their "very sweet smells." They dallied for
several days before the *Half Moon* pushed upstream to find the
route to the Moluccas, passing by "that side of the river that is
called Manna-hata." During the next several days, Hudson and

his crew attempted to communicate with the local peoples who congregated along the shore or rowed alongside the ship in their canoes. More than once, Hudson plied the natives with liquor to get them to reveal the location of the western sea. He was amazed at the abundance of food and the sturdy construction of the dwellings in the numerous villages, as well as admiring the "great quantity of maize or Indian corn, and beans of last year's growth, and there lay near the house for the purpose of drying, enough to load three ships, besides what was growing in the fields." The crew then sailed upriver through a land they felt was "the finest for cultivation that I have ever in my life set foot upon, and it also abounds in trees of every description." After about 250 kilometres, coming near to the present city of Albany, the river narrowed and became too shallow for the *Half Moon* to navigate. Hudson reluctantly turned the ship around and floated back downstream to the ocean, thinking about how he could spin his failed venture into something positive to tell his employers.

Nearing the mouth of the river, Hudson proposed further exploration but was threatened "savagely" by his crew. Changing his plans, he steered "strait across the ocean" and put into port—not in Amsterdam, but in Dartmouth, England—in the fall. He dashed off a letter to his employers, the Dutch East India Company, describing his voyage and requesting additional funds to undertake another voyage the following year. Not surprisingly, the directors were not amused. They demanded that Hudson return the *Half Moon* to Amsterdam immediately. But as he was reluctantly readying his ship for departure, he was arrested by the English government for "voyaging to the detriment of his country" and was ordered not to leave England. There was a rumour going about that he had made a great discovery for the Dutch, and the English did not want to lose the information. Hudson was commanded to appear before the king in London, and a guard was placed at the door to his home. The Dutch consul, van Meteren, fuming, fired off a report to Amsterdam decrying the actions of the English government. "The English are inconstant, rash, vainglorious, light and deceiving, and very suspicious, especially of foreigners whom they despise," he claimed. "They are full of courtly and affected manners and words, which they take for gentility, and wisdom."

Although the VOC soon dismissed Hudson's discoveries as being of no value, less than a year later some individual Dutch merchants not affiliated with the company were intrigued by the possibility of trading for furs. They "again sent a ship thither, that is to say, to the second river discovered, which was called Manhattes."

Van Meteren published his assessment of Hudson's voyage, proclaiming the discovery to be Dutch. He described "as fine a river as can be found, wide and deep, with good anchoring ground on both sides" and said that the land was inhabited by a "friendly and polite people" who were eager for mutually beneficial trade. What they had to trade was what drew the interest of Amsterdam merchants on the lookout for new opportunities. Any merchants who were shut out of the VOC monopoly trade, who preferred greater control over their investments and who were no longer intrigued by the failed waterway to the East Indies, which would have been under the control of the VOC anyway, were attracted by van Meteren's claims of "many skins and peltries, martins, foxes, and many other commodities." A sea route to Cathay or the Indies was all well and good for dreamers, but the promise of immediate and guaranteed returns from an industry that was much closer and safer was as good as gold. A vast region of land unoccupied by any European power lay between New France to the north and English Virginia to the south.

These attractions meant that in the years after Hudson's voyage, independent Dutch mariners and merchants sailed the rivers, explored inland, probed the coast, established relations with peoples of the coast and the interior and constructed a number of primitive huts and trading factories as far inland as present-day Albany. Within a few years of Hudson's voyage, the natives were trading the "soft gold" of beaver furs at independent Dutch trading posts along the three rivers near Manhattan: the Hudson, the Connecticut and the Delaware. Since no roads led into the dense forests, rivers were the great arteries of travel and commerce, and the land staked by the Dutch at the southern tip of Manhattan Island was to become the epicentre of trade, solidifying Dutch territorial claims and giving rise to one of the world's great commercial cities. Here traders began by bartering manufactured trinkets for beaver pelts. Fur was exceedingly valuable in Europe for lining coats, collars, capes and muffs. Beaver fur was particularly useful, because underneath the outer long glossy coat was a denser layer of soft, tightly growing shorter hairs that, in a toxic and dangerous industrial process, could be made into felt, a substance that could be, in turn, made into durable, warm and fashionable hats. The traders also found Hudson's boasts of the land's agricultural potential to be accurate, and within a few years a ramshackle collection of huts had been constructed at the southern tip of the island and the land cleared for farming.

When the English captain and explorer Thomas Dermer cruised to the mouth of the Hudson River in 1617, also looking for the fabled northwest passage to the spiceries, he was shocked to discover "divers ships of Amsterdam and Horna who yearly had there a great and rich trade." He was even more astonished to discover "some Hollanders that were settled in a place we call Hudson's River, in trade with the natives." It was the start of a long association of the Dutch with this new land.

· 3 ·

THE TWELVE-YEAR PEACE BETWEEN SPAIN AND THE
United Netherlands from 1609 to 1621 inspired the commercial activity by private merchants in America. During the peace
far-thinking members of the States General deliberated on how
to damage Spain when hostilities resumed. They planned to
finance a war of independence by tapping private capital, using
the web of commercial networks and the host of skilled mariners
and navigators that had been developed and nurtured through
trade. "The vehicle seized upon was grandiose in design," the
historian Thomas J. Condon writes in *New York Beginnings: The
Commercial Origins of New Netherland,* "and incorporated a West
India Company which, through subsidization, would become a
partner of the state in the war against Spain. Ranging over the
vast sweep of the New World, the company would aim to choke
off the life strength of Spain at its roots. To do this the efforts of
the company were to be directed into the twin channels of war
and trade—in that order and with no fine line drawn between
the two." On June 3, 1621, the States General granted an initial
twenty-four-year charter to the Dutch West India Company,
modelled after its flourishing and famous eastern counterpart,
which was then under the auspices of Jan Pieterszoon Coen's
draconian and bloody vision. This company's governing council was called the Nineteen, or the Lords Nineteen, consisting
of powerful merchants, financiers and politicians who headed
and represented the five chambers or subscription centres that
provided the capital to launch the venture. Private trade in New
Netherland would not be permitted after 1623, when the company's monopoly would begin.

The Dutch West India Company was chartered with two
main objectives: piracy and a productive (that is, profitable)
settlement of its North American territories, which would also
serve as a base for further pirate raids on Spanish shipping.

The company would make money for its investors and speculators both by trading in the West Indies and North America
and by attacking and seizing Spanish ships in those regions.
"The incorporated West India Company," the States General
declared, "ought not to enter, in the beginning, into a dispute
with the subjects of neighbouring Kings and Princes, but much
rather observe good correspondence and friendship towards
them." Nevertheless, one of the company's first undertakings
was to outfit a military assault on the Spanish sugar plantations at Bahia in 1623–24 that involved twenty-three ships and
more than three hundred men. In 1625 the company attacked
and plundered San Juan, Puerto Rico, and in 1628 Admiral
Piet Hein sallied forth with a mighty squadron and ambushed a
sixteen-ship Spanish silver fleet with cargo valued at over eleven
million guilders, allowing the company to pay a 50 per cent dividend that year. Over the next decade the company financed
the operations of more than 700 ships and 67,000 men, who
returned triumphantly with over 500 prizes of enemy shipping
that fetched over 40 million guilders at auction. Clearly, early
investors were amply rewarded by this new business venture.

The company also established trading posts in West Africa,
the Antilles and other islands in the Caribbean, and Surinam
and Guyana in South America, as well as conquering the Portuguese colonies in Brazil. Throughout the 1620s the company
likewise sought to consolidate its hold on central-eastern North
America, a region that promised not only to be profitable for the
fur trade but also to serve as a way station or base for West India
Company ships en route to the plundering grounds in the Caribbean. The first twenty-four families of company colonists sailed
from the Netherlands with Captain Cornelis May aboard the
Nieu Nederlandt in 1624. They scattered into the remotest regions
of the vast, sparsely inhabited land, which was mainly populated
by native Americans of various tribes, principally the Lenape

and the Mahicans. These hardy and exceptionally brave souls built from the wilderness "some hutts of Bark," trading forts, or factories, along the major rivers. More settler/employees arrived the following year, and they were soon sending to Amsterdam furs valued at 27,000 guilders per year. Some began farming on Manhattan, "a convenient place abounding with grass." Cattle roamed the fields while windmills, sawmills and rough wooden barracks rounded out the settlement of New Amsterdam. "Had we cows, hogs, and other cattle fit for food (which we daily expect on the first ships)," wrote one enthusiastic colonist, "we would not wish to return to Holland, for whatever we desire in the paradise of Holland, is here to be found."

The company's directors did not share this settler's enthusiasm for the land. The new settlement was supposed to be a trading outpost, not a beachhead of Dutch colonial expansion. The provisional orders governing the actions of the employees firmly placed the company's interests first: the settlements would be run as trading posts, ruled by a governor appointed by the directors; decisions would come from head office, not from the ground up. The settler/employees were "to obey and to carry out without any contradiction the orders of the Company then or still to be given, as well as all regulations received from the said Company in regard to matters of administration and justice." They would fulfill the needs of the company by living where they were directed to live; planting crops as dictated by the company; providing labour on the fortifications and other essential buildings, such as the governor's house, as needed; and performing military service when required. After six years, these adventurous pioneers might be given some land to do with as they chose, so long as they obeyed company directives. It would not be quite the idyllic plantation on the edge of paradise that many longed for: labourers in the primary settlement on the southern tip of Manhattan Island, called New

Amsterdam, as one of their first tasks were directed to construct a rudimentary star-shaped earthen and palisade fort. They gave it the thematically appropriate, if uninspired, name of Fort Amsterdam.

The citizens of this peculiar company town on the edge of the North American wilderness were a rough lot. They were fed "hard stale food, such as men are used to on board ship," and took shelter in run-down hovels where they "huddled rather than dwelt." Drunkenness, fighting, theft, assault, murder and rape were frequent crimes reported among the mostly male population. One in four establishments in New Amsterdam was a grog house or beer and tobacco emporium. Considering that the population consisted mostly of indentured servants, employees and slaves owned by the company, the chaotic and immoral behaviour of the citizens had only one source: the company, which, despite its apparent disgust with the settlement and its people, made a hefty profit from its monopoly on the sale of beer and liquor to them—a profit that was second only to its profit from furs. Squalor, filth and disorder reigned supreme.

Under a series of mostly incompetent and corrupt governors, and as a result of the company's subtle pressure to restrict development, the colony was slow to flourish. Company directors in the Netherlands feared that settlement might actually be bad for business, as settlers would demand services such as schoolteachers, church ministers, a legal system and military defence—all of which cost money. Farming and conflict with the natives over land might disrupt the flow of valuable furs. The company instead preferred the population to be kept low in numbers and directly employed by them. A few independent people might operate a small farm or engage in their own personal trade, so long as they sold their furs or produce to the company and bought all their goods at the company store. One early governor, Peter Minuit, who became famous for allegedly buying all of Manhattan for sixty guilders' worth of trade goods, was recalled to Amsterdam because he was not effective enough in curbing the growing private trade in furs. This was a trade that nearly all the settlers participated in to augment their meagre wages, despite the company's best efforts to put a stop to it.

By late 1630 New Amsterdam had a population of only four hundred. It was run down and dilapidated, the fortifications were in disrepair and the five company farms were "vacant and fallen into decay; there was not a living animal on hand belonging to the Company on said Bouweries." The town had already been eclipsed by the younger community of Boston, in New England; it had failed to thrive under the neglect and parsimony of the company, and many feared the entire enterprise would be lost to the English, whose North American colonies of Virginia and New England were vital and expanding. (Because of the English Civil War, Puritans had fled to America to found their ideal society, swelling the English population dramatically within a handful of years.) Reluctantly, the company loosened its restrictions on the number of new settlers while keeping a firm grip on their civil liberties and freedoms. New arrivals, though ostensibly free citizens, had to acknowledge the sovereignty of the Dutch West India Company by paying yearly fees or taxes.

Within two decades, New Amsterdam resembled a prosperous Dutch town with its gabled roofs, windmills, a stone church, several large stone houses, an expanded fort, a governor's residence and a school. But since their chief objective was to generate money for their employers, the governors of New Netherland did not respond eagerly to the settlers' desire to create a civil society. They were heavy-handed in ordering settlers around—removing and promoting them at whim—and taxing them so much that one early settler complained that "under a king, we could not be worse treated." Many lived under a pall of discontent, and as a result the community and outlying settlements did not thrive. The historians George J. Lankevich and Howard B. Furer noted in *A Brief History of New York City* that "although physically the town was 'after the manner of Holland,' in terms of its ambition and profit it was very un-Dutch." That is to say, initiative and energy were in short supply. This lack of vitality might seem astonishing, considering that the town and colony were run by a joint stock corporation with the sole objective of generating profits; but is it so odd that a people whose personal freedom and upward mobility were restricted might not leap to their appointed tasks?

One brutal governor in the early 1640s, an Amsterdam merchant named Willem Kieft, managed to start a war with the native peoples of the lower Hudson Valley after demanding tribute from them. His ill-conceived revenue-generating scheme resulted in a horrific massacre of the natives, the deaths of dozens of colonists and the destruction or abandonment of company outposts outside New Amsterdam, which itself was then inundated with refugees. A council of eight leading citizens of the colony sent a report to the Nineteen in Amsterdam outlining the disastrous predicament in which Kieft's intemperate actions had placed the enterprise: many "skulk, with wives and little ones that still survive, in poverty together, in and around the Fort at the Manhattas where we are not safe for an hour."

In 1643 Kieft hired a band of English "Indian fighters" led by John Underhill to attack all the surrounding native villages. They tortured and killed 1,600 natives and brought dozens of captives back to Fort Amsterdam, where Kieft reputedly "laughed right heartily, rubbing his right arm and laughing out loud" while the soldiers brutalized and killed them. One of the prisoners died most horribly when his captors "threw him down, and stuck his private parts, which they had cut off, into his mouth while he was still alive, and after that placed him on a mill-stone and beat his head off." Not surprisingly, Kieft's brutality and greed "in a short time nearly brought this country to nought." The actions of Kieft the merchant-warrior were in direct opposition to the wishes of the overwhelming majority of the people living in New Netherland. Yet, it was these people who suffered most from Kieft's aggression once the inevitable reprisals came. This type of war, whereby the company's property was destroyed and its ostensible customers and suppliers were exterminated, was bad for business.

When news of his actions was reported to Amsterdam by dissatisfied colonists, Kieft was swiftly recalled. Leading colonists also fired off strident missives demanding a greater say in the affairs of the colony and corporate outpost. Moreover, they petitioned the States General for a civil governing structure similar to that in place in towns in the Netherlands, that is, a responsible government independent of the company.

Kieft's replacement would be given the task of returning the settlement of New Netherland and the town of New Amsterdam to profitability. The new governor faced two incompatible visions: to stockholders, the company was a commercial enterprise to generate profit; to the inhabitants of New Netherland, the settlement was their home, and they wanted someone to organize and regulate their society. New Amsterdam had always been run as a company town, with restrictions on what people could do, how they could make a living, where they could live, what goods they could purchase or import or export, what services they could employ and so on. Taxes were high and services meagre. The company feared the unregulated and uncontrolled actions of its employees. Relaxing the rules, however preferable that would have been to the colonists, was not in the company's immediate interest. The man the Nineteen sent out to replace Kieft as governor of the ultimate company town was himself, not surprisingly, the ultimate company man.

· 4 ·

PIETER STUYVESANT WAS A SERIOUS, INTELLIGENT MAN with squinty eyes and an imperious demeanour. His clean-shaven, fleshy face was dominated by a protuberant nose and a large, blocky chin. In his famous portrait, he stares defiantly, his balding head covered with a tight, dark cap, long locks of curly hair dangling to his shoulders and his lumpy face set off by a starched white collar wrapped tightly around his neck. The attire we see defined his personality and his approach to life: rigid, unyielding, self-righteous and stern. Proud of his university education—a rare occurrence in those days—he was an admirer of culture and education, and preferred the Latin form of his name, Petrus, instead of the plain Pieter. Stuyvesant carried on a voluminous correspondence with one of his friends entirely in verse. He was not a man to back away from his life's harsh obstacles or realities; he never let setbacks get in the way of his objectives, even when those setbacks were as dire as having his right leg blasted off by a Spanish cannonball at the age of thirty-two. He would come to be defined by the silver-banded wooden peg leg that replaced the one he lost in service to the company, which he would loyally serve for most of his adult life.

Stuyvesant was born around 1612 in a tiny town in the flat farmland of Friesland, in the northern Netherlands. Although his father was a stern Calvinist clergyman, the young Stuyvesant strayed from the strict morality of his upbringing while attending the University of Franeker. Seducing his landlord's daughter (or some similar scandal) forced Stuyvesant's departure before he had taken a degree in philosophy. Undaunted, and with irrepressible energy, he immediately cast about for suitable venues for his talent and ambition. At that time, the tall ships crowding the harbour of Amsterdam, their masts and sails stretching skyward, were departing and arriving daily from distant places all over the world. The young man chose the West India Company, enlisting as a lowly clerk. Aboard a ship for the first time in his life, he sailed away to the Caribbean Sea. His officers, impressed with Stuyvesant's zeal, energy and devotion to duty, quickly promoted him as he moved about the company's holdings. He specialized in logistics, communication and transportation between Brazil, the Caribbean and New Amsterdam. Combining natural leadership qualities with a lack of deference to authority, Stuyvesant both gained followers and made enemies. Fortunately for him his chief enemy, Jan Claeszoon van Campen, the senior military and political officer of the company's Caribbean operations, died in 1642. Stuyvesant, just thirty years of age, assumed van Campen's position as governor of Aruba, Bonaire and Curaçao (the Dutch West India Company's American headquarters).

In April 1644 Stuyvesant led a fleet of twelve battleships carrying more than a thousand troops across Caribbean waters to the Spanish-held island of St. Martin, part of the Antilles chain near Puerto Rico. The island had been wrested from the West India Company's control several years earlier during the ongoing struggle between the decaying Spanish Empire and the emerging Dutch Republic, a conflict that also involved the English, French and Portuguese. In recent decades this Caribbean struggle had dwarfed even the battles between these same powers in Indonesia. Great fleets had sallied forth from Europe, disgorging armies of disciplined troops onto American shores. In 1630 a Dutch fleet of 67 ships carrying 1,170 cannons and 7,000 men arrived off Pernambuco (now Recife, Brazil) and

swiftly conquered it. During the following years, the West India
Company conquered numerous other Portuguese strongholds
and extended its control of Brazil's northeastern coast. Another
great battle, the siege of Bahia, involved a Portuguese fleet of
86 ships and over 12,000 troops. Chaos ruled as the struggle
for dominance continued throughout the mid-seventeenth century. Trade and travel were undertaken at the mercy of unruly
privateers, pirates and national navies. The stakes were high:
control over the plantation economies of Brazil and the Caribbean, combined with control over the slave trade from West
Africa, was a potent cocktail for profit—provided one could
ignore or justify the resulting terrible cost in human misery.
The conditions for the average sailor were ridiculously harsh:
disease-ridden, malnourished wretches died by the thousands
in the tropical heat and malaria-infested harbours. Stuyvesant
saw it all, and used his iron will to command order from this
chaos. He connived to supplant his adversaries while simultaneously squeezing profits from the land owned by the company,
using the vast numbers of slaves brought from West Africa to
Brazil. With the free labour being provided by the slave force,
the company traded in sugar, salt, horses, tobacco and dyewood,
as well as plundering Spanish treasure galleons.

In his April 1644 assault on St. Martin, Stuyvesant was not
lucky. Spies had informed him that the Spanish forces on the
island were sparse and ill-prepared. After landing his company
troops and buttressing their fortifications on the beach below
the Spanish fortress, he demanded the Spaniards' immediate
surrender. They had no intention of surrendering; indeed, they
had been recently reinforced and supplied, and responded with
vigorous cannon blasts. Stuyvesant nevertheless ordered his
men to the attack, digging in their cannons for a long siege. As
the impetuous commander clambered up on the earthen ram-
parts of his defence to urge his men on to greater glory against

the hated Spanish, a cannonball from the fort hurled through the gunpowder-clouded air towards him and smashed into his right leg below the knee, shattering it. Collapsing to the ground in agony, Stuyvesant nevertheless ordered the continuation of the siege. But it was hopeless. His men were driven back, and his mangled body was carted back to his ship, where a surgeon probed the ghastly wound. It did not look good. The leg would have to go.

Seventeenth-century surgical techniques provided little comfort or assurance of success. Without the advantage of targeted anaesthetic, and armed with unsanitized saws and knives, surgeons relied on speed and a great deal of luck when amputating limbs. Death was as likely an outcome as success, particularly in the West Indies, where the stifling humidity and scorching heat provided a ripe environment for infection. Stuyvesant pulled through—as much a testament to his iron will as to the surgeon's skill. Delirious and feverish after the procedure, he nevertheless wrote to his superiors in the West India Company: "Honorable, Wise, Provident, and Most Prudent Lords," he began, before informing them that he "did not succeed so well as I had hoped, no small impediment having been the loss of my right leg, it being removed by a rough ball." The "small impediment," as he put it, would not let him focus on his administrative tasks, though he tried his damnedest to ignore the infernal pain and sickening pus of the raw stump, which was wrapped in stained and damp bandages. The wound was not healing properly, so Stuyvesant's physicians advised him to return to a more temperate climate before infection set in. Reluctantly he agreed, leaving his post as head of operations in the Caribbean. He had been in charge for less than a year, and he feared for his career; departing in August, he arrived in Amsterdam in December 1644, after a dreadful voyage spent in fever and pain.

Back in Holland, in the home of his sister and brother-in-law, his injury began to heal. The household also included his brother-in-law's sister, Judith Bayard, the thirty-seven-year-old daughter of a Calvinist minister, who took on the role of nurse during his convalescence. By that age in her life, she was considered a spinster and had probably given up all hope of marriage, but Stuyvesant fell in love with her. She did, after all, speak several languages; she was a fine singer and had a cultivated taste in music and fashionable dress instincts. The couple were married after less than a year, in August 1645, and prepared for a life together in the New World. This time, though, Stuyvesant would take up a new challenge farther north: he would be the director-general of New Netherland, where the Dutch West India Company hoped he would quell the disturbing push for independent government and deal with the mess left by Willem Kieft. The company was impressed with Stuyvesant's devotion to duty and his heroic sacrifice of a leg for them; but he was also a man not inclined to question the natural order of things, and they knew where his loyalties lay. The Nineteen felt a stronger director-general would put a halt to the ever-increasing letters of dissent reaching the States General, as the colonists—many of them their own employees—agitated for political rights. The company planned to fight for its monopoly rather than give in. For his own part, Stuyvesant apparently learned to view the loss of his leg as a clarion call to fulfilling his destiny: surely he had been spared probable death because the Lord had a greater purpose for him.

In August 1647, from the deck of their ship, Stuyvesant and Judith spied the place they would call home for the remainder of their lives. From afar, New Amsterdam appeared to be a quaint town of windmills, gabled roofs and sprawling farms. But the pretty picture of the growing town concealed a rot that threatened to tear the place apart. It was a shambles, one that might have caused a man of lesser moral certainty to quail. But Stuyvesant . . . was Stuyvesant. It was his duty and a challenge to set this place right.

The after-effects of Kieft's "land-destroying and people-expelling wars" were everywhere to be seen. The hundreds of soldiers and indigent colonists, employees of the company, wandered about aimlessly. Their ramshackle dwellings littered the muddy streets and clogged the interior courtyard of the dilapidated Fort Amsterdam. Stuyvesant wrote that the fort was "resembling more a mole hill than a fortress, without gates, the walls and bastions trodden underfoot by men and cattle" that wandered freely, grazing through the compound and settlement. There was no proper dock, and drinking establishments had sprouted like mushrooms after a rainstorm. The people, like their settlement, had "grown very wild and loose in their morals."

Although he had planned to completely reorganize and reform the colony in three years and then move on to his next assignment, Stuyvesant, soon known in New Amsterdam as "the General," was to rule there for the next seventeen years. He made many changes, ushering the ramshackle outpost through its time of growing pains and into a thriving settlement. He enacted laws forbidding the sale of liquor on Sundays, introduced fines for knife fighting and imposed strict penalties for other misdemeanours and crimes. His punishments usually involved incarceration, hard labour and a diet of bread and water. The punishment for two sailors found ashore after failing to return to their ship on time was "to be chained for three consecutive months to a wheelbarrow or a handbarrow and put to the hardest labour, strictly on bread and water."

Stuyvesant issued edicts and ordinances to clean the filthy community and to establish official streets, eliminating the winding, uneven alleys and serpentine goat paths by moving houses and realigning property lines. He set speed limits for wagons and paved the major thoroughfares with cobblestones. He then set his eyes on the unruly and "ubiquitous hogs," cattle, goats and horses that roamed the community at will, foraging from the garbage that was strewn liberally in the streets. Residents were soon fined for tossing their "rubbish, filth, ashes, oyster-shells, dead animals or anything like it" into the newly cleaned and straightened streets. Butchers could no longer fling the offal from carcasses out their front doors; animal dung had to be cleaned up by the owner of the animal that produced it; and outhouses were ordered cleaned and maintained so that the cess no longer overflowed, because it "not only creates a great stench and therefore great inconvenience to the passers-by, but also makes the streets foul and unfit for use."

"The General" outlawed wooden chimneys and thatched roofs, established fire wardens, mandated leather firefighting buckets to be placed at strategic street corners and required "genuine Amsterdam ells, measures and weights to be used in all commercial exchanges." He created a monetary system that included a standard value for wampum shells and made it illegal not to accept them as legal tender. Stuyvesant then established official market days on Tuesdays and Saturdays, organized a jail and police patrol and created official garbage dumps. Not yet done, he ordered the construction of a great dock for unloading and loading ships' cargoes. But he also resisted establishing poor relief, refused to finance orphanages and hospitals and would not mandate public schools, despite the great demand. Stuyvesant did, however, liberally use public funds to maintain and enlarge the fort and the church, and he ordered that a great ditch or planked canal be run through the town. Although there was much grumbling about changing the old ways, Stuyvesant undoubtedly made the town a better place to live.

It was his paternalistic authoritarian style that irritated people the most; he made decisions and enacted taxes, sometimes unpopular ones, without consultation or warning. To many he was nothing other than the head of the company, a man who looked after its needs first and foremost, which was to a certain extent true: Stuyvesant was loyal and steadfast in protecting his employer's interests, but not exclusively so. Many of his improvements to the settlement and the colony cost money, money that otherwise could have been sent back to the company's headquarters as profit. Perhaps most galling to the colonists, however, was his maintenance and enforcement of the company's monopoly in all the colonists' trade activities, including their dealings with the native peoples. The place could not thrive with these shackles on human initiative, many complained.

When it was suggested that only company employees should be forced to obey the regulations of the director-general and his hand-picked council, Stuyvesant fumed. "We derive our authority from God and the West India Company, not from the pleasure of a few ignorant subjects," he coolly informed them. Another commentator observed wryly that anyone who openly opposed Stuyvesant "hath as much as the sun and moon against him." The director-general was prone to violent rages and threatening tantrums when anyone challenged him, and some colonists believed he was slightly mad or unhinged, so strong were his passions and his desire to keep power to himself. Passionate also about his religion, he went to great lengths to curtail religious freedom in the company's colony and to compel the inhabitants to observe the tenets of the Dutch Reformed Church. His policies targeted and persecuted Jews, Lutherans, Baptists and Quakers until the company directors in Amsterdam, belatedly responding to public opinion, demanded that he accommodate other views, in keeping with the tolerant practice in the Dutch Republic at the time.

For years Stuyvesant deftly strode a narrow line regarding
the obvious conflict of interest between his company, his country and the colonists. He relished his position of authority, the
respect it bestowed, the money it brought him and the lifestyle
it enabled. For seventeen years he managed this balancing act
with a firm hand, pushing the colony forward with one hand
and holding it back with the other. Only a man of Stuyvesant's
mettle, unflinching and wily in the ways of managing people,
could have held it all together for so long—running a colony
of thousands of people, with their unfathomable and complex
dreams, ambitions and schemes, and containing them by using
the governing structure of a joint stock corporation. Over the
years, however, an ever-increasing number of the colonists were
no longer directly employed by the company, and these people
resented its power over their lives.

Stuyvesant's efforts regarding the freedom and rights of
New Amsterdam's inhabitants, however, were noteworthy in
illustrating his lack of enthusiasm—his obstruction, resistance
and continuous conflict with his "subjects." He preferred the
time-tested military dictatorship model, tempered with the
type of corporate efficiency that worked wonders in the African slave trade and other company operations farther south.
The trouble began with the first speech he made after he and his
entourage, including several advisers and three shiploads of soldiers, stepped ashore. Festooned in breastplate with his sword
belted at the hip, his stump thrust defiantly to his side, Stuyvesant addressed the assembled townsfolk, informing them of his
plans for the settlement, the company settlement. He would
treat them "as a father to his children, for the advantages of the
Privileged West India Company, the Burghers, and the Country"—presumably in that order; and presumably they would
learn to see the wisdom of his ways.

· 5 ·

ADRIAEN VAN DER DONCK FIRST CAME TO NEW NETH-
erland in 1641 as a recently graduated lawyer, about twenty-two
years of age. He had completed his degree at the University of
Leiden, an intellectual centre at the heart of the philosophical
and legal debate surrounding the Dutch Republic's efforts to
throw off the Spanish yoke. It was the Netherlands' Golden Age,
and the republic's worldliness and prosperity conspired to ease
the rigid bonds of conservative society and admit new ideas and
ways of doing things. A swift talker and superb self-promoter,
van der Donck had talked his way into a respectable position as
a sort of travelling sheriff and prosecutor for Kiliaen van Rensselaer, the patron of the enormous semi-independent estate of
Rensselaerwyck, up the Hudson River near present-day Albany.
The kind-eyed idealist imagined that he would be the upholder
of justice in the far-flung, sparsely populated regions of van
Rensselaer's estate, a dispenser of law to the people.

His employer, however, had other notions. Van der Donck
travelled around the estate, granted by the Nineteen under a
special licence, revelling in its beauty and natural splendour. He
frequently took matters into his own hands without consulting
his employer, who remained in Europe. He chose a new farm
site for himself, dismissing the one assigned to him, refused to
collect rent from tenants he considered too poor to pay and did
not bother cracking down on the black-market sales of beaver
skins that provided much-needed income to the estate's impoverished tenant farmers. Van Rensselaer admonished van der
Donck in letters, pointing out that his duty was "to seek my
advantage and protect me against loss," not to champion the
interests of the settlers. "From the beginning you have acted
not as officer but as director," van Rensselaer complained. But
he was far away—indeed, he had never visited his estate in New
Netherland and had no intention to do so—and van der Donck

continued as he saw fit. But when his three-year term ended, van Rensselaer did not renew it. Van der Donck packed up and moved south to New Amsterdam to seek his fortune in the true heart of the Dutch colony.

Van der Donck loved his new home. He acquired a large tract of land north of Manhattan, on the mainland, married a young English woman named Mary and began to hire people to farm the land for him. He continued his studies of the local native peoples and the flora and fauna and eventually published his knowledge and opinions in *A Description of New Netherland*. Most importantly, though, he earned a reputation as a troublemaker. He hired himself out to represent people in legal matters against the Dutch West India Company. He was arrogant, outspoken and tenacious. He ingratiated himself with the governor, Willem Kieft, on the one hand, hiring out his services as a lawyer to help run the colony, while on the other hand he took an ever more prominent role in crafting what became the increasingly tenacious letters of protest to the States General in The Hague, advocating rights for individuals "according to the custom in Holland." He fought for a permanent council of advisers and was soon advocating for Kieft's removal from office.

During this time, while Kieft blithely destroyed years of the New Amsterdam colonists' hard work and decades of reasonably stable relations with the native peoples, van der Donck stumbled upon what would become his life's work: the need for responsible political representation for the people. "As it was," writes Russell Shorto in his history of New Netherland, *The Island at the Center of the World*, "there was no judicial system; or rather, the system was Kieft. There was no body of case law; he settled disputes however he chose. There was no appeal. Kieft and the other directors of the colony weren't given a mandate to oversee the establishment of a political and legal system; instead, the company shipped them off with a single tool: military dictatorship." While this government by corporate dictate had its merits for far-flung commercial outposts perched on the rim of strange and dangerous foreign lands, New Amsterdam had already evolved beyond this narrow corporate outpost style and was, according to Shorto, "fast becoming a full-fledged society." It begged for a governing structure free from the iron grip of the Dutch West India Company. Kieft's great concession to inclusive government was to appoint a two-member governing council that would represent the people's interests: one member he personally chose from the citizens, the other was himself. One of the members of this new council was given two votes, whereas the other had only a single vote. It is not hard to guess who Kieft appointed to the position with two votes. And, with decisions being carried by majority vote, Kieft's council of advisers was little more than a joke, an insult to the people whom he and the company considered to be little more than serfs. The mediaeval political structure of the colony was one that could no longer contain the expanding spirit of the community.

Like many in the growing body of settlers who wanted to make their home in America, van der Donck was annoyed at the poor state of the settlement. It was clearly failing to achieve its potential on many levels. The idealist had found an outlet for his passion for the new land and his belief in the freedom of peoples to determine the course of their own future, ideals that had been instilled in him during his university years in Leiden. As Dutch citizens, were the settlers not entitled to the same legal rights here as in Holland? No other monopoly trading outpost had ever been concerned with these issues, since most were staffed by employees serving out their time before returning home. In New Amsterdam, most of the residents really wanted to stay and make the new land their home, and the disgruntled masses of merchants, tradespeople and farmers found their voice in van der Donck. But the company had powerful representation in the government and was not about to let its monopoly be so easily challenged. The problem would be solved, the Nineteen reasoned, not by more autonomy but by a firmer hand.

In the days and weeks after Stuyvesant first strode from his ship in August 1647, he immediately began his overhaul of the company settlement. He made New Amsterdam—the regional corporate headquarters, as he saw it—into a valuable asset. He also set about dealing with the problem of the treasonous fellows who had been drafting documents calling for greater self-government in the colony. Throughout much of Stuyvesant's reign, the young lawyer van der Donck was a thorn in his side. Van der Donck and Stuyvesant—who were only eight years apart in age—did not start out as enemies; indeed, van der Donck initially ingratiated himself with his stern new boss. The community was small, and everyone lived within walking distance of each other, so good relations were necessary to smooth the conduct of daily business. Van der Donck was very proficient in English, his wife being from England, and helped Stuyvesant in his dealings with the bordering English colonies— an important service because by the 1640s, New Amsterdam was emerging as the central hub of North American shipping, even functioning as the entrepôt for the English colonies to the south and north.

By 1648 van der Donck and his co-agitators had persuaded Stuyvesant to accept some limits to his absolute authority and succeeded in securing from Stuyvesant a board of nine advisers to help guide the director's decisions regarding the common good of the colony. Van der Donck revealed his true affiliations and long-time involvement in the politics of reform only after Stuyvesant confirmed his post on the board. He became the president of the council and devoted himself to politicking for its cause, travelling to the outlying farms and villages, meeting merchants in taverns and strolling the harbour to discuss business with ship captains. While building support and learning about the desires and wishes of the citizens, van der Donck was also compiling a list of grievances in a tract advocating civil rights for the residents of New Amsterdam. These sentiments ran deep in the Dutch tradition of responsible municipal government, one that was free from arbitrary taxes, corruption and political and mercantile favouritism. A proud man like Stuyvesant made co-operation difficult, however; his ultimate responsibility was to the company. The situation created obvious conflicts over which common good had to be served.

Van der Donck wanted the Dutch government to take over the settlement, effectively ending company rule. There were two opposing driving forces within the Dutch Republic at this time. Stuyvesant represented one force: the merchant kings, the slavers and the warriors, men who could be brutal expansionists, loyal to their company and country and frequently confusing the two loyalties in their quest for dominance over global trade and their commercial and military war against the hated English, Spanish and Portuguese. Van der Donck represented the other force: the thoughtful, Renaissance-inspired philosophers and legal thinkers who championed natural law and the rights of individuals to self-determination. His position was naturally at odds with Stuyvesant's ultimate job: to run New Netherland for the financial benefit of distant shareholders. Citizens' rights occupied a second tier at best.

The friction between the two men grew as the years passed. Stuyvesant even considered van der Donck's behaviour treasonous; he could not understand why van der Donck persisted in writing petitions and holding public meetings after he had been given a prominent position on the governing board. He understood the world in terms of power, and thus thought van der Donck wanted to depose him and claim the power for himself.

Van der Donck was equally baffled by Stuyvesant's intransigence and increasing animosity. "These persons had been good and dear friends with him always," van der Donck claimed, "and he, shortly before, had regarded them as the most honourable, able, intelligent and pious men of the country, yet as soon as they did not follow the General's wishes they were this and that, some of them rascals, liars, rebels, usurers and spendthrifts, in a word this and that, hanging was almost too good for them."

Stuyvesant had van der Donck arrested and expelled him from the council, keeping him in jail while deliberating over the matter of the "mutinous and insulting" actions of the board. He had charged van der Donck with treason, a crime warranting the death penalty. The stakes had been raised, and no one was going to back down. Stuyvesant, however, released van der Donck when he realized that too many prominent people in the community opposed him. If Stuyvesant blatantly flouted Dutch law, he could be denounced as a tyrant. But as soon as van der Donck was released, he went back to work agitating for citizens' rights. Civil rights were in the spirit of the age: in 1648 peace had been declared throughout Europe, ending the Thirty Years' War, and Spain had officially recognized Dutch independence. The need for the West India Company to be a licensed syndicate for piracy was greatly decreased—in fact, it was now illegal—and having a corporate military-style governor over one of the republic's greatest colonies was beginning to be seen as an anachronism. The company was, after all, chartered primarily to tap private capital in the assault on Spanish shipping in the Caribbean.

On July 26, 1649, van der Donck and the councillors signed the "Petition of the Commonality of New Netherland" and he put the final touches on the "Remonstrance," an eighty-three-page formal complaint grounded in legal principles that were the foundation of the Dutch Republic. The latter was van der Donck's crowning achievement, the culmination of years of work. He and two other members of the council sailed across the Atlantic and presented their case to the Dutch government in The Hague. Van der Donck spoke eloquently during his "Address to the High and Mighty Lords States General of the United Netherlands, by the People of the New Netherland." He claimed that the settlement had been crushed, smothered and held back by the incompetence and corruption of the West India Company and that the people should be brought under the authority of national government to alleviate the "very poor and most low" state it was now in. Stuyvesant, he claimed, was a "vulture destroying the prosperity of New Netherland" and was reviled by "all the permanent inhabitants, the merchant, the burgher and peasant, the planter, the labouring man, and also the man in service." The colony had not reached its potential, and would not, unless the people were granted economic freedom and local government and lower taxes. The English colonies, he pointed out, were "fully aware that our country is better than theirs," but with the company in charge, stifling growth and development, "it will lose even the name of New Netherland, and no Dutchman will have anything to say there." The "Remonstrance" complained of the lack of schoolhouses, churches, orphanages and other government services, which the company would not supply. The company, the petition claimed, should be stripped of all authority because "this country will never flourish under the Honorable Company's government."

Prompted by the "Remonstrance," the States General took action in 1650 with a provisional order to the West India Company to create a more liberal form of government, in accordance with the Dutch tradition, and to encourage more immigration, which the company had restricted. Meanwhile, van der Donck went to great effort to generate positive interest in the colony such that "formerly New Netherland was never spoken of, and now heaven and earth seem to be stirred up by it and every one tries to be the first in selecting the best pieces of land there." Two years later, in 1652, the States General ordered the company, despite its arguments and connections to powerful individuals, to set up a functioning and responsible municipal government. Stuyvesant was commanded to return to Holland in order to answer for his actions. Van der Donck was to personally deliver the States General's letter to Stuyvesant when he returned, after years away from his home and family, and his position on the board of nine was to be reinstated.

· 6 ·

IT WAS A MONUMENTAL AND EPOCHAL DECISION, ONE that could have changed the history of North America and the world, but for the vicissitudes of war. Before van der Donck could sail across the Atlantic, Dutch and English fleets clashed in the English Channel. It was the beginning of the First Anglo-Dutch War, which was fought mostly over global trade. The Dutch West India Company, now holding the upper hand, persuaded the States General to rescind its earlier directive. With Holland fearing an English invasion, freedom, long dreamed of in New Netherland, was again denied. "Van der Donck's activism," Russell Shorto writes, "which only weeks before had been lauded as the full flowering of Dutch legal progressivism being applied, in a test case, to the nation's overseas province, suddenly looked positively dangerous." The company's charter was not revoked, and Stuyvesant was not recalled. With a war starting, the company's original purpose, as an agent to fight foreign enemies, was significant once again. But the States General did at least uphold the requirement for the company to establish a functioning municipal council.

The Nineteen, vindictive in their victory, took advantage of the situation. They refused to allow van der Donck to return to

New Netherland—after all, the colony had been reaffirmed as their monopoly preserve, and he was a troublemaker who had nearly cost them their charter and their power. Only after much negotiation was he granted a passport to return to his home and family, at the end of 1653, and only after he had renounced the right to play a role in government and agreed to give up practising law in the North American colony forever. The company would allow him to live in its corporate holding so long as he was neutered. His cause seemed forever lost; van der Donck described himself as "wholly disheartened and cast down."

After crossing the Atlantic, he continued agitating for civil rights, but behind the scenes. Stuyvesant had to take action on some reforms, such as collecting standard business licence fees, filling official government positions like that of sheriff and building an official city hall. Given the war in Europe and the resulting potential for an attack on New Amsterdam, Stuyvesant also ordered work to commence on a great palisade wall that stretched over seven hundred metres around the old fort and eventually gave rise to Wall Street. In spite of these initiatives, the citizens felt that the company was too tight with its purse strings when it came not just to municipal but also to military infrastructure. The settlement's defences were poor, and Stuyvesant knew this well, but even his frequent demands to the company's directors for more troops, ships and equipment went unheeded. These things cost money, and they were not to be approved without imminent need. The colonists knew they were under-defended and frequently complained about the situation, but Stuyvesant, though sympathetic, was caught in the middle. Fortunately for New Netherland, the war never reached North America; a peace treaty with England was signed in 1654.

The conflict between the colonists and the company, however, continued. Stuyvesant had not given the limited municipal government any taxing authority, so it depended on the company to fund its civic initiatives. The company and the municipal government jointly ran the colony, but the partnership was not a happy one. Edwin G. Burrows and Mike Wallace write in *Gotham: A History of New York City to 1898* that the two incompatible councils, one representing the people, the other the company, were "constantly bickering over precedence and maneuvering for petty advantages with no clear-cut division of duties between them." The company feared any changes to its profitable arrangement and wanted the colony to remain a factory centre, a corporate holding, rather than becoming an independent colony. After all, it had started the colony decades earlier and saw no need for any independent institutional structure. Whenever the Dutch Republic was at peace, however, the commercial government became an anachronism, and the demands of the permanent population of non-employees grew more strident.

"To cast the struggle between the West India Company and the leaders of the commonality in terms of a contest between the forces of tyranny and the forces of democracy," writes Thomas J. Condon in his book *New York Beginnings,* "or between a grasping commercial company and a struggling group of freemen, fails to do justice to the dimensions of the historical problem involved." But while the company was not entirely malevolent, its greatest failing was that it did not engender any sense of loyalty in the colonists. Many of the settlers were not even Dutch-speaking—some were born in North America, others were fleeing the oppressive societies of New England with their grim theocratic laws and world view. Others yet were from Germany, France or other places in Europe. It has been said that eighteen different languages were spoken in the early Manhattan settlement. One of the results of this multicultural gathering was that the people's loyalty was fluid and difficult both to contain and to direct, being pulled in so many different directions.

In outsourcing civic responsibility for its citizens to a monopoly corporation, the States General of the United Provinces of the Netherlands paid the price in lost loyalty. The colonists were not loyal to the company, particularly since it was headquartered across a vast ocean, in the same way that they were loyal to their community. They felt betrayed by their nation, which continued to foist an unwanted, perhaps even hated, corporation upon them, and they lost the will to fight their nation's enemy. So, when Colonel Richard Nicolls and the English frigates threatened New Amsterdam in 1664, the colonists had little interest in resisting. They did not want to lay down their lives, endanger the lives of their families or gamble their farms or businesses in defence of an obstructionist monopoly, and perhaps die or lose their property to defend the interests of the West India Company and its domineering governor, Stuyvesant. This was particularly so when the English seemed to promise them many of the things for which they had unsuccessfully fought the Dutch company over the years.

On September 8, 1664, Stuyvesant and his small garrison, compelled by the will of the people, marched out of Fort Amsterdam with their "drums beating and colors flying" and formally surrendered to Nicolls and the English force. The Dutch company troops boarded ships and soon set off for Europe, leaving England as the uncontested political power in the erstwhile Dutch colony. Nicolls, the new political master, toured his new holding, pleased with his accomplishment—he had taken the entire colony without firing a single shot, giving England jurisdiction over not only the former New Netherland but the entire east coast of North America. He promptly announced that, henceforth, Fort Amsterdam would be called Fort James; Fort Orange, inland along the Hudson River, would be known as Fort Albany; and the town of New Amsterdam, and indeed all of New Netherland, would now be New

York. When he heard the news, King Charles II of England wrote to his sister in France, "You will have heard of our taking New Amsterdam. 'Tis a place of great importance . . . we have got the better of it and 'tis now called New York." At that time the entire colony had a population of about nine thousand, of which several thousand lived in New Amsterdam on Manhattan Island.

Less than a year later, in February 1665, Charles II declared war on the United Provinces, using the now decades-old massacre at Ambon as the rallying cry. This was the start of the Second Anglo-Dutch War. The two nations' great fleets geared up for another round of battles, and Stuyvesant received a perfunctory order from the Nineteen to return immediately to Europe. He must have known he was being set up to take the blame for the ignominious surrender of New Netherland to the English, and he took defensive action. When he boarded the ship for Amsterdam, the erstwhile director-general had armed himself with documents attesting to his character as "an honest proprietor and patriot of the province and a supporter of the reformed religion." The community leaders of the Commonality of New Netherlands, his legal jousting partners for the past decade, had decided to let bygones be bygones and came together to jointly defend their surrender to the English. Capitulation, they claimed, had been their only option: "The Honourable Petrus Stuyvesant, then Director-General of New Netherland did, immediately on the arrival and sojourn of the English frigates, employ every possible means to encourage and animate the Burghers of the City of New Amsterdam and the people of the outvillages, especially on Long Island, to all possible resistance; certainly, to defend the city and fort of New Amsterdam as long as it was capable of defence, but that neither the one nor the other could be prevailed on to do so, because it was impossible, with any hope of a good result."

Nevertheless, when Stuyvesant stalked off the ship in Amsterdam, the West India Company publicly accused him of cowardice and incompetence, and blamed him for the loss of the colony to the English. These accusations he vehemently rebutted in the States General. The company he had served his entire adult life had turned on him, claiming that he had "allowed himself to be rode over by Clergymen, women and cowards, in order to surrender to the English what he could defend with reputation, for the sake of thus saving their private properties." As it had done with van der Donck, the company denied Stuyvesant the right to return to its corporate landholding across the Atlantic, keeping him in exile from his wife and children and from the place he had come to regard as his home. Whether he appreciated the irony of his predicament is not known. When he finally did win from the States General his right to return, Stuyvesant retreated to his farm on Manhattan Island and retired from public life to a quiet, respectable prosperity with Judith and their children. During the seventeen years he ruled the vast tract of North America for his corporate masters, he had come to realize that his interest no longer lay with the West India Company or with Holland. He lived for four more years in New York, until his death in 1672 at the age of sixty.

At the Treaty of Breda that ended the Anglo-Dutch war in 1674, the States General gave up the right to reclaim New Netherland from England in favour of regaining Surinam (Dutch Guiana), which English forces had recently captured; slaves and sugar plantations were of greater value to the company at the time. In the bargain the Dutch Republic also gained the nutmeg island of Run, which the VOC had recently conquered from the English and wanted to keep. What was to become the most famous city in the world was bargained away for a tiny and barren nutmeg island in Indonesia and some

South American slave-dependent sugar plantations. Almost a century later, in 1764, the original Dutch West India Company collapsed under its debt load. After refinancing and reorganizing, it soldiered on until 1791, when the Dutch government assumed its stock and the authority over its remaining territorial possessions in the Caribbean and South America.

ALTHOUGH HAUGHTY, stubborn and protective of his authority, Pieter Stuyvesant was not a violent man. He appears to have cared for the people of New Netherland and was sympathetic to their needs, but he believed they needed a firm hand and were not to be trusted with responsibility or authority. He made New Amsterdam a clean, orderly and lawful place, but restricted trade and immigration so that its population grew slowly compared with that of the surrounding English colonies. Overly regulated, its citizens never fully unleashed their potential. Although he had the interests of the community at heart, Stuyvesant remained a corporate director, ultimately beholden to his masters and the shareholders. It must have been difficult, balancing his obligations to the company, the legal owners of the entire colony, and the people whom he regarded increasingly as his compatriots.

He could never fully embrace either obligation. In the early years, the colony needed a man of forceful character to bang it into shape, but Stuyvesant was too proud, irascible and stubborn to know when it was time for him to step down. He was hampered by his naturally conservative instincts and his loyalty to his employer, a company that seemed particularly blind to the implications of its policies in a global economic sense. For years the West India Company had restricted the colonists' freedoms and had never provided enough for their military defence. These quarrels between the citizens and the company had settled into a bitter resentment.

Oddly, before he surrendered New Netherland to the English, in the articles of transfer Stuyvesant insisted on a clause stipulating that the citizens "shall keep and enjoy the liberty of the consciences in religion" and other freedoms under the new English rule. As a result, New York under the English resembled the Dutch Republic in its cultural and religious tolerance and was not at all like the surrounding English colonies. The merchant king of New Netherland moulded New Amsterdam into a bustling, cosmopolitan port, ideally situated for future growth; at the same time, he sucked the life out of it by smothering it. Like a flame denied oxygen, New Amsterdam under the company's rule dwindled into smouldering coals until, enlivened by a fresh breeze, it became New York.

Jan Pieterszoon Coen, merchant and warrior, despised the English and fought ruthlessly to secure a monopoly in spices for the Dutch East India Company.

A volcano ominously erupts on Gunung Api in the Banda Islands, coinciding with the arrival of a Dutch East India Company fleet, in this early seventeenth-century engraving.

The famous port of Batavia, now called Jakarta, was founded by
Jan Pieterszoon Coen in 1619 because he despised the cloying,
fetid airs of Bantam where the Dutch East India Company
headquarters had been located.

The chaotic and
bustling spice markets
of the Moluccas
are depicted in this
seventeenth-century
engraving.

Pieter Stuyvesant, the stern and paternalistic director-general of the Dutch West India Company, ruled all of New Netherland from his fort in New Amsterdam from 1647 until he surrendered to the English in 1664.

't Fort nieuw Amsterdam op de Manhatans

One of the earliest engravings of the budding Dutch West India Company settlement of New Amsterdam on Manhattan Island, originally included in Adriaen van der Donck's *A Description of New Netherland*.

This 1664 colour print by Johannes Vingboons shows New Amsterdam at the moment of capture by English troops in September. The English renamed the town New York.

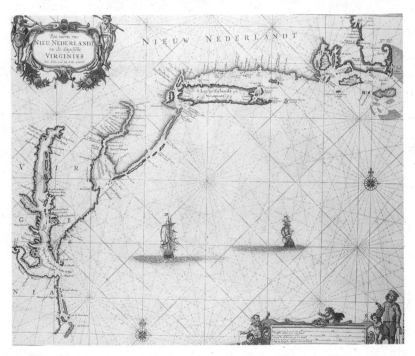

This 1667 *Chart of New Netherland and the English Virginias from Cape Cod to Cape Canrick* by Pieter Goos shows the region claimed by the Dutch West India Company as well as the English colonies to the north and south.

Robert Clive, the brilliant military genius who rose from being a clerk to lead the English East India Company to enormous territorial gains in the dying days of the Mughal Empire in the mid-eighteenth century, is shown in this classic painting by Sir Nathaniel Dance.

This mid-eighteenth century print titled *A Perspective View of Fort St. George on the Coromandel Coast, belonging to the East India Company*, shows one of the most important company trading and military outposts in India.

In this famous and somewhat fanciful eighteenth-century painting titled
Robert Clive and Mir Jafar after the Battle of Plassey, 1757, by Francis Hayman,
Clive is shown graciously negotiating for the future of Bengal and its
thirty million inhabitants. It was the first major territorial conquest of
the English East India Company.

Chapter 3

"Consider the situation in which the victory
of Plassey placed me. A great prince was dependent
on my pleasure; an opulent city lay at my mercy;
its richest bankers bid against each other for my smiles;
I walked through vaults which were thrown open
to me alone, piled on either hand with gold and
jewels. Mr. Chairman, at this moment I stand
astonished at my own moderation."

ROBERT CLIVE, C. 1772

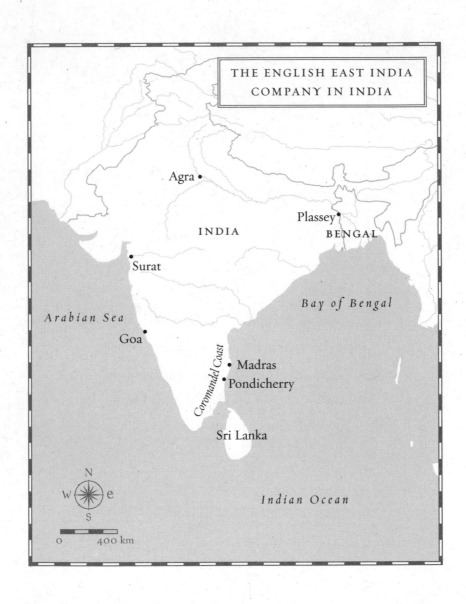

THE ENGLISH EAST INDIA
COMPANY IN INDIA

Agra

Plassey

BENGAL

INDIA

Surat

Arabian Sea

Bay of Bengal

Goa

Coromandel Coast

Madras

Pondicherry

Sri Lanka

N
W   E
S

Indian Ocean

0   400 km

Companies at War

· 1 ·

AFTER THE MASSACRE AT AMBON IN 1623, THE FOR-
tunes of the English East India Company stagnated. Panicked
English merchants throughout the East Indies now feared for
their lives: what would prevent the Dutch East India Company, the VOC, from instigating further atrocities or massacres
of the English? Although the hated Jan Pieterszoon Coen had
departed for Europe, who knew the mind of the new governor
general, Pieter de Carpentier? Within a few years virtually all
employees of the English company had fled the region, except
for a skeleton base at Bantam. This exodus, coupled with a general economic decline, caused shipping to and from the Eastern
markets to plummet by over 60 per cent. By the end of the
1630s the company, horribly in debt, began to sell off its assets,
ships and buildings. Only a modest trade with India sustained it
during these lean years.

Several years earlier, in the early 1600s, William Hawkins had led a diplomatic mission to the Mughal Emperor Jahangir, carrying a letter from England's King James 1 requesting the right to establish a trading outpost in Surat on India's northwest coast. The company's trade in India began slowly and tentatively, but throughout the seventeenth century trade with India kept ships busy, departing London for the East and returning with exotic cargoes. The start of the English Civil War in 1642 and the subsequent decade of unrest made maritime travel increasingly dangerous and was disastrous for commerce. Then, in 1649, Oliver Cromwell ordered King Charles 1 beheaded and proclaimed a commonwealth, and the company's royal charter ended. Soon rival traders began to outfit ships to sail to India. Cromwell urged the company to continue its shipbuilding and overseas trade, but without the benefit of a monopoly a decline in the company's fortune was inevitable. It struggled as Cromwell vigorously pursued legal claims against the VOC for the damage to English shipping stemming from the massacre at Ambon. He did, however, succeed in gaining 85,000 pounds in compensation for the company and 4,000 pounds for the families of the tortured and murdered English merchants.

In mid-January 1657 Sir William Cockayne, the governor of the company, convened a meeting of the remaining investors to highlight the company's unsound financial position. Revenue was down, with no near-term prospects for improvement. Expenses had been slashed but to no avail, and the company's debt was mounting. Cockayne proposed a liquidation of the remaining assets and a shutdown of the entire enterprise: "It is resolved to appoint a sale of the island, customs, houses and rights in the Indies." In previous years most of the valuable assets had already been sold off to sustain the waning business. The great fleets that once graced the Thames, bringing the heady spices, perfumes and textiles of the world to Europe, would cease to sail to those distant shores. Before the business could be wrapped up, though, Oliver Cromwell and his Council of State, startled into action by the imminent demise of one of the nation's premier business enterprises, drew up a new charter for the company, which passed on October 19.

But the company would not be the same organization. Although its monopoly would again be enforced and the company would again be exempt from the law forbidding the export from England of silver, the prime currency of the Eastern trade, its financial structure was to be more like that of the VOC: while it would be a joint stock enterprise, its capital would become permanent rather than temporary. Previously the company had been more like a shell organization that tried to coordinate a series of independent ventures, rather than a company as we know it today, with an overarching direction or strategy. Each expedition had been financed independently and had profited or lost independently. The bookkeeping was complicated, raising new capital for each ship that sailed was tedious, and competition among the company's own ships prevented the formation of a unified strategy against the VOC. If a profitable toehold was to be established for the Eastern trade, a structure similar to that of the Dutch company was needed, including the ability to use all available capital to pursue common goals, such as strong fortifications, co-operation between ships, the construction of joint factories and effective defence forces. To succeed, the new English East India Company would need both an organized strategy for logistics, support and defence and the money to finance it. The new corporate structure promised to solve these issues, and within months London investors had come up with over 750,000 pounds in new capital. For the first time in decades, the company's future looked bright.

When Cromwell died the following year, the charter was again thrown into limbo. But with the restoration of the monarchy two years later, the new king, Charles II, issued a new royal charter to the company, giving it extraordinary powers it had never possessed before—empowering it to wage war, administer justice, engage in diplomacy with foreign princes, acquire territories, raise and command armies and capture and plunder ships violating its monopoly. Like the VOC, the English East India Company had now acquired many of the powers of a state. Its mandate, however, was to deploy these new powers in the service of the shareholders rather than of the state. Though only a fraction of the VOC's size, the English company was now effectively a state within a state—at least, it could operate this way outside Europe.

The company prudently decided against pursuing a new private commercial war against the VOC in the Spice Islands and instead refocused on India, where it had enjoyed modest success. Spices would no longer be the primary goal of the enterprise— access to cheap spices direct from the source was controlled by the VOC, whereas India offered new and valuable commodities such as silks, indigo dye, cotton textiles and saltpetre, the vital ingredient in gunpowder that was in perpetual short supply in Europe and would drive the company's fortunes for over a century. Surat officially became the company's new headquarters, and the few remaining personnel in Bantam were transferred to Surat. Not that conflict between England and the Dutch Republic had ceased—only a few years later, in 1664, Richard Nicolls commanded Pieter Stuyvesant and the Dutch West India Company to hand over the city and port of New Amsterdam to English troops.

Throughout the remainder of the seventeenth century, the English company's trade and profits were modest but steady, and they increased with its time in India. By the early eighteenth century, the company had established three distinct "presidencies" in the Indian subcontinent: at Surat along the northwest coast, Madras along the central east coast and Calcutta in the northeast. The VOC had a strong presence in India, but the subcontinent was enormous and the Dutch company had no capacity to monopolize the commerce or even to war against its rivals. Although the two companies were engaged in some intrigue and squabbling over access to saltpetre, this was not direct warfare, as had occurred over spices.

Saltpetre—crystals formed in the earth from bacterial action on animal dung and urine, with the assistance of heat—formed with particular vigour in the sewage-sodden soils of the agricultural heartland of Bengal, around Calcutta, where the extraordinary heat and prolonged dry season produced great quantities of the highest quality. "East India," according to one seventeenth-century merchant, "gloryeth as much in this [saltpetre] as in its spices." By the end of the seventeenth century India was the primary source of supply for almost all of Europe, and by the eighteenth century many European companies had agents, warehouses and social or commercial relationships with the various saltpetre producers in India. Because of its heavy weight, saltpetre was used as ballast before ships set sail, and their other valuable cargo was piled on top.

Indian saltpetre to a large extent fuelled most of the European wars from the mid-seventeenth century through the eighteenth century. In *Rival Empires of Trade in the Orient, 1600–1800,* Holden Furber writes that throughout the second half of the seventeenth century and into the eighteenth century the English East India Company's "sales, with their steadily rising receipts from Bengal saltpetre, reflected an ever more warlike Europe." The historian Jagadish Narayan Sarkar comments in the *Indian Historical Quarterly* that "saltpetre was so much in demand in England that there was a standing order from the Company's authorities there for an annual supply." In spite of the wild price fluctuations for saltpetre (depending on the state of war), the English and Dutch companies reaped vast profits from their mercantile activities and paid huge dividends to their shareholders and taxes to their respective governments.

Competition intensified in the early eighteenth century. In addition to the Dutch and English East India companies, there were French, Danish, Swedish and Austrian companies vying for Indian saltpetre. Although they could never exclude the others as they had in Indonesia, for most of this time the Dutch dominated the industry. They had the largest warehouses, the most experienced people and the most efficient barge transport system (saltpetre was too heavy for overland transport). English factors, or company agents, recorded their predicament in the early days with a touch of jealousy: "The Dutch manage things better," wrote one wistful factor, while another claimed that "the Dutch are insolent and feare not to break all contracts."

Soon, however, another rival company for the India trade began operations in France. La Compagnie des Indes Orientales, chartered in 1664, had grown to prominence in southern India. By the early 1700s the French company had become entrenched in Chandernagore in west Bengal and Pondicherry along the Coromandel Coast, near the English company's outpost in Madras. The French, English and Dutch companies began challenging each other as the Mughal Empire's central authority waned. Their intrigues with Indian princes brought them to the edge of outright war. The crumbling of the Mughal Empire did, however, bring great opportunities for the European traders.

· 2 ·

YOUNG ROBERT CLIVE WAS NOT A GOOD STUDENT, AND his parents despaired for his future. A long line of modest landowners in Shropshire, the Clive family possessed an enormous, ancient manor house in need of repair, and Robert's father practised law to augment the estate's income. The family had high expectations for Robert, their oldest child. Born in 1725, he had five younger sisters and one younger brother. But their big brother proved to be an intractable prankster and was expelled from several prominent schools. A natural leader, audacious and brash, he dreamed up schemes to amuse himself and was drawn to the moral grey zone of society. On one occasion he organized a group of youths into a gangster-style protection scheme to extort money from shopkeepers.

Shrewd, self-satisfied and wry, Clive had a talent for sensing weakness in others and the confidence to act on his intuition, even when the odds seemed against him or the penalty for failure was extreme. He also possessed a strong sense of duty and loyalty to his comrades: for example, when the directors of the East India Company voted him a valuable ceremonial sword for his bravery, he refused to accept the gift unless his commanding officer was likewise honoured. Extremely generous and free with his money, he was a man to whom the normal rules of society did not seem to apply. He followed his own conscience and dealt with the consequences later. It would have been difficult to imagine that this impetuous and carefree youth, careless about the consequences of his actions and prone to questionable adventures, would one day establish the English East India Company's military and political supremacy over large parts of the Indian subcontinent and lay the foundation for the British Raj. The official portraits of Clive show him, in later years, decked out in the ceremonial regalia of a fabulously wealthy lord, weighted down with the responsibility of maintaining social standing. These portraits do not hint at the spark of unpredictable energy that animated his youthful exploits and won an empire for his employers.

At the age of seventeen, Clive was enlisted by his parents in the English East India Company to serve as a clerk overseas. It

was well known that fortunes could be made in this way, not by
serving as a clerk, but by the many more shady or semi-official
opportunities that lay outside the narrowly defined role of a
clerk. Survival was the wild card. Shipwreck, disease, misadven-
ture were very real threats—while the chance of going to an early
grave was less than it had been in the company's early days, it
was still considerable. Clive departed England in a small fleet of
company ships with a naval escort to sail past the coasts of France
and Spain, and witnessed one of his sister ships on the convoy
smash to pieces on the rocks near the Cape Verde Islands. Only
a small contingent of survivors were hauled from the surf. Not
long afterward, his own ship ran aground along the coast of Brazil. The damage was severe but no lives were lost, and the ship
had to be repaired from keel to masts during a nine-month delay.
Clive, gaining focus as he got older, did not waste this time in idle
diversions. He devoted himself to learning Portuguese, and was
quite fluent by the time he arrived in Madras on June 1, 1744,
nearly a year and a half after leaving home.

By the time of Clive's arrival, the English East India Company had thrived such that it had surpassed the Portuguese and
was soon to eclipse the Dutch East India Company as well. The
political situation in India was tense, partly as a result of ten-
sions in Europe. The second half of the seventeenth century and
the early eighteenth century saw a continuous series of conflicts
in Europe involving Sweden, Denmark, France, the Netherlands, Spain, Portugal, the Holy Roman Empire, Russia, Poland
and the Ottoman Empire in an endlessly shifting round of alliances. Scarcely a handful of years passed when a war was not
being fought somewhere on the continent. The Dutch Republic and France had been at war from 1672 to 1713, and French
commerce had taken a beating. But with the recent peace
between Holland and France, commercial activity expanded, as
did commercial jealousy, animosity and competition.

In 1705, after ruling for almost half a century, the Mughal emperor Aurangzeb died at the age of eighty-eight. The Mughal dynasty was descended from the Mongols, an invading force that had swept into India from Central Asia in the sixteenth century. Throughout that century, the Mughal armies marched and conquered, slowly extending their rule over most of what is now India, Pakistan and parts of Afghanistan. When Aurangzeb died, his empire began to disintegrate as local rulers who had chafed under his heavy-handed rule seized the opportunity to assert their independence. Central authority waned, and the imperial government was increasingly unable to maintain the peace. Travel and trade became more and more subject to the whims of local lords and bandits, and corruption ballooned as the hierarchy disintegrated. "In the absence of a strong government," writes Stephen R. Bown in *A Most Damnable Invention: Dynamite, Nitrates and the Making of the Modern World,* "the companies began to arm themselves and maintain small professional standing armies that they hired out to local rulers to settle regional power struggles."

After years of increasingly acrimonious squabbling, the French company, then headed by Joseph François Dupleix, sought to control India by building on the ruined foundation of the Mughal Empire. The historian Henry Dodwell writes, in *Dupleix and Clive: The Beginning of Empire,* "in Europe they [the companies] were mere private corporations; in India they were political entities . . . The real question at issue was whether or not to embark on a struggle which would determine the possession of India, but no one perceived this." The scene was set for epic change, from the chaos of a crumbling central power to the superior military technology of the company troops. There were always problems. In order to secure regular shipments of saltpetre, silk and cotton, company agents had become knowledgeable about and involved in the politics of the region: how to pay or avoid taxes, whom to bribe and to whom to address complaints. After decades of having a business presence, the traders had deep political and social connections within both the government and the leading merchant families. The European companies were lured into local politics to protect the trade and give some stability to their business activities. They also earned some income leasing their corporate troops out to local rulers to keep the peace, which inevitably drew them even deeper into struggles with local princes, and also with each other.

Trade and international politics were too linked to remain disconnected for long. The French company in particular was almost an arm of the state. It was founded by the state, funded by the state, and its dividends were guaranteed by the state. The king and his senior ministers freely meddled in company affairs and felt no compunction about using it to further their foreign-policy goals. The French company was much less a trading monopoly than either the Dutch or English companies, which still existed principally to make money for the shareholders, however peculiarly and ruthlessly they went about that goal. One of the English company's obligations to maintain its monopoly was that it supply the English Crown with five hundred tons of saltpetre annually, at favourable rates, or it would face crushing export duties on silver bullion, the currency of the Eastern trade. Thus it was buying its monopoly with an annual gift of cheap saltpetre to the English state. But the English East India Company was content to quietly profit from its enviable monopoly position and to avoid further entanglement with international politics. It was not directly under any government control and faced no pressure to assist in foreign wars—until the 1740s, when the company's directors asked the government for a favour: would it agree to send warships to clear French shipping from the Indian coast?

It was into this world, just as events began to heat up, that young Clive arrived, never imagining his own epoch-altering role in the coming struggle. Though apparently a hard-working lad, Clive was already disillusioned with his role as a desk-bound clerk in these early years. In one letter home he wrote, "The world seems vastly debas'd of late, and Interest carries it entirely before Merit, especially in this service . . . I should think myself very undeserving of any favour, were I only to build my foundation on the strength of the Former. I don't doubt but you'll make use of all possible means for my advancement." While urging his parents to work for his advancement, Clive himself eventually chose a far more active role in securing his future. A slight, sickly young man who occasionally suffered from depression and seizures, he nevertheless adjusted readily to his new role as man of action.

· 3 ·

THE UNEASY NEUTRALITY BETWEEN THE FRENCH AND English companies in southern India ended abruptly at the outbreak of the War of the Austrian Succession in 1744. The English government readily acceded to the English company's request for military help from the Royal Navy; after all, the French company was really an arm of the state and therefore had to be attacked along with all the other targets. Royal Navy ships arrived in India in 1745, attacking and capturing several French company ships. A French national fleet arrived soon thereafter and, following a series of tit-for-tat attacks (the English and French companies' main commercial centres almost rubbed shoulders—Pondicherry was only 130 kilometres from Madras), the commander of the English fleet ordered his ships north to Bengal to refit. This left the company outpost at Madras undefended. In fact, the settlement never had real defences because their construction costs would have been payable out of company profits and thus had been neglected. Dupleix, the French governor general at Pondicherry, was pleased when the French fleet sailed north along the coast and began to attack Madras on September 7, 1746. A crafty man of about fifty, he had lost most of his personal fortune in the Royal Navy's earlier attack and was eager for revenge.

Not only was the English East India Company outpost at Madras poorly defended, it was also poorly manned. Only about three hundred company men were stationed in the town. This was less than a quarter of the number of French troops, and most had no military background or experience. The local ruler, or nawab, had forbidden Dupleix to attack the English but had no forces ready to enforce his commands. After two days the fort surrendered; apparently the liquor stores had been blasted and the men, after guzzling the spirits, refused to fight—for which one can hardly blame them, poorly paid and vastly outnumbered as they were. In the confusion of the surrender negotiations, however, the young clerk, Robert Clive, "in the habit of a Dubash [local interpreter] and blackened," made a daring escape with several other Englishmen. They travelled by foot about 150 kilometres south, to the English company's last remaining outpost along the coast, Fort St. David. When the French attacked Fort St. David, they had a surprise: they were challenged by nearly ten thousand troops, the forces of the nawab. The much smaller French company forces nonetheless routed them, and the fort was saved only by the timely arrival of the Royal Navy fleet returning from Bengal.

There were only a few other insignificant skirmishes before the war ended in 1748. Madras was returned to the English company as part of the peace settlement, but the taste of excitement provided by the brief conflict changed Clive's career—no longer would he succumb to the tedium, boredom and predictable routine of a clerk. He requested a change in his posting.

"Mr. Robert Clive, Writer in the Service," reported his governor at Fort St. David, "being of a martial disposition, and having acted as a volunteer in our late engagements, we have granted him an Ensign's Commission upon his application for the same." Clive, ever his own cheerleader, ingratiated himself with his superiors, writing to the company directors in London to brag of his "great courage and bravery" and to request a promotion. He was given the position of steward, a potentially lucrative post that gave him a commission on the sale of all provisions and victuals for the company's employees in the region and offered some opportunity for private trade. It was a good position for someone so young and inexperienced.

With the peace, the dreary life of merchant trading again descended upon the Indian coast. But the hostilities had forever shattered the tenuous peace that had been enjoyed in the past. The scheming intensified, and the competing companies eyed each other suspiciously, searching for the latest threat. The short conflict had revealed to Clive something of immense value that was not widely appreciated, something that he would later use to devastating effect: the weapons and training of the French and English companies' soldiers were vastly superior to those of the local forces. Clive began to see the companies in a new light— not merely as innocuous traders but as formidable military powers. Although numerically superior, the local armies were little better than unruly mobs armed with primitive weapons of poor quality. "How very ignorant we were of the art of war in those days," Clive recalled. "Some of the engineers were masters of the theory without the practice, and those seemed wanting in resolution. Others there were who understood neither, and yet were possessed of courage sufficient to have gone on with the undertaking if they had known how to go about it. There was scarce an officer who knew whether the engineers were acting right or wrong, till it was too late in the season and we had lost too many men to begin an approach again." But practice makes perfect, and Clive became aware that their own troops could engage far greater numbers of local soldiers and expect to win; that without having intended to achieve such a goal, the French and English companies had become powerful regional military forces, able to effect change far beyond trade. The troops served the companies' interests but also became one of the most valuable commodities they had to sell to local rulers, particularly rulers whose interests were in alignment with the companies' long-term business interests.

After the peace of 1748, most of the English company's employees, if not Clive, hoped for a continuation of undisturbed and profitable trade, which was after all their reason for being in India. Dupleix and the French company, however, had other ideas. Although the two nations were officially at peace, in India their two companies were to be at war. While the Mughal Empire crumbled, local princes had been asserting greater power, and by 1740 many of them were de facto independent nations or kingdoms. One of the most powerful of these princes was Asaf Jah, ruler of the Deccan, the region where Madras and Pondicherry lay. When Asaf Jah died in 1748, Dupleix saw an opportunity to extend his own power and influence. He began to scheme with the contenders for the throne and eventually managed to place his candidates in power: Salabat Jang on the throne of the Deccan, and his local subordinate and deputy, Chanda Sahib, in the Carnatic along the Coromandel Coast.

English company officials in India were caught in a conundrum: their directors in London urged trade and profit, not expensive military adventures involving the dynastic squabbling of Indian princes. But Dupleix's actions made it apparent that following a course of non-interference and peaceful trade might result in the French placing in charge sympathetic rulers who would not only favour the French company but who might be encouraged to expel the English company altogether, resulting in a French company monopoly. The English might be shut out of India by the French, as they had been shut out of the Spice Islands by the Dutch a century earlier.

Their only option was to support a rival ruler, and they soon conspired to set their own puppet ruler on the throne of the Deccan: Muhammad Ali, the younger son of the deposed ruler of the Carnatic. Clive resumed military duties, as a captain, during the struggles. When the combined armies of Muhammad Ali and the English company were besieged in the fortress of Trichinopoly by Chanda Sahib and his French allies, a plan was put forward to relieve the siege by launching an attack on Arcot, the capital city of the Carnatic, which had been left undefended, and thereby force Chanda Sahib to march to its defence. Clive begged for the command—a risky gamble that would leave the company's bases at Madras and Fort St. David open to attack and possibly pave the way for French supremacy along the coast if the plan failed.

Clive and his meagre force of about two hundred English company troops and three hundred mercenaries marched inland through both sweltering jungle and withered scrub, crossing rivers and winding their way into the hills. They covered a difficult one hundred kilometres in six days of forced marching over treacherous terrain through the burning heat of August, and then through more days of pounding monsoon storms that turned the parched dust into a quagmire of mud. Spies had informed Clive to expect an opposing force of about a thousand to be defending the fort in Arcot, a town of around 100,000 inhabitants, so Clive was surprised to find it deserted. His ragtag force of exhausted and filthy irregulars wound through the dirty narrow streets, past the curious eyes of the onlookers and up to the stone fort in the centre of the settlement. The fort's garrison had fled during the night, under "the combined influence of superstition and cowardice," having fallen prey to rumours exaggerating the size of the force marching against them. A natural leader, Clive immediately ordered the French flag taken down, and he unfurled the one he had brought for the occasion: not, as might be expected, the flag of his company or of England, but the pennant of Muhammad Ali. The town and fort, he announced, had now been taken as a holding of the legitimate ruler of the Carnatic. He forbade his men to loot, accept bribes or take "gifts" from the people as payment for their defence: he needed no other enemies. Even studious neutrality would be a boon, and his polite respect bought him that, at least.

Clive now set his men to work rebuilding and repairing the dilapidated defences of the fort, fortifying themselves against the inevitable counterattack. For the next fifty days, he and his band endured an all-out siege before being relieved by reinforcements. But he was not idle during the siege. Under cover of darkness he launched lightning forays into the enemy encampments, fended off numerous assaults against the gates, faced relentless sniping and artillery fire and endured inadequate food and stale water. Two of the men standing next to Clive were blasted dead, and only luck preserved him from a similar fate. Finally, over ten thousand troops commanded by Chanda Sahib's son Raza encircled the fort and dispersed throughout the winding, narrow streets of the town. Clive received honeyed bribes and violent threats to abandon the fortress: great riches, free passage for his men; terrible suffering and torment should he refuse. Yet still he held firm, perhaps suspecting the terms would not be honoured, or hoping for reinforcements from Madras or from the English company's allies. More likely he held firm out of sheer bull-headed stubbornness and a rigid sense of honour: he had said he would take and hold the fort, and so he would, and damn the consequences.

In Madras it was reported to the council that "Clive thinks himself able to defend a breach should the enemy make one; his only apprehensions therefore are his people's falling down through fatigue; that he thinks no less a force than 1000 Blacks and 200 Europeans can attempt to relieve him, as the enemy's situation is strong and their numbers increase daily." On November 14, 1748, an auspicious day, the assault began: it was the Muslim holy day of Ashura, mourning the martyrdom of the prophet Muhammad's grandsons. Many of the troops in the attacking army were Muslims who believed that death in combat would send them directly to paradise. As the first light of day crept over the horizon, a swarm of men launched themselves at the gates of the battered fortress, carrying hundreds of great scaling ladders. In the forefront of this charging mob lumbered dozens of armoured battle elephants, their enormous heads encased in metal plates for battering.

The attackers' success seemed assured, until Clive ordered explosives to be set off and his sharpshooters to continue firing their rifles at the hapless beasts. Roaring in agony and frustration, the elephants wheeled into the midst of the charging infantry, stamping and flinging men aside in their mad quest to escape. Still the attackers charged at the gates, heedless of the flying bullets, and launched a raft of men across the moat. Clive aimed one of the great guns down and fired into the mob, causing the men to panic and capsize the raft, drowning most of the attackers. The French commander and his troops apparently remained out of the melee, observing the carnage and destruction, but aiding little. Raza called off the attack and fled to a nearby fort to contemplate his defeat. A few hours later English company reinforcements arrived from Madras, accompanied by several thousand Maratha cavalry under Morari Rao, one of the nominal allies of Muhammad Ali.

But there was to be no rest. With his reinforced company army now numbering nearly a thousand and augmented by six hundred Maratha horsemen, Clive went on the offensive. He swept over several nearby forts and then defeated Raza's army of nearly five thousand, which was marching with French company reinforcements. Key to the victory was the defection of hundreds of sepoys from Raza's army. For the next several months Clive continued to lead his small army to a series of victories throughout the region, using the techniques that would bring him even greater renown in the coming years and secure for his company vast riches and tens of millions of subjects. Speedy movement across the land and surprise direct attacks with no hesitation, capped off by bribery to subvert the loosely loyal contingents of local armies, enabled Clive to virtually wipe out the power of the French company in the region and assure the succession of Muhammad Ali to the throne of the Carnatic.

Meanwhile, in Madras, Clive's subordinates were managing his affairs and had made him a small fortune. The young, rich hero rented a comfortable house and immersed himself in making the social rounds in the small settlement. These rounds included meeting the young sister of one of his friends, Margaret Maskelyne, who had recently arrived from England. Margaret was seventeen, and Robert was now twenty-eight. They married weeks before departing for England in February 1753. Cultured, beautiful and charming, she seems not to have been a partner in her husband's machinations and daring exploits. One of Clive's biographers reported that "Clive was always affectionate with Margaret and apparently faithful, although there is no evidence that he ever consulted her on his plans or that she had any influence whatever on his actions." They stayed together until the end of his life.

Clive left behind a company that was a formidable military force in southern India. Even at this stage in his career, on the long sailing voyage home, he was already working to develop his heroic legend. When not otherwise engaged with the attentions of his new bride, he was deep in conversation with Robert Orme, his comrade and later hagiographer, discussing the details of his many battles, triumphs, heroism, gambles, close calls and escapes from death. Orme was preparing a history of the English East India Company's exploits in India. Clive, being of average height and not particularly handsome, with small eyes, a bulbous nose and a squarish face, would take some crafting to mould into a hero. He instinctively knew that to achieve the pinnacle of his wild ambition, he would need more than deeds. Deeds were fine, even necessary, but to achieve his objective he would need a legend, and just as importantly in eighteenth-century England, he would need a fortune.

· 4 ·

WITH EUROPE AT PEACE, THE TALES OF CLIVE'S HEROIC actions for the English company in India were soon widespread. Clive was now famous. He had earned a reputation, according to an Indian governor, of being a "well-known invincible." Prime Minister William Pitt the Elder called him "the Heaven born general." But in spite of his good fortune and national acclaim, illness dogged Clive. Poor food, stagnant water, sleepless nights, a bullet wound, living outdoors in scorching heat and drenching rains during forced marching, not to mention the stress of battle and command, would surely take their toll on anyone, and Clive was no exception. He was plagued by fatigue, fevers and abdominal pain, probably malaria and dysentery, and perhaps other ailments. He developed a reputation among his compatriots for being moody and suffering bouts of gloomy depression, during which he brooded on suicide and which alternated with periods of spirited fury and restless energy. By contrast, historians have also uncovered records suggesting that he was quiet and responsible. Some have suggested that Clive was manic depressive, or bipolar. These illnesses and depressions were to accompany him for the remainder of his life, recurring after periods of intense strain, stress and frenetic activity. He began to use opium to alleviate the pain during his low periods.

Clive and Margaret bought a large estate house in England and settled into a quiet life while he recovered from his tenure in India. In March 1754 Margaret gave birth to their first child, Edward, and Clive entered into an agreement with the company to return to India as soon as he had recovered. Also at this time, for unfathomable reasons, he decided to try and win a seat in Parliament. He spent nearly five thousand pounds in bribes, according to the custom of the era, only to lose the contest (as well as about an eighth of his considerable fortune) on a technicality. He then signed on with the company to be deputy governor at Fort St. David for a period of five years, with a clause to succeed as governor of Madras when the incumbent died or retired. In April 1755 Clive and Margaret boarded a ship for the long voyage back to India. Before he reached his posting in eastern India, however, his ship stopped at Bombay on the west coast. Once again Clive went into action, helping to capture a fort held by pirates. He was also plunged immediately into the politics, the scheming and the jockeying for power that was increasing throughout India.

Clive and his entourage arrived at Fort St. David and learned potentially disastrous news: the French company was continuing its political machinations to ingratiate itself with local rulers in the interior (an agreement between the two companies stipulated that they would refrain from political involvement along the Coromandel Coast, the region of Clive's previous victories). Not only that, but the old nawab of Bengal had died, and his grandson, Suraj-ud-Dowlah, had inherited the position and promptly attacked the English company at the town of Kasimbazar. The arrogant English factors there had insulted Suraj-ud-Dowlah and challenged his authority, perhaps even backing a rival claimant to the throne or at least giving the claimant sanctuary in their fort in Calcutta. They also began working on reinforcing their fort, as if anticipating action.

Violent and insecure, the young nawab could not accept this challenge to his authority without risking a loss of respect. He had heard rumours of war from Europe and had many French company soldiers training his armies. In June 1756, when the English traders refused to stop fortifying Calcutta and hand over the traitor, the nawab attacked, at the head of a large French-trained army, and conquered the English company's fort at Calcutta. Calcutta was one of the company's most valuable settlements, a prosperous trading centre renowned for its cotton and saltpetre. Upon entering the city, Suraj-ud-Dowlah apparently commented that "the English must be fools to oblige him to drive them out of so fine a city." Like the Carnatic, Bengal was a province of the great Mughal Empire, and the new nawab, while maintaining a façade of allegiance, was in reality asserting his independence, preparing for a time when there would be no Mughal emperor in Delhi.

At the same time, the rumour around Madras was that a mighty French national fleet of nineteen ships of the line had set out from France for the French company settlement at Pondicherry, carrying thousands of soldiers. The fleet's ultimate purpose was unknown. If the rumour was true, what possible reason could there be, other than to press an attack against the English company? The English at Fort St. David were also bedevilled with another fantastical rumour, a tale that proved to be one of the enduring myths from British India: the Black

Hole of Calcutta. When he captured the English Company fort, Suraj-ud-Dowlah apparently ordered 146 Englishmen dumped into a pit only five and a half metres wide and four metres long, with only tiny barred openings providing air. In the steaming heat of the pit dozens perished, crushed by their comrades. Historians have concluded that probably only half that number died and that the nawab was likely not directly responsible. Whether true or not, the tale of the Black Hole of Calcutta gained wide renown as an example of the perfidy, barbarism and cruelty of the nawabs and of Indian rule in general, and provided later justification for the British as "civilizers."

Clive was practically begging to go to the rescue of Calcutta. Stalking around Fort St. David, fuming and anxious, he wrote a letter to the board of directors in London claiming that the "loss of Calcutta is attended with the greatest Mortifications to the Company and the most barbarous and cruel Circumstances to the poor Inhabitants." He was the leader of the punitive force, an appointment that ruffled some feathers because he was viewed as only a "company" soldier rather than a professional officer in the nation's armed forces—the company's Madras council had chosen him over Colonel John Aldercron, who was in charge of some national troops then present in the town. A touchy and proud man, Aldercron bickered and sowed jealousy between the professional soldiers and sailors and the company service. Apparently Clive and Aldercron could not work together, and the quarrelling nearly resulted in losses in the years ahead. Making enemies within his own ranks was something Clive seemed particularly good at. He could be boastful and arrogant, and frequently stole the limelight from others. He paid no heed to diplomacy towards his own countrymen in higher positions, something that would haunt him years later.

Writing to the directors in London, Clive confidently predicted his victory and claimed that he would not be satisfied "with the retaking of Calcutta only: and that the Company's Estate in these parts will be settled in a Better and more lasting condition than ever." He maintained he would "recov[er] Calcutta and the Company's losses, Rights and privileges." In Madras, he received instructions that must have given him great relief in their vagueness and latitude for personal discretion: "pursue such measures as you shall judge most conductive to the Company's benefit," he was told. Clive departed in December 1756, with five Royal Navy ships, heavily armed ships of the line commanded by Admiral Charles Watson, three company warships and several other smaller ships transporting nearly two hundred soldiers, including infantry, artillerymen and nearly a thousand local sepoy troops and general camp workers. "This expedition, if attended with success, may enable me to do great things," Clive wrote to his father. "It is by far the grandest of my undertakings. I go with great forces and great authority."

Before launching his attack, Clive regrouped his forces and sent an arrogant but formal letter to the nawab stating that "we have for these ten years past been constantly fighting—and it has pleased God Almighty to make me successful." He then went on the offensive, taking a few smaller forts and suffering some heavy losses, before he and his men marched on Calcutta, triumphantly entering the city on January 2, 1757. A month later he defended it against a mighty army of the nawab, who tried to retake the city. The nawab's army was reported to consist of two hundred horsemen and thirty thousand infantry. Even considering the likely exaggeration, it was a force that dwarfed Clive's detachment of several thousand. Nevertheless, Clive ordered his men to attack on February 5 and routed the grand but bewildered army, sending horses and elephants in a panicked flight into their own ranks, which broke and ran in terror. Clive wrote to his father afterward, "Our success was very great . . . we killed 1300 men and between 5 & 6 hundred horse with 4 elephants. This blow has obliged the Nawab to decamp and conclude a peace very honourable and advantageous to the Company's affairs." But the city of Calcutta was in ruins, utterly desecrated—its buildings burned, its trees cut down. The cost of the damage was estimated at over two million pounds.

The peace was short-lived. Suraj-ud-Dowlah's great army had not been defeated, merely scattered. And hearing the news of war in Europe from his French allies—a war that had started in May 1756—the nawab strengthened his alliance and prepared to continue his struggle against Clive. Clive, meanwhile, had also received the news of the outbreak of what we now call the Seven Years' War in Europe. The struggle for Calcutta was therefore no longer merely a corporate battle, but an extension of the larger European conflict. Accordingly, Clive felt it was within his rights, perhaps his duty, to march his army upriver and, under cover of several Royal Navy warships that silenced the French artillery guns at Chandernagore, to attack a fortified French trading outpost in March.

Clive again had some royal troops under his command because his corporate army was too small—this was the beginning of the commingling of private and public interests that would later characterize the East India Company. He presciently recognized the potential for a conflict of interest in the future: "it had been better for the service," he wrote, "they had never come and I had the like number of Company's in their room." These were the soldiers of his nation, certainly, but they were not the soldiers of his company. Having to rely on them, indeed even having them in India, muddied the waters of command. He would never have complete control over them, and they would never respect him in the same way they would respect regular officers. In fact, their presence pried open the great door of compromise and introduced a higher authority into Clive's world, one that diminished his own power by the sheer immensity and intractability of the ancient hierarchies and sources of social power that it introduced.

Although there was no immediate personal or corporate profit to cover or offset the considerable expense of Clive's attack on the French outposts, the assault was certainly a major blow to the company's primary competitor in India. Clive himself recognized it when he proclaimed, with his usual lack of humility, that he had dealt "an inexpressible blow to the French Company everywhere." When the news reached London, stock in the English company soared by 12 per cent. The English East India Company was on the verge of both its greatest victory yet and its greatest profits. And Clive, who sent off numerous letters to the directors in London regaling them with his heroism, exploits and overriding duty and loyalty to the company, would again be put forth as the instrument of conquest.

· 5 ·

THE BATTLE OF PLASSEY IS A DEFINITIVE TURNING point in the history of the world. On the face of it, it was a simple affair, though the known details are vague and difficult to sift from the myths that arose in its wake. In the three months after the French defeat at Chandernagore, the nawab Suraj-ud-Dowlah regrouped his dispersed army, augmented it with a strong French contingent and marched towards Calcutta. According to Clive's hagiographer, Robert Orme, Clive was "surprised at their numerous, splendid and martial appearance."

This could be taken as an understatement, since what he saw arrayed before him was something of a nightmare. In all, the army was about fifty thousand strong and included up to eighteen thousand cavalry, heavy artillery and a contingent of armoured battle elephants draped in scarlet cloth. This force grandly arrayed itself across a jungle and mangrove plain known as Plassey, about twelve kilometres north of Calcutta. Hundreds of standards fluttered in the wind and the drums beat loudly as the multitudes arranged themselves into divisions. These troops, under French tutelage, appeared more disciplined than any Indian horde Clive had yet encountered. His force consisted of just over a thousand European troops and an infantry of about 2,200 sepoys and a few small guns. He had no cavalry at all. Defeat seemed a foregone conclusion. Yet Clive was well aware of both the strengths and the weaknesses of his own force and the weaknesses of the opposing hordes. He gambled that the vast forces arrayed across the plain would prove undisciplined and perhaps even disloyal; that they would be poorly paid, poorly provisioned, poorly commanded and poorly organized. His own advantage, on the other hand, was that his army was small enough for him to personally command, using to full advantage his reputation for assured victory—and his troops' certainty that if they fled they would all perish.

Nevertheless, the odds on this day seemed stacked against Clive. He hesitated, calling a council of war to debate the options, wondering "whether in our present situation, without assistance, and on our own bottom, it would be prudent to attack the Nawab, or whether we should wait till joined by some country power?" Probably he was waiting to gauge the results of his intriguing with high-placed leaders within the nawab's army. One famous version of the story has Clive receiving a letter from one of the nawab's confidants named Mir Jafar and then, after reading it, strolling in the shade of some giant trees in contemplation before firming up his mind. On June 21 it rained heavily, and when the sun rose the next day, Clive took action: brash, decisive, foolhardy action. Perhaps he feared not living up to his reputation or falling short of the destiny he had laid out for himself. In any event, he attacked.

The unexpected move startled the nawab, and his forces merely watched as Clive's troops advanced and entrenched themselves in a stand of mangrove. On June 23 the forces engaged in battle, with little of significance happening other than Clive's small cannons blasting and killing hundreds of infantry—until the moment Clive had been awaiting: the defection of a great portion of the nawab's army, led by the treacherous Mir Jafar. Clive had promised him great offices if the English company succeeded. As the nawab advanced, Jafar retreated. Clive's guns peppered away at the French forces as they slowly marched forward. Then, as Clive had predicted, the elephants refused to march into gunfire. They panicked, the French stood back from the battle and the cavalry stood their ground when their commander was shot and killed, undermining their morale. A torrent of rain, lightning and thunder soaked the battlefield in the afternoon, an event Clive had anticipated; he had ordered his men to cover their ammunition and guns. The guns of the nawab and his French artillery were soaked. Believing Clive's to be as well, the infantry advanced. Their advance slowed and then halted in the hail of bullets. Suddenly Clive ordered an audacious bayonet charge. The infantry turned and fled, dropping everything in their haste, abandoning their camp, their dead and wounded, their supplies, weapons, equipment and provisions. It turned into a total rout.

An amusing and inaccurate painting of the battle shows a heroic Clive in the vanguard of his army, astride a charging horse, boldly exhorting his men to victory on a battlefield littered with the abandoned detritus of the nawab's humiliating flight. There were only a few hundred dead on the nawab's side, and just a handful on the company's. Clive's was not a military victory, but a victory of chance, treachery and diplomacy. Clive, however, claimed it as a superb military victory and pronounced himself a great general. It was the sort of boast that was beginning to irritate people—claiming an ever greater share of the limelight for himself while barely recognizing the contributions of others or acknowledging the important role of fate or luck.

The spoils of war for Clive and the company were immense. According to the agreement they had reached beforehand, Clive installed the treacherous Mir Jafar on the throne. Marching into the opulent chamber in one of the nawab's principal palaces, Clive observed the conspirators clustered about Mir Jafar; none sat upon the throne until Clive graciously indicated to Mir Jafar that now was time for him to assume his seat. Clive then offered a handful of gold coins to the new nawab as a symbol of his respect and submission.

Mir Jafar granted Clive a *jagir,* or land grant, along with all its revenues, of all the land surrounding Calcutta. The *jagir* yielded 27,000 pounds per year, funds extracted from the local populace and paid to Clive in rent from the company. In addition to his annual *jagir,* Clive also possessed some 300,000 pounds of plundered loot, or "gifts" for his services. Mir Jafar's other payments for securing his position were equally staggering: 160,000 pounds personally to Clive; another 500,000 or so pounds to be distributed among the company's army and navy, additional gifts worth tens of thousands of pounds each to many other company officials and an ongoing annual fee of 100,000 pounds to the company to cover its military expenses. In November 1758 Clive was appointed governor of Bengal by the directors in London. Now he was also a landlord, and a sort of feudal lord ranging over his company's most profitable trading centre. This type of arrangement was not unusual. Others certainly made fortunes from similar arrangements, but Clive's take was unparalleled and bound to cause problems later on. What right did he have to amass such wealth for fulfilling his duties as a company employee, particularly when British national troops had aided in some of the battles?

Clive's struggle was not over. Over the next several years he rushed around putting down insurrections and consolidating the company's gains. In this ongoing war between the French, English and even Dutch, their companies no longer used their meagre forces to augment the armies of local rulers, but had taken up the battle wholly on their own. The English company could not actively work to change local politics and remain merely a trading enterprise. "Either all must abstain from intervention in Indian politics," writes Michael Edwardes in *Clive: The Heaven-Born General,* "an impossible eventuality after Plessey—or one must prevent any other from becoming a 'country power' . . . For the British, the consolidation of their position as a 'country power' and the reduction of the Dutch and French to mere trading status went hand in hand."

With Clive's many victories military and political, the company was set to become one of the strongest powers in India. Historian James P. Lawford, writing in *Clive: Proconsul of India,* notes that Clive was now "a soldier statesman who saw a battle not as an end in itself, but only as one aspect of a policy for attaining a political objective." The company established Bengal as its core stronghold and the seed from which British India would steadily grow. After conquering Bengal, the company controlled access to Bengal saltpetre, the greatest source of the most vital military ingredient in the world, and under that company, and later the British government, saltpetre was cut off entirely from hostile nations during times of war. The first to feel the squeeze were the French. France's sudden and unexpected loss of Indian saltpetre in 1758 and her forced reliance on poorer-quality domestic gunpowder have been proposed by historians as key factors influencing the French to sue for peace in 1763, ending the Seven Years' War. The French company henceforth was allowed to trade at certain factories but would never again be permitted to host any troops.

But all was not well. As Philip Lawson has commented in *The East India Company: A History,* "the trading mandate that had governed the Company's existence since the seventeenth century disintegrated. Where commerce had once reigned supreme there now appeared territorial and political power in India with all its vexed responsibilities for the Company." These sentiments were echoed by the contemporary observer John Nicholls in his *Recollections and Reflections,* published in 1822: "This Empire has been acquired by a Company of Merchants; and they retained the character of exclusive trader, after they had assumed that of sovereign . . . Sovereign and trader, are characters incompatible." The company was starting to face responsibilities it was ill-equipped to handle as a trading corporation. Clive's victories had given it the beginning of an empire to govern, but how to govern? Even Clive seemed aware of the enormity of the company's new responsibilities, and perhaps also of its growing conflict of interest. In a letter he wrote to William Pitt in 1759, Clive observed: "But so large a sovereignty may possibly be an object too expensive for a mercantile company; and it is feared that they are not of themselves able, without the nation's assistance, to maintain so wide a dominion." Corruption began to run rampant as company officers, commanders and traders, holding near absolute power, degenerated into rapacious plunderers. The wealth of millions of Indians was slowly seeping away to quietly fill the pockets of grasping and greedy company officials and employees.

Britain's acquisition of the embryonic empire in Bengal was to prove far more costly and complex than could have been imagined. Indeed, the initial celebration and soaring stock prices that followed the news of Clive's victory at Plassey were soon dampened by subsequent events, for Clive left an unstable and volatile political situation in India when returning to England in 1760. The ongoing struggles between the various nations' companies in India mirrored the national struggles in Europe. These struggles, played against the backdrop of the decaying and crumbling Mughal Empire, perhaps made it inevitable that whichever company was victorious would have to keep expanding and destroying all its competitors—or risk being destroyed itself if it failed. The English East India Company had lost control over its destiny.

· 6 ·

AFTER FOUR EXHAUSTING YEARS OF WARRING WITH the French and the Dutch and trying to bring stability to the chaos threatening to overtake parts of India, Clive decided to return to England for a rest. He was now thirty-five years old. His annual *jagir* was more than the entire original capital of the English East India Company when it was founded in 1600. Ironically, because his personal wealth was so large, Clive dared not risk transporting it to London himself; neither did he dare to use his own company's services. Instead he commissioned the services of the enormous Dutch East India Company, the VOC, as a sort of exchange bank, depositing the sums with them in India and claiming the credit for them in England. He was now one of the most affluent individuals in England, a nation where enormous wealth was concentrated in the hands of a very few privileged aristocrats. Clive marked his return in 1760 with a great display of his riches. He bought numerous large houses and desirable estates for his family, strewing money about the land as if his wealth were limitless, which for him it basically was. He was called to a royal audience and met King George III; he was granted a peerage in Ireland and thereafter was known as Baron Clive of Plassey; and he got himself elected to the House of Commons (in order to keep a hand in influencing political developments in India). Some of his friends were elected as well, money being of no concern to one of the wealthiest men in the nation. He also received an honorary degree from Oxford. However, Baron Clive quarrelled with powerful people in Parliament, arousing their enmity, envy and even hatred. Creating spectacles with his lavish and ostentatious display of wealth, he was caricatured as a swaggering "nabob," a derogatory twist on the term for an Indian ruler, and one that was appended to any merchant with a vast fortune and pretensions to aristocracy.

Clive began a lengthy and dangerous dispute with the chairman of the English East India Company, Lawrence Sulivan, and other members of the company's board of directors. Sulivan had bridled at Clive's suggestion to Pitt that the revenues from Bengal should be directed to the government rather than to the company. He threatened to block Clive's receipt of the income from his landholdings, the *jagir,* around Calcutta. Although the nawab had given over the *jagir* to Clive personally, the company had not voted to officially approve his right to it. Despite his astronomical wealth, Clive needed the annual 27,000-pound *jagir* payment to maintain his extravagant lifestyle. "My future power, my grandeur," he wrote, "all depend upon the receipt of the *jagir* money." Money, and the respect engendered by its copious display in eighteenth-century Britain, was an essential ingredient in forming Clive's larger-than-life persona. In 1763 Clive marshalled his resources to depose Sulivan, but the chairman won re-election and immediately tried to block Clive's receipt of the *jagir* money. A legal battle ensued, and Clive sought to use his influence in government to pressure the company to pay him. At the same time he wrote letters to the Mughal Emperor Shah Alam II, India's paper ruler, to seek confirmation of his due.

While Clive wasted his time on these frustrating squabbles, the company's troubles in India grew larger. Its council in Calcutta replaced Mir Jafar, whom Clive had placed on the throne, with a new nawab "in a proper and public manner, that he as well as the country may see that he receives his government from the Company" and began to extort ever-greater sums from the territory in exchange for its role as kingmaker. But even the richest province in India had a limit to its wealth. Eventually armies were raised against the company by the Mughal emperor and other local princes in an attempt to destroy the English company. The cost of the wars escalated, consuming an increasing share of the profits. And not all the battles favoured the company troops. The situation was again tenuous: certainly the French had been defeated, but might the company be ousted from its golden perch by local, perhaps more legitimate, rulers? The company's stock plummeted. The British government feared for its lost tax revenue and diminished international prestige. Perhaps the hero of Plassey could turn the situation around?

Clive and his supporters certainly thought so, but only on the condition that Sulivan be deposed and Clive's *jagir* be confirmed for ten years. The shareholders complied, placed Clive in charge of three thousand additional troops and granted him additional powers in Bengal: he would only have to share power with a council of four, and the selection of the four councillors was left up to him. Growing bored and quarrelsome in England, Clive was eager for a triumphant return to India: there, scheming and warring and high stakes made life's gambles far more interesting than dealing with pasty-faced bureaucrats and politicians in foggy England, where his struggles seemed irritating and pointless. In India he would again be a man of action, a controller of destiny in a place where great events were transforming the world, not just another bickering member of England's political class.

Clive sailed to Calcutta in 1765, arriving to hear the shocking news that Major Hector Munro had won a fantastic victory for the company: he had defeated the combined forces of the rebelling nawab, a neighbouring prince in Oudh and the titular emperor Shah Alam II. Munro's armies were continuing to advance. Clive felt that the company had already gone too far for a trading enterprise and that its operations in Bengal were a mess. It was too much of a gamble, he thought, too risky and dangerous to keep marching on Delhi like Spanish conquistadores. Chaos threatened northern India. Clive issued orders to halt the company's army from continuing its advance on Delhi and recalled the troops. He returned the land to the ruler of Oudh. "To go further," he wrote to London, "is in my opinion a scheme so extravagantly ambitious and absurd that no governor and council in their senses can adopt it, unless the whole system of the Company's interest be first entirely new-modelled." He seems to have begun to anticipate the problems that would soon arise from the company's military adventuring in India. The manpower to assume the government of such a great number of people, many times the population of England, simply did not exist. Conquest, Clive knew, had to be done with the collusion and subservience of local rulers, even if those rulers would no longer have any real power apart from the company that had placed them on the throne and that had the ability to remove them from power if their behaviour and actions did not please. The company could be all-powerful, but the veneer of legitimacy had to be maintained.

On August 12, 1765, Clive met the Emperor Shah Alam II and presided over a hasty ceremony in a casual setting around a dining table in Clive's travelling command tent. The emperor, with a scrawl of his pen, gave the company a "firmaund from the King Shah Aalum, granting the dewany of Bengal, Behar and Orissa to the company, 1765." With this official overlordship over nearly thirty million people the company was now an imperial power—the beginning of British rule in India. "We are sensible that, since the acquisition of the dewany, the power formerly belonging to the soubah of those provinces is totally, in fact, vested in the East India Company. Nothing remains to him but the name and shadow of authority," Clive wrote to his directors in London. "This name, however," he noted, "this shadow, it is indispensably necessary we should seem to venerate." He was uncharacteristically acting like a governing statesman and less like a plundering barbarian or conquistador—he had, after all, made a vast fortune doing what he was now trying to prevent others from doing in his wake.

Private greed, boundless ambition and fluid morals had led to the company's success in conquering Bengal, but these characteristics were no longer valuable in governing the territory. Clive was an intelligent and astute man, not without honour and a sense of duty and obligation; he knew the corporate culture would undermine and destroy the company's gilded position if it did not change. Its long-term profit depended on immediate change. It would not be easy, challenging entrenched positions of entitlement, shattering dreams of power and wealth among a group of people for whom those things represented the entire reason for their being in India—their chance to leap social and material boundaries and return to England far above their previous station, an opportunity not available under any other conditions. Chances were, Clive would be resented and resisted as a hypocrite.

Nevertheless, he set about improving the civil administration: he forbade company officers from accepting "gifts"—bribery or other forms of graft—despite his own substantial gift of the *jagir* that would be plumping up his fortune for years to come; he increased salaries; he tried to limit the company's monopoly so as not to constrict and strangle the local economy; he introduced a

pension fund for the company's army and seeded it with a substantial donation of his own; and he reorganized and streamlined
the army, weeding out corruption where possible and creating
three separate brigades, each of sufficient force to confront any
other single army fielded by an Indian prince.

Disobedient officers who challenged Clive's reforms were
arrested, placed on ships and returned to England. Clive fired
people who disagreed with him and removed their duty-free
trade passes. He was not delicate in how he went about his rapid
and dramatic changes, and he seemed not to care how he was
perceived—it was now part of his duty, and he would see it done.
One of his own council members was so startled at his dictates
that he wrote, "Clive is really our king. His word is law and he
laughs at contradictions." But the work tired Clive and broke
his health. Depressed and ill, he departed for home in February 1767, having spent only twenty-two months in India and
leaving much work undone. The corruption was only mildly
dampened, perhaps only driven from view.

· 7 ·

EVER FREE FROM SELF-DOUBT, CLIVE WROTE TO HIS
friend and hagiographer Robert Orme in 1767, a year before he
left India for the last time, that "Fortune seems determined to
accompany me to the last; every object, every sanguine wish is
upon the point of being completely fulfilled and I am arrived at
the pinnacle of all I covet, by affirming the Company shall, in
spite of all the envy, malice, faction and resentment, acknowledge they are become the most opulent company in the world,
by the battle of Plassey." But he would soon have cause to rue his
earlier optimism.

Clive had accomplished great things, and he knew it. Nevertheless, he wanted others to know it too, and he was still

working on polishing the myth of his grandeur and destiny, of a man protected by providence, not aware that it was about to be shattered by detractors envious of his meteoric rise. Clive was preoccupied with managing his image—perhaps to create a justification for his incredible accumulation of wealth. Surely he knew that the tales Orme had spun were not entirely accurate, but he wanted great things from life, and participating in a little stretching of the truth seemed harmless. In doing so, however, Clive never worried about trampling on the aspirations of others; he could rise like a comet—meteoric, bright and fast, transcending the rigid boundaries that separated and ordered British society—but he ruled out this same trajectory for others. He angered the people he had bested and the people whose fortunes had been stunted by his attempts to limit corruption. He angered people because he was arrogant and outspoken. There were many who would love to see him fall.

When Clive arrived in London, he was not well. Describing himself as "sick and weak," he probably suffered from a combination of ailments, a cocktail of illnesses contracted in India that likely included malaria, gallstones and an unknown "nervous complaint" as well as recurrent bouts of depression. He self-medicated with opium. Irritable and short-tempered, he did not resettle well into his former life as Baron Clive. He alienated some of his long-time comrades before dashing off to Europe for nine months of travel and recuperation, returning to London late in 1768. When he arrived, he was once again embroiled in company and national politics. His personal, political and business enemies circled. The people he had offended, insulted, thwarted and challenged lay in wait.

In India, it was becoming apparent that the company was incapable of governing its vast new territories. As it staggered into the role of government, it could not shed its original self-interested grasping mentality. It had access to incredible treasure in the form of taxes, but it had acquired responsibilities as well—this revenue could not, as some wanted, be siphoned from Bengal as profit. Running a country, as the company was belatedly learning, is not a profitable venture for shareholders. Taxes in Bengal rose by 20 per cent, placing a terrible burden on the local populace. Much of the amount raised was plundered by corrupt company and local officials; in no way was it deployed for the benefit of Bengalis. It was merely a system of extraction, taking from many people to enrich a handful of well-placed company officials. As Holden Furber writes in *Rival Empires of Trade in the Orient, 1600–1800,* "faced with the consequences of Plassey, the British governing classes became convinced that the company's activities should be made to benefit the 'public' as well as the company and its servants. By the 'public' these eighteenth-century gentleman meant the 'nation' in the sense in which they understood that term; they were not thinking of distributing the company's profits to the poor but rather of reducing the national debt." If India were to be plundered, the British state should share in a greater amount of the proceeds. Were not royal troops and officers of the Royal Navy involved in the battles won by Clive and others for the company? Why should the company derive all the benefits, when public funds had been expended? That these privileged few nabobs should return richer than anyone, and challenge the established hierarchy in doing so, was becoming a serious irritant.

Despite Clive's promise of opulence and riches for the East India Company and the return of ever-increasing numbers of swaggering nabobs, the company's fortunes were not so rosy. Managing an empire amid the political chaos and opportunism that was post-Mughal India proved not to be universally profitable for the company. Most of the profit seemed to bypass it and accrue to the nabobs. Military engagements with various Indian princes consumed vast profits and threatened the company's landholdings, and rumours of French political meddling were again on the rise, causing a precipitous drop in the price of its stock. A devastating famine in Bengal, exacerbated by incompetent rulers and the plundered resources of the state, caused millions to starve to death. Perhaps a third of the population died, severely damaging the economy for years and resulting in more losses for the company. In Britain, these problems were placed, not inappropriately, at the feet of the nabobs who were lampooned in the press—particularly Clive, who was portrayed as boorish, uncultivated and unscrupulous.

In 1772 a politically motivated parliamentary inquiry into the conduct of the company, and of Clive personally, unearthed many sordid details of their actions in India. Episodes of bribery, corruption, trickery and other deceptive behaviour came to light. The evidence against Clive was supplied and amplified by his numerous critics. James P. Lawford writes in *Clive: Proconsul of India* that "the one-time absolute ruler of vast provinces, the arbiter of the fate of millions, had to submit to the cross-questioning of a virtually unknown chairman and of a man actuated only by malice; he had to listen while all that he had achieved was questioned and belittled." Occasionally Clive's own testimony raised eyebrows, as occurred when he described the great mountains of treasure laid before him for his choosing after the Battle of Plassey: the jewels, gold and silver bullion, coins, priceless art and antiques. In a speech in his own defence he implored the gathered parliamentarians to "consider the situation in which the victory of Plassey placed me. A great prince was dependent on my pleasure; an opulent city lay at my mercy; its richest bankers bid against each other for my smiles; I walked through vaults which were thrown open to me alone, piled on either hand with gold and jewels. Mr. Chairman, at this moment I stand astonished at my own moderation." One can only imagine the parliamentarians' response to this audacious claim.

But Clive was an astute and intelligent man, a schemer, persuader and great orator. He calmly answered his critics while defending his actions in India, proclaiming himself offended and insulted that he was being treated "more like a sheep-stealer than a member of this House." His old enemy Lawrence Sulivan he marked out for particular attention, describing him and other London-based company directors as a cluster of gluttonous swine, "devouring turtle and all kinds of viands out of season and in season, and swilling themselves with whole hogsheads of claret, champagne and burgundy." Despite his theatrics and a masterful defence against the charges of corruption, greed and dishonesty, Clive could not deflect a proposal by a detractor and ally of Sulivan's, Major-General John Burgoyne, "that all acquisitions made under the influence of military force or by treaty with foreign princes did of right belong to the State." Burgoyne asserted that restitution was therefore the only right course. He continued that Clive "had illegally acquired the sum of 234,000 pounds to the dishonour and detriment of the State." His argument went that "it was impossible that any civil or military servant, in treating with a foreign Prince or state, could lawfully bargain for, or acquire property for himself." This rationale seems perfectly logical today, but at the time it was all too common to accept "gifts" in the Eastern trade. Clive remarked that "Presents in India are coeval with the Company. As soon as we began to raise fortifications the Company's chiefs began to receive presents . . . There has not been a commander of his Majesty's Squadron, nor a commander of His Majesty's Land Forces, nor a governor, nor any chief who has not received presents."

Nevertheless, Clive sensed disgrace and financial ruin. In his final speech in the House of Commons, he took a cringing, placatory approach to his defence. He pledged his innocence and claimed it was unjust "to punish a man for what he could not know he could be guilty of." He spoke of honour and of how his will would not be broken: "I have only one thing more, that is a humble request to the House. I make it not for myself, but for them. The request is this, when they come to decide upon my honour, they will not forget their own." He retired in nervous tension to one of his many mansions to await the verdict that could ruin everything he had accomplished, a verdict that could not only claim all his wealth but also destroy his legacy— the legend of the great Clive, the invincible Clive, the Clive who truly deserved his position and status.

After waiting for one nerve-wracking day, he was acquitted and even offered slight praise: "That Lord Clive did, at the same time, render great and meritorious services to this country." But for him, the year-long fight had been demoralizing. A famous portrait of this aging merchant king, done in 1773 by Sir Nathaniel Dance, shows a slightly paunchy man weighted down by the heavy finery of his garments. His eyes droop and his mouth is straight; his jowls sag, and there is no sparkle in his gaze, giving the general impression of a glum toad. Clive retired from public life in May 1773, and a few months later departed for France by himself, not returning to London until late June. He remained depressed and in physical pain, and in November 1774, a year and a half after his public ordeal, he stabbed himself in the throat with a penknife in his London manor, leaving no note or explanation. He was forty-nine years old and was survived by his wife and four children.

One of Clive's many biographers, Michael Edwardes, has observed that "Clive's 'rapacity' has been condemned by Victorian moralisers, modern 'radical' historians, and Indian nationalists. The privileges and profits demanded and obtained by him and by others were no more than the perquisites of power which Indian rulers and their supporters accepted as of right." Clive truly believed that he deserved his vast fortune, that he had done no wrong in plundering a foreign land—the vast bulk of his fortune, indeed that of all the nabobs of the era, had not been derived from successful and honest trade, but rather from corruption and bribery. He could hardly be blamed for his cynicism about other titled and wealthy English families, who no doubt had derived their status and wealth from equally unsavoury actions in the near or distant past. Clive probably did restrain his plundering after the Battle of Plassey; he could have taken even more than he did, there being no one to stop him. He also could have kept all the treasure to himself and not shared it with his officers or contributed to the company soldiers' pension fund. Clive has never been accused of personal cruelty or violence, merely of grandiosity and of accumulating great wealth from crumbling empires that presented opportunities for his vast ambition.

THE 1772 parliamentary inquiry into the English East India Company began the slow unravelling of the company's powers. Despite vigorous resistance by its shareholders and supporters in Parliament, Lord North's Act of 1773, arising from the airing of the company's dirty laundry during the inquiry, changed both the way the company would operate and the way in which Bengal would be ruled. The act brought the British government officially into the affairs of India. The English East India Company would no longer be an entirely independent entity. Its powers were severely curtailed: no longer could it declare war; no longer could it make decisions that affected both national and international affairs. The part of India it controlled would now have a governor general, a council and a supreme court.

A decade later, in 1784, Pitt's India Bill introduced further controls on the company's behaviour, giving Parliament a voice in all decisions relating to India's political, military and commercial affairs through a board of control. By the late eighteenth century, the company's monopoly began to be viewed as anachronistic by the new breed of free traders of the burgeoning Industrial Revolution, who saw India as a destination to ship manufactured goods to rather than as a source of imported silk, saltpetre and spices. Nevertheless the company continued to expand, exerting its military dominance in Singapore, Malaya, Burma and Hong Kong. Although more of the subcontinent came under British control, it was not the company's army that did the conquering, but the king's, particularly under Arthur Wellesley, the future Duke of Wellington, who subdued great swaths of the Indian interior and placed millions more people under the company's control.

That control was being eroded, however: in 1813 the board of control assumed authority over the company's commercial functions and eliminated its monopoly. Twenty years later, all the company's special rights regarding trade with China were likewise curtailed, and its role was limited to the administration of the territories of India and the training and deploying of a mighty cadre of civil servants. As its influence waned, the power and control of the British government waxed, until the more than two-century-old enterprise existed only as a quasi-governmental agency, just as the Dutch East India Company eventually became an arm of the government of the Netherlands in Indonesia.

On November 1, 1858, after British troops crushed an Indian uprising, Queen Victoria assumed the title of sovereign, and later empress, of India. By that time, the Company of Merchants of London Trading into the East Indies had long since abandoned its commercial origins, although it still held titular commercial sway over a fifth of the world's population. Not until January 1, 1874, was the company officially dissolved by the East India Stock Redemption Act, ending its long, dramatic and somewhat romantic history.

It would be overly simplistic to say that the company's incredible success in the mid-eighteenth century flowed directly from Robert Clive's military victories. But his tremendous abilities and his scheming brilliance certainly enabled the defeat of the French company and resulted in the early territorial gains that formed the beachhead for its later expansion. Clive did not leave an empire but rather the framework of an empire, a skeleton that was filled out by others in the coming decades. He was in the right place to exploit dynamic shifts in the alignment of world commercial and political patterns. Before Clive arrived in India, the English East India Company was a moderately successful trading enterprise, just beginning to worry over the French company's manipulation of local political struggles between Indian princes. When he died, the company was emerging as the holder of a mighty empire on the far side of the world, the conqueror of the richest province of one of the world's most populous and wealthy kingdoms, and on its way to becoming one of the greatest corporations in history.

Robert Clive, in his intuitive brilliance in perceiving the fragile political makeup of post-Mughal India, was one of the world's great merchant kings. He had the confidence to not shy away from the very large challenges and opportunities that were placed before him. Not only did his mind foresee opportunity and possibility amid political chaos and daunting odds, but his arrogance—his sense of personal entitlement, his chutzpah— was probably the trait that enabled him to change the world, for better or for worse.

Chapter 4

"Since my life is in constant danger not only from the
hostility of wild tribes but from men often unwilling to submit
to discipline, since my strength is exhausted and my health
dissipated battling the hardships I have had to endure, I feel
that that natural time, the hour of my death, is for me more
uncertain than for most men, and therefore I make my will."

ALEKSANDR ANDREYEVICH BARANOV, C. 1809

The Lord of Alaska

ALEKSANDR BARANOV AND

THE RUSSIAN AMERICAN COMPANY

· 1 ·

IN A FORMAL PORTRAIT PAINTED AT THE TIME OF HIS retirement in 1818, Aleksandr Andreyevich Baranov, "the Lord of Alaska," as he was sometimes known, is a balding, trim man. He is dressed in a formal black coat offset by a creamy-coloured silk neck scarf, over which a medal of distinction hangs prominently. He clasps a quill in his right hand, which is positioned over a partially scrawled parchment, as if the portraitist had suddenly disturbed Baranov in the act of completing his accounts or official correspondence. His gaze is direct and unflinching, his chin and lips firm as if his jaw were clenched, his posture relaxed and confident.

Overall, the portrait conveys the impression of a man of moderate distinction who begs to be told the truth, perhaps already knows it, and merely desires the telling to be personal. He seems a kindly father figure, trustworthy, patient and understanding. His lips curl ever so slightly upward, as if in inner contemplation of a private joke or in mildly amused resignation at the state of the world. He had ruled Russian Alaska for twenty-eight years; now, at seventy-two years of age and with his tenure at its end, he did not know what to do with himself.

During his time in the domain of the Russian American Company, on the eastern frontier of the Russian Empire, Baranov had earned a reputation for decisiveness bordering on ruthlessness, for even-handed severity in punishment, even while earning the deep respect and loyalty of many of his men. He led by example, and he kept his promises to them, donating his personal money when circumstances demanded and paying for the education in Russia of children he considered gifted. He had abandoned his first wife and children in Russia years before he departed for Russian America, but he always provided for them financially—even for the son and daughter he had adopted as foundlings. He was a hard worker and did not shield himself from the dangers faced by his men. The promotions and rewards he granted were based on merit and achievement, regardless of the recipient's parentage or racial background. At times, he used Russian American Company funds to cover indemnity payments to orphans and widows or for native men lost on voyages, like a lord magnanimously rewarding service, even in death—actions that were seemingly at odds with his decision to compel the men to service in the first place. During his tenure, the company pushed south along the northwest coast of America so that it maintained a presence as far as what is now the boundary between the U.S. state of Alaska and the Canadian province of British Columbia. Although he tactfully headed off the northward advance of British and American mariners and fur traders, he failed to establish Russian control over the Columbia River. He even presided over the founding of a Russian company settlement in California, but failed to found a similar outpost in Hawaii, which he had considered annexing as an outpost of the Russian Empire.

But Baranov's kindly and intelligent eyes and bland expression belied his darker traits. He was not averse to brutality in pursuit of his objectives; he used people unflinchingly and placed them in danger when he felt the need. Stubborn and determined, he frequently threatened his employers with his resignation when his demands were not met. Admired and beloved by some, he was feared and loathed by others. He survived two attempts, a decade apart, by his men to murder him. His treatment of Kodiak Island natives bordered on the inhumane and was certainly illegal according to Russian law. He also made war on his competitors for years, until his company was granted an official government monopoly.

As a corporate holding, at arm's length from the Russian government, Russia's American colony was built by Baranov and expanded, with his boundless energy and imagination, to become an enormous territory roughly equivalent to today's Alaska. He began by aggressively warring with the native tribes. In 1804 he bombarded a Tlingit village for six days from aboard a Russian warship, forcing the residents to accept the authority of the Russian American Company. He dislocated thousands of native peoples from their homes and reordered their activities to suit the needs and interests of the company. In the process, he reduced them to serfs in their own land while extracting vast quantities of furs and other natural goods for his board of directors and noble shareholders in St. Petersburg. But when he was forced from his position as head of the Russian American Company in Alaska, a shadow hung over his departure. He was facing politically motivated charges, an investigation and a possible trial back in St. Petersburg. It was a long and adventurous life for the eldest son of a humble storekeeper born in a remote, backward village along the Finnish border.

The Lord of Alaska was born in the tiny village of Kargopol in 1747 (around the time the young English trader Robert Clive first requested a transfer to the military branch of the English East India Company at Fort St. David). He was born in a sparsely settled region where the forest was broken by countless small lakes and ponds and where roads were muddy tracks. His father occupied the lowest rung of the trading hierarchy, so low that he was denied membership in the local merchants' guild; he was barely above the peasants in status. Although there was no school in the region, Baranov somehow learned to read and write a little and to keep accounts. A curious and enterprising boy, at the age of fifteen he fled south to Moscow, the business centre of the nation, to see the rumoured wonders of the world for himself. It was a shock to him, wrote Hector Chevigny, in his colourful and slightly fanciful 1942 biography *Lord of Alaska,* "to realize there could be so many people in the world, so many houses not built of logs, such huge markets, so many churches with their multi-colored domes, so many and such huge bells to fill the air at all hours."

In Moscow the energetic lad gained employment with a German merchant and spent the next decade or so learning all he could of commerce, bookkeeping, languages and, most importantly, reading and writing well. He avidly pursued studies in literature and science. He was also introduced to the rigid class structure of Russian society, in which nobles and merchants were segregated and his own lowly status could never be fully overcome. He rose to the rank of clerk before returning to his birthplace, where with his new capital he sought to establish himself as a higher-status merchant. But the return was a mistake. Although he married and had a daughter, he was not any happier in Kargopol now than he had been as a boy. After several years, in 1780, at the age of thirty-three, he left for Siberia with his younger brother Pyoter, filled with dreams of making his fortune. He never saw his wife or daughter again, though he always provided for them generously.

In Siberia, Baranov and his brother worked as itinerant traders and tax collectors in Irkutsk, a prosperous town of around six thousand inhabitants, saving their money until he, Pyoter and two other partners opened a glass factory, using local raw materials. It was Baranov's idea, gleaned from his readings while in Moscow. Glass then being an expensive import to the remote region, the enterprise was an immediate success, and Baranov was given an official commemoration from St. Petersburg for his accomplishment of helping to improve industry in Siberia. But even after eight years in Irkutsk, he had not been invited to join the local merchants' guild because of his low class. Frustrated with this discrimination (which was probably the reason for him always treating his employees according to their abilities, not their class), his restless spirit stirred again. He also chafed at the obligation to make decisions jointly with his partners—he wanted to be the boss, even if it meant less money and more risk. So again he fled, for a further frontier, dragging his younger brother along to the sparsely inhabited region north of the Sea of Okhotsk. He planned to establish trading outposts for furs among the Chukchi, a feared and violent people. A prominent merchant named Grigorii Ivanovich Shelikhov, then just returning from founding a Russian colony on Kodiak Island in Alaska, tried to persuade Baranov to join his venture as a manager. Baranov refused, not wanting to subjugate his independence to the designs of another.

His expedition began with great promise. Since the discovery of Alaska a few decades earlier and the rush to plunder its velvet booty of sea otter and fox furs, the domain of the Chukchi had been mostly abandoned by Russian traders. As a result, the quantity of furs had increased after many years of overhunting. Loading a giant raft with trade goods, the Baranov brothers poled north down the Lena River, over two thousand kilometres into Yakutsk, where they purchased reindeer as beasts of burden and continued north. After two years of trading, by 1790, they had amassed a small fortune in sable furs and were heading south when a large band of Chukchi ambushed them and stole the bulk of their cargo. Leaving his brother behind on the Sea of Okhotsk to defend what remained of their goods and furs, Baranov rushed south along the coast on horseback to report the theft to an old acquaintance, Johann Koch, who was the regional military commander at the village of Okhotsk, then Russia's only Pacific seaport.

Here fortune intervened. Confronted with bankruptcy, and without the means to secure new capital to start over, Baranov faced the real prospect that his shares in the glass company in Irkutsk would be forfeited to pay his creditors, which would leave his family destitute. He was pondering his next move when he received an unexpected offer. Shelikhov was in town, overseeing the launch of his ship to Alaska. He again made the trader an offer to head the thriving colony of Kodiak Island and, indeed, all of Shelikhov's business interests in the new land. Shelikhov wanted someone ambitious and trustworthy, someone charismatic and interested in expanding the enterprise; someone who could take charge of an increasingly volatile situation and deal with the incursions of foreign (chiefly British) traders and the possibility of privateers. They negotiated an open-term appointment, but the forty-three-year-old Baranov knew that it would continue for years. The ship was leaving within weeks, and Baranov had to decide quickly. Given his financial predicament, he really had no choice. Reluctantly, he agreed.

He could hardly fault the terms: he would be called the chief manager, an important title, with 210 shares in the Shelikhov-Golikov Company; he was to have absolute authority over Shelikhov's operations in Alaska, with the stipulation that "if the local circumstances prevented following the government regulations or if the best interests of the company and fatherland were served otherwise, I am not prevented from taking action which I deem fit." He was also given authority to be the representative of the Russian government in Alaska, to judge crimes, settle disputes and accurately record all explorations and the placement of copper territorial markers. He was to found new satellite colonies and improve and expand the operation as he saw fit. The money would be enough to pay off his debts and secure the livelihood of his Russian family.

Baranov boarded the ship *Three Saints,* along with about fifty other recruits for the colonial-commercial venture, and sailed east for Alaska in the fall of 1790. It turned out to be a terrifying near-death experience, the most dangerous and wildest adventure of his life.

· 2 ·

RUSSIAN TRADERS AND PRIVATE EXPLORERS HAD BEEN sailing the Pacific east to the distant shores of North America for about fifty years, ever since the epic voyage of Vitus Bering known as the second Kamchatka expedition. This expedition had been inspired by the progressive reforms of Peter the Great and continued by his widow, Empress Anna Ivanovna.

The second Kamchatka expedition was one of the most ambitious scientific and exploratory expeditions ever undertaken. Based on Bering's sober proposal to follow up on the inconclusive results of his first voyage in search of America a decade earlier, the second expedition was designed to show Europe the grandeur and sophistication of Russia. By the time Bering saw his final instructions in 1731, they had swollen to such grandiose proportions that he scarcely recognized them. He would be at the head of a virtual army of exploration: a few thousand scientists, secretaries, students, interpreters, artists, surveyors, naval officers, mariners, soldiers and skilled labourers, all of whom had to be brought to the eastern coast of Russia across eight thousand kilometres of roadless forests, swamps and tundra, along with tools, iron, canvas, food, books and scientific implements.

Once he arrived in Kamchatka, Bering was supposed to build two ships and sail east to America, charting the North American Pacific coastline as far south as California, in addition to charting the coasts of Kamchatka and the Arctic Ocean and establishing astronomical positions throughout Siberia. Concurrently, he was to build another three ships and survey the Kuril Islands, Japan and other areas of eastern Asia. These were his most reasonable and practical instructions. His orders also called for him to populate Okhotsk with Russian citizens, introduce cattle raising on the Pacific coast, found elementary and nautical schools in the distant outpost, construct a dockyard for deepwater ships, and establish iron mines and ironworks for smelting ore. Not surprisingly, despite Bering's Herculean efforts, these tasks would not be completed for generations.

On June 5, 1741, Bering's two ships slid out of the makeshift dockyards at Petropavlovsk, lurched into the grey, choppy waters and hoisted sails. As the *St. Paul* pushed east through the fog, Bering spent much of his time laid up below deck with an energy-sapping illness. The officers thus began running the ship without consulting him or informing him of their decisions. For almost a month, it was a dreary and uncertain voyage; the voyagers saw nothing but sky and sea until July 16. Then, their first view of America: a mighty, snow-dusted spire shrouded in fog. It towered over a vast range of smaller mountains, snug against the coast as far as the eye could see, with endless forests of green emerging into view through the mist. It was St. Elias Day, and they named the peak accordingly. The mountains, the naturalist

Georg Steller observed, "were so lofty that we could see them quite plainly at sea at a distance of sixteen Dutch miles . . . I can not recall having seen higher mountains anywhere in Siberia and Kamchatka."

All the officers and mariners cheered and congratulated each other on discovering the new land. But Bering, roused temporarily from his cabin for the event, showed no elation when he strolled on deck. Surveying the scene and hearing the faint roar of distant breakers crashing against the shore, he shrugged his shoulders, returned inside and later noted glumly, yet prophetically, "we think now we have accomplished everything, and many go about greatly inflated, but they do not consider where we have reached land, how far we are from home, and what may yet happen; who knows but that perhaps trade winds may arise, which may prevent us from returning? We do not know this country; nor are we provided with supplies for a wintering."

Bering's fears proved to be prophecy. After exploring several islands, encountering a variety of native peoples and its passengers realizing the enormous size of the new lands to the east, Bering's ship was wrecked on an island off the Russian coast. Scurvy took hold during the voyage and killed many of the crew as well as Bering himself. The island where they spent a wretched winter eking out a miserable existence is now known as Bering Island, after the doomed captain. During the long, dark months of that winter, the shipwrecked mariners observed several of the unique creatures that were endemic to either Bering Island, the Aleutian Islands or coastal Alaska, including the massive, now-extinct northern manatee, sea lions and fur seals, which "covered the whole beach to such an extent that it was not possible to pass without danger to life and limb."

The most populous creature they observed, and the most important in the history of the Russian American Company, was the sea otter, a friendly, communal animal that lived close to shore all along the coast. "Altogether in life it is a beautiful and pleasing animal," Steller wrote, "cunning and amusing in its habits . . . Seen when they are running, the gloss of their hair surpasses the blackest velvet. They prefer to lie together in families, the male with its mate, the half-grown young and the very young sucklings all together. The male caresses the female by stroking her, using the forefeet as hands, and places himself over her; she, however, often pushes him away from her for fun and in simulated coyness, as it were, and plays with her offspring like the fondest mother. Their love for their young is so intense that they expose themselves to the most manifest danger of death. When their young are taken away from them, they cry bitterly, like a small child, and grieve so much that, as I came to know on several occasions, after ten to fourteen days they grow as lean as a skeleton, become sick and feeble, and will not leave the shore."

The sea otters were playful creatures that elicited amusement from mariners until someone realized that their skins were extremely valuable. Their furs were worth a fortune in China, and throughout the summer the men hunted thousands of them and stripped them of their skins. Hardened by years of harsh life in Kamchatka and the dreadful sufferings of the past winter, the hunters saw the otters as their ticket to a life of ease and went "raging among the animals without discipline or order," clubbing them, drowning them and stabbing them until the large herds had all but disappeared from the eastern side of Bering Island. In the spring they constructed a makeshift boat from salvaged planks, loaded it with mountains of otter skins and sailed west, back to the Asian mainland. Bering had, along with dozens of his unfortunate mariners, perished miserably of scurvy during the winter. The survivors, however, brought back the tale of their incredible voyage—and of the fortune that awaited others hardy enough to brave the journey.

· 3 ·

THE FUR HUNTERS WHO EXTENDED THE REACH OF Imperial Russia across the Pacific Ocean, and who eventually became the nucleus of the Russian American Company, lost little time in exploiting the valuable resources of the new land. When the first mariners returned from Bering's ill-fated voyage, the tales they wove of the wealth of sea otters in the Aleutians and Alaska had an immediate impact. The following year a shipload of hunters returned with a cargo of sixteen hundred sea otters, two thousand fur seals and two thousand blue foxes. Soon thousands of hunters annually crossed the Bering Sea in their quest for the velvet booty. Financed by merchants as far away as Moscow, traders became rich overnight, prompting even more to enter the bonanza. Within fourteen years, Bering Island's treasure of sea otters, sea lions, fur seals and foxes was gone. The hunters moved farther east, where they occasionally engaged in bloody battles with the coastal natives, after which they forced them into servitude as hunters.

Soon the hunters' forays became a vicious wild-west-style slaughter as they moved from island to island, attacking and capturing natives and engaging in massive harvests of sea otters. One expedition in 1768 returned with forty thousand seals and two thousand sea otter pelts, fifteen thousand pounds of walrus ivory and vast quantities of whalebone. Expeditions began venturing farther along the coast so that voyages lasted up to two years and the crews, a mix of Russians and indigenous Siberians, established semi-permanent depots or settlements. On the Asian mainland the settlement of Okhotsk grew busy as the depot of the American trade, hosting the sailors and their families as well as the semi-annual influx of merchants who brought in packhorse trains from Irkutsk laden with supplies. After making the exchange, they trundled, under the protection of guards, west into the heart of Asia with their American furs. Chinese merchants ran caravans out of Kiakhta on the Mongolian-Russian border, a 2,100-kilometre journey across Mongolia and the Gobi desert from China.

After several decades of invasion and plunder, the various trading companies coalesced around a handful of conglomerates, backed by capital from Moscow. The Shelikhov-Golikov Company was the most significant conglomerate, with ambitions to dominate the fur trade and control all of Alaska. In 1767, when Grigorii Shelikhov was about twenty years old, he had met Ivan Larionovich Golikov, a disgraced financier who was several years older and who was serving a term of exile in Irkutsk. Shelikhov had worked in all areas of the fur trade, from sales at Kiakhta to production in Okhotsk, when he teamed up with Golikov. With Golikov's financial knowledge they started a strong enterprise of great scope. Shelikhov's wife, Natalia, tall and charming, was also shrewd in business and eager for success. After hearing of Captain James Cook's third voyage along the North American Pacific coast, the Russian entrepreneurs were inspired to expand their enterprise in Alaska with a permanent colony. After two years of planning, in 1783 Shelikhov and his wife were set to lead this group to Kodiak Island in a pilgrimage that included three ships carrying two hundred men, dozens of cattle, seeds for cabbages and potatoes, and tools. They had grand plans, some might say delusions, and took with them a blacksmith, carpenters, navigators and farmers. Shelikhov imagined cities flourishing along the coast, where music and art blended with commerce and agriculture, where fine houses and churches lined paved streets and public squares.

Although it was illegal for Russian traders to use violence against native Alaskans—this was a crime against the state ostensibly punishable by death—Shelikhov planned right from the outset to do exactly this to establish a foothold for his colony, counting on the great distance from Russia to keep his secret. He chose Kodiak Island, despite a history of violence with native people there that made most Russian ships avoid it. His ships landed in the summer of 1784, in what is now called Three Saints Bay (named after one of Shelikhov's ships), and quickly launched an assault against a native fortress. Over the next few months, Shelikhov and his settlers attacked and killed many natives, taking hostages and building fortresses and stockades around the island as well as exploiting intertribal rivalries to gain additional manpower for the conquest of the region.

Shelikhov followed his vicious assaults with placatory gifts and unexpected fairness. Captured islanders were surprised to be treated with respect and dignity; the women were not exploited but encouraged to marry colonists, and many were urged to live near the Russian settlement. Once the company had established a toehold, Shelikhov tried to make friends. He built a small school to teach native children the Russian language and other basic skills, such as carpentry, that might make them useful to the new company colony. When he and Natalia sailed away in 1786, the colony was well underway.

Over the next several years Shelikhov, his wife and Golikov schemed and lobbied government officials in Irkutsk and St. Petersburg to grant them both a monopoly and state financing for their enterprise. They made exaggerated claims for their accomplishments as well as appeals to patriotism. One powerful and united company would be better able, they argued, to defend their territory from the encroachment of British, American and Spanish traders. But rumours of Shelikhov's brutal methods on Kodiak Island had begun to trickle back west to Russia, no doubt spread and amplified by agents of the other powerful trading enterprises operating in Alaska. Shelikhov was a boaster and an exaggerator, claiming that he had converted all the Aleut Islanders to the Orthodox faith and had added over fifty thousand subjects to the empire, as well as making other outrageous claims that were so patently false that they hindered rather than helped his cause.

Although it was still the era of the great monopolies in Europe, Russia's empress, Catherine the Great, was not interested in obtaining new lands on the distant fringe of her already expansive and sparsely populated domain. "It is one thing to trade," she claimed, "quite another thing to take possession." She turned down Shelikhov's requests, and he retreated east to Irkutsk. All was not well with the Shelikhov-Golikov Company: although the colony was running smoothly and furs were being returned across the Pacific to its warehouses, the trade with China was closed—it had been so for years, because of a diplomatic dispute. The Alaskan furs were building up in warehouses, and as a result most of the company's competitors had cut expenses and temporarily abandoned the trade. It was easier for them to do so, since they had no colony to maintain. Shelikhov's money was running out; his managers in Alaska had not been proactive enough, so the colony was stagnating rather than expanding.

Shelikhov had already replaced one manager, and now the second, a Greek named Evstrat Delarov, was also proving to be a disappointment. Shelikhov had earlier tried to hire Baranov for the position; indeed, historians have speculated that Baranov may have been one of the investors in Shelikhov's enterprise. Wondering what to do about his ineffectual manager at Kodiak, Shelikhov was probably delighted when Baranov arrived in Okhotsk, momentarily destitute and open to possibilities that he had dismissed only a few years earlier. As we have seen, he lost no time in offering Baranov a position.

· 4 ·

BARANOV HAD NEVER BEEN TO SEA AND KNEW LITTLE of what to expect from a long ocean voyage. If he had imagined it with some trepidation, he would have at least been mentally prepared. He boarded the ship to Alaska in August 1790, with high hopes and dreams, but was soon facing a set of unusual difficulties. Crammed into the hold of the small ship were cows and sheep, milling about, defecating, mooing and baying in terror and confusion. Goods were crammed into every available space: boxes of tools and work materials, cloth, nails, fuel, bales of tobacco, bricks of tea, great sacks of sugar, salt and flour—mundane but necessary provisions that could keep for years. The overburdened old ship lurched and wallowed in the swells, its aging timbers moaned and protested under the strain and water leaked in to such an alarming extent that the passengers were pumping round the clock. They could barely rouse themselves from their befouled bunks, so sick were they with the motion of the ship.

The ship's water casks were improperly filled, and the precious liquid drained away into the bilge. The captain ordered water rations cut, while storms bucked the ship about the wild ocean. Soon the dreaded scurvy had sapped the vitality of dozens: their teeth fell out, their breath became rancid, and strength left their limbs. When the lookout finally spied the island of Unalaska through the fog and mist, it was nearly too late. Dropping anchor there, the men rushed ashore for fresh water, but a storm moved the anchor at night and the *Three Saints* was dragged towards shore, where its already decaying timbers scraped against rock, parted and let the water in. The ship let out a sigh as it settled. As the storm increased in severity, the passengers and crew rushed to unload the precious cargo—their very lives depended upon it. They ferried the supplies ashore on rafts and in small boats while the *Three Saints* was picked apart and its planks tossed up on the gravelly beach. The fifty-two men disconsolately settled in for the winter on the barren, windswept island, hunkering down in some dugout dwellings abandoned by the natives.

Once he was on land, though, Baranov was filled with excitement and energy. At forty-four years of age, he was by far the eldest of the group; indeed, many considered him far too old for this harsh life. But he explored all winter, hiking constantly and observing the new land, learning the language of the Aleuts and practising how to sail a small boat and hunt sea otters. And his group survived the winter. In the spring, all but five of the men loaded themselves into three sea-lion hide boats and pressed on, through the cold and rain, to cover the 1,100 kilometres to Kodiak Island; the other five remained to guard the remains of the cargo. Baranov did not like sea travel. Exhausted by the journey, he broke down with fever and remained weak and ill for over a month after the boats arrived at Kodiak Island in June 1791. When he recovered, he was stunned by what he saw: heavily forested, snow-capped mountains thrust skyward right from the water; it was a majestic, desolate, harsh and awe-inspiring scene.

The following spring, the home-going men sailed away in one of the two remaining ships, leaving Baranov with 110 men, most of whom, Baranov noted, were lacking in ambition and enterprise. Certainly they were not troublemakers, as Shelikhov had chosen them for their docility, but they needed direction and order. Baranov soon imposed a quasi-military structure on the settlement, including strict obedience to orders, periodic inspection of the bunkhouses and ceremonial musters in which the men stood at attention to observe the raising and lowering of the Russian flag. Gambling was prohibited, and alcohol consumption was limited to milder liquids made from fermented berries (although Baranov kept a secret still for his personal use). Prostitution was prohibited, and strict regulations governed relations between the Russian men and native women, in effect requiring a form of monogamous marriage, partially financed by the Shelikhov company. Baranov enforced laws respecting the native custom that children belonged to their mothers, a custom that meshed nicely with his own and his company's interests in having the men remain in Russian America. Men who grew attached to their female partners and children frequently stayed on much longer than their legal five-year contract required, and many of them settled permanently.

Baranov improved the standing of his settlement with the nearby natives, the Alutiiq. He learned their language and customs and followed them, toured all of Kodiak Island to meet the people and negotiate with them, and enlisted hundreds of them to hunt sea otters the following spring. Those resisting his urgings to work were coerced to provide from each settlement "several persons of both genders"—which was of course illegal, but he trusted that news of the practice would remain buried. He had the authority to enlist native labourers only "provided every one of them is paid fair wages for his work." Although he technically had no legal authority to punish either Russians or Alaskans, he frequently used the lash to maintain discipline in the distant outpost. For him, the natives were employees, customers, competitors and, in some cases, "second-tier" persons, much like Russian serfs. But Baranov was not all dour and full of the lash. He was also fond of music, dancing and singing, and the barrack-like communal lodging houses were frequently enlivened by energetic celebrants, including Baranov himself, who was an eager participant in festivities.

Baranov moved the entire settlement to a more sheltered and convenient location, working hard to ensure that the new town was "beautiful and pleasant to live in." He also began building new forts or outposts on the mainland, where different native groups lived, and persuaded them to maintain good relations, coaxing them with goods and promises of trade. He even took as his wife Anna, the daughter of one of the prominent chiefs. He had a comfortable two-storey house built for himself and Anna, and soon they had a son. Baranov met with English traders, including the famous British mariner George Vancouver, who was then creating a monumental chart of the entire region from California to Alaska for the British government.

But there were always troubles. The Aleuts and Alutiiq of the Kodiak region, who were essentially under his command, sometimes met with war parties of slave-raiding Tlingit from farther south. The men of Baranov's colony were constantly in conflict with other Russian traders in a low-level yet violent struggle. Baranov persuaded many of the natives not to trade with his competitors, and on occasion urged them to attack rival trading outposts. Throughout the 1790s he accomplished much with very little support, keeping everyone fed and managing to placate the quarrelling factions. But he was in constant fear of mutiny by labourers and of attacks from arrogant higher-class Russian naval officers that Shelikhov had hired, and on one occasion he was stabbed by a drunken malcontent in one of the work barracks when he chastised employees for stealing company supplies of liquor and tobacco and for refusing to work. His authority was undermined by the cadre of priests who secretly sent letters back to Russia denouncing his leadership, claiming he was immoral and encouraged drunkenness and other activities, such as singing. Having reached the limits of his tolerance, he threatened to resign when Shelikhov dared to criticize him: "Since coming to work for you I fear I've lost that which I value most—my good name. You had best find a successor. I am getting old and my senses are dulling... My energy is failing me. The next time I ship furs, however, I come with them unless you change your attitude toward me and send me men capable of labour instead of parasites picked up just to round out a figure." But before he could leave, he was caught up in events that would keep him in Russian America the remainder of his life.

While Baranov toiled away in Alaska in the 1790s, slowly building an orderly, efficient and profitable enterprise along a mostly uncharted coast, his titular boss, Shelikhov, was working to place the business on the soundest footing he could imagine in Russia: a monopoly. In 1792, trade with China was again opened to Russian merchants through the isolated outpost of Kiakhta, and Shelikhov was well placed to take advantage. For a good price, he quickly sold off the great store of American furs he had been amassing and began to pay off the company's debts. Things were good: he had kept his colony alive, and Baranov was proving to be all he had hoped for: sober, ambitious, enterprising and expansion-minded, and aware that he was not merely running a mercantile enterprise, but was also representing Russian culture. Now, if only the pesky competition could be eliminated so that the Russians could present a united front against the dangerous and potentially violent native peoples and interloping British and American traders.

Shelikhov continued to work on gaining government support for his enterprise, or at the very least getting a restriction on other companies joining the competition—too many ships sailing to Alaska would drive the price of goods down in China. As luck would have it, he had a new supporter in the court of Catherine the Great—a distant relative, twenty-year-old Platon Zubov, Catherine's most recent lover. Shamelessly indulging Zubov, Catherine allowed him to sell favours for his own enrichment. Through this avenue, Shelikhov secured a partial monopoly on his activities in Russian America: no competitor would be allowed to establish an outpost or settlement, or indeed even to trade, within 500 versts (about 530 kilometres) of his and Golikov's operations. Shelikhov and his wife

Natalia celebrated for a time, but were dismayed with the arrival of more of Zubov's "good" news. Zubov had tirelessly lobbied for several other of Shelikhov's past requests: ten missionaries, a supply of Siberian exiles to ease his labour shortage, and the right or privilege of buying Russian serfs as agricultural workers. In the past, Shelikhov had boasted of his need for missionaries to tend to the spiritual needs of the colonists and spread the Christian faith to the natives. Indeed, he had lied about already having built a church to house them, and promised to pay for their upkeep. He had of course expected government financial aid, but none was forthcoming, so the gifts of serfs and priests were more of a mixed blessing, and one wonders if that was indeed the intent.

But Shelikhov and his wife rose to the occasion. They would be sending more than 150 new people across the Pacific to Alaska, and set to work acquiring the ships, arranging the financing and organizing for this influx of settlers and employees. With the limited government monopoly in place, the colonists and missionaries would be reliant on Shelikhov for all communication with Russia, something over which he had complete control. And he had the doughty Baranov to handle any complaints in Russian America. When the delegation of workers and missionaries arrived in Irkutsk in May 1794, Shelikhov and Natalia met them with smiles and a warm welcome, particularly for the government official that had been sent from St. Petersburg to oversee the well-being of the priests and serfs and ensure that Shelikhov kept his promises.

Nikolai Petrovich Rezanov was a young and handsome noble from a distinguished Russian family that had lost most of its ancestral wealth. Highly educated and urbane, Rezanov had been in the military before studying law and joining the Bureau of Petitions. He accepted an invitation to stay as an honoured guest of the Shelikhovs in their large home, where he was introduced to their attractive, energetic and adventurous daughter, Anna. So enamoured were they with each other that Anna joined the travelling party of around four hundred as they barged and rode their horses thousands of miles east to Okhotsk on a journey that lasted months. As they slowly wended their way over the mountains, Shelikhov regaled Rezanov with tales of the valuable lands in Russian America and of their value to Russia, of the need to prevent the British from claiming it all and of the great achievements of his colony, all done for the betterment of the empire, naturally.

The rude, dirty and chaotic settlements Baranov was banging into shape across the distant waters were little more than rudimentary factories for the extraction of furs, populated with surly workers and potentially violent indentured natives. In Shelikhov's telling, however, they were quaint European villages eager for priests, teachers and greater links with Russia. After the ships set off from Okhotsk, bringing to Baranov an unwelcome and entirely unexpected human cargo, Shelikhov, Rezanov and their small party worked their way back to Irkutsk. While awaiting the winter snows to make travel easier for the long journey east, Rezanov and Anna fell in love and were married in January 1796. They set off for a new life together in St. Petersburg. As part of Anna's substantial dowry, Shelikhov and Natalia had settled upon her a significant number of the shares of the Shelikhov-Golikov Company, a clever move that ensured Rezanov would not forget his interest in Russian America once he was back in the capital. Six months later, Shelikhov was dead from a heart attack at the age of forty-eight.

On Kodiak Island, Baranov was furious at being saddled with the responsibility for the priests and demanded to be relieved after his five-year contract so that he could return to Russia. Natalia at first delayed and then begged him to stay on, and then further delayed sending his replacement for years, citing the chaos that Shelikhov's death had precipitated. She had taken over the management of the enterprise and was embroiled in legal squabbles with the merchants of Irkutsk. The charges eventually reached St. Petersburg, where she fortunately had an ally in her son-in-law, Rezanov. The merchants of Irkutsk trading with Russian America were resisting all of Natalia's efforts to get them to join their resources for a common end, despite additional pressure from the Russian government to form the United American Company. They wanted their independence, and as a result they hated Natalia. Rezanov, who had assumed a position of power as a respected adviser under the new czar, Paul, persuaded him of the need for a colonial corporation in the mould of those created by other European powers: the Dutch East India Company, the English East India Company and the Hudson's Bay Company. It was a tried-and-true model for success. This monopoly would serve "to soften the manners of the savages by bringing them into continuous contact with Russians . . . and the Russian way of looking at things," Rezanov advised. Russian America, despite nearly half a century of unofficial occupation, still had no government. Rezanov proposed that the entity be called the Russian American Company.

On July 8, 1799, Czar Paul I decided in favour of Rezanov and the new Russian American Company. All competing companies had one year to either be absorbed or wind up their operations. The czar also changed the long-standing ban on nobles engaging in commercial activity by allowing them to invest in, but not manage, the new monopoly. Natalia and her children were all ennobled for their role in promoting Russian culture in the wilds of America. Rezanov was appointed procurator general of the senate, and became the only official government representative on the board of the Russian American Company.

Members of the aristocracy and senior government officials flocked to invest in the new company, as did merchants and traders. In 1800 the head office of the enterprise was moved from Irkutsk to St. Petersburg, to be closer to both the government and powerful investors. It was a good year to invest; in its first year, the value of company stock spiked nearly 300 per cent. Baranov owned a substantial number of shares, and when he heard the news he must have chuckled in satisfaction at his good fortune at not pressing for his resignation. Now he did not want to leave his new home, for it was also the home of his two children, Antipatr and Irina, and a wife with whom he had grown comfortable. With the monopoly in place, he would no longer be distracted dealing with pesky competitors and could devote himself solely to the task of expanding the Russian American Company's trade network, spreading Russian culture and promoting Russia's political dominance. He was elevated to the position of manager, or governor, in charge of the Russian American Company, which had monopoly jurisdiction, political and commercial, over all of Russian America.

· 5 ·

THE POWERS OF THE RUSSIAN AMERICAN COMPANY were similar to those of the other famous trading monopolies of the era and included the right to maintain armed forces, make treaties and agreements with other nearby powers and, of course, conduct commercial activity as a monopoly. The company would own all the property within its jurisdiction, save the purely personal property of its employees, and control all other activity. Its domain was to be enormous—from the Arctic as far south as the 55th parallel, and from Siberia east to the Pacific American coast and then inland to an as yet undefined distance.

The company's initial charter was to last for twenty years. It was to be a government within a government, and Baranov was to be the undisputed boss over what was basically a medium-sized kingdom. Although thousands of native people would laugh at the notion that Baranov was now their overlord, the company already had nine outposts other than Kodiak, which by now had about forty wooden buildings, including a church.

Russian power in America increased after the formation of the Russian American Company because the various local peoples could no longer play off the competing Russian business enterprises against each other. "After 1799," writes historian Lydia Black in *Russians in Alaska, 1732–1867,* "there was no room for maneuvering, and political independence in external affairs was lost to all nations within the immediate control of the Company." The balance of power had shifted, and the company continued to expand its operations southward into the sea-otter-rich territory of the warlike Tlingit. When Baranov first visited Sitka Sound in 1797, he found it to be an ideal spot for a company base. The large, sheltered inlet was located among intricate, forest-lined fjords dotted with innumerable islands. The climate was rainy and the vegetation lush, made possible by mild ocean currents. Gargantuan stands of hemlock, spruce and cedar blanketed mighty mountains; the soil was rich for agriculture and the waters good for fishing. Most importantly, the region hosted a multitude of sea otters, which were becoming hard to find farther north. But this was, of course, not an empty wilderness: it was the heartland of the Tlingit. The beaches were lined with giant cedar longhouses situated behind rows of totem poles. Hector Chevigny writes: "Their civilization was definite, their arts developed to the point of formalism; they practiced democratic government yet upheld grades of aristocracy ... Like piratical Vikings they put to sea in long, perfectly fashioned canoes, seating thirty warriors armed with helmets, breastplates, and shields. They wandered hundreds of miles from their bases, to Puget's Sound and the Columbia River, up to the Aleutians and even along the Bering coast, in search of booty and slaves to labor in their villages or to offer as human sacrifices." Invading this territory would certainly cause trouble, and had not been possible when Russian enterprises were competing with one another.

Baranov feared that if he failed to push his operations farther south, the British would move in, claim the territory and dominate the trade; his intelligence reports suggested that a number of foreign ships were visiting the region every year to trade for valuable pelts. "It is safe to assume," he wrote, "that in the last ten years the English and Americans have sent to that region ten ships annually and we may also assume each carried away an average of... two thousand skins... At the current Canton price of forty-five rubles apiece this amounts to four hundred and fifty thousand rubles... And such shipments to Canton have a very depressing effect on our own market... If we want to prevent the ruin of our own business by the English and Americans some such step must be taken. Above all, it is imperative that we move nearer them to watch their actions." The British and American traders were also dealing in guns, and the raiding parties of Tlingit coming north were now far more dangerous. The Napoleonic War in Europe was weakening the British and Spanish, so it was time for the Russian American Company to reach south and establish control. Baranov set his eyes on Sitka Sound, where the company could establish a new base and settlement.

In the winter of 1799 Baranov threw himself into the Herculean task of planning the advance, and in May 1800 his ships and hundreds of men set off on the company's most ambitious expansion attempt into a new market. In total, Baranov commanded more than 1,100 men in small boats (about 100

Russians, 700 Aleuts and 300 natives of various other tribal groups). Storms sank some small ships, and a Tlingit night raid killed perhaps thirty men before they even reached Sitka. When Baranov met with Skayutlelt, the ranking chief of Sitka Sound, he was given permission to build a company fort on a prime beach. But the deal did not meet the unanimous approval of the sound's residents. The elderly chief was criticized by others of his clan for daring to let Russian invaders settle in the sound. While Baranov's labourers worked to transform the giant trees into walls for the fort, native war parties patrolled nearby. Within months, the fort was complete. Its base was about twenty metres long by fifteen metres wide, with walls half a metre thick, topped by a second storey that extended outward from the first, and included watchtowers at two corners. The settlement had a smithy, a cookhouse, barracks and fields cleared for agriculture and domestic animals. Baranov called it Archangel.

Weary from his exertions and the chilly weather, the fifty-two-year-old Baranov prepared to return north to Kodiak, leaving about thirty Russians and perhaps four hundred Aleuts to man the fort until he could return with reinforcements. On the voyage, nearly two hundred of his Aleut hunters perished from eating tainted shellfish. He faced a near-mutiny upon his return to Kodiak, one that was urged on by priests and some swaggering naval officers, abetted by the fact that they had not received supplies from Okhotsk in two years. Baranov subdued the mutineers just as the long-delayed news arrived of his appointment as head manager of the Russian American Company. Realizing that he was now quite wealthy due to the rise in value of his shares, he donated substantial sums to fund a school. He also received recognition for all his hard work for the company and the nation: a medal from the new czar, Alexander, "for faithful service in hardship and want and for unremitting loyalty."

His triumph, however, was soon tainted by news of tragedy. Later that summer he learned that his settlement and fort at Sitka had been attacked by Tlingit warriors, armed with American guns, and had been "reduced to ashes and the people annihilated." There were only forty-two survivors out of hundreds of colonists he had left there only months before. The Tlingit had then plundered more than four thousand sea otter pelts from the storerooms. During the summer of 1800, Tlingit warriors also attacked other Russian American Company outposts along the coast, killing nearly six hundred people. The company's losses were stupendous, as was the loss in lives, including those of men whom Baranov had known for years. And then there was the company's loss of access to the best remaining sea otter habitat.

Baranov was certainly buffeted by extremes of news. Just after learning of this devastating setback for the company, he heard that St. Petersburg had elevated his rank to that of collegiate councillor—equivalent to a colonel in the army, or a captain in the navy. If he so chose, he could demand to be addressed as "Excellency." For a man of humble birth and education, it was an astonishing elevation that would make his job of governing Russian America significantly easier. To his board of directors he wrote, "I am a nobleman, but Sitka is destroyed. I cannot live under the burden, so I am going forth either to restore the possessions of my august benefactor or to die in the attempt."

Vowing revenge on the Tlingit, Baranov promised to retake Sitka and keep it with the same obsessive determination that had propelled him to carve a profitable business enterprise out of a collection of malcontents, under-supported by a head office on a distant continent and plagued with internal disputes and power struggles. He schemed with British sea captain Joseph O'Cain to acquire arms and ammunition, and worked tirelessly to get the money he needed for wages and equipment by sending hundreds of Aleuts south to California with O'Cain in a bizarre profit-sharing scheme that surely would not have passed muster among his board of directors in St. Petersburg. The furs would be captured with Russian American Company personnel; O'Cain's large ship would then transport them across the Pacific Ocean, and O'Cain would sell them in Canton, under the American flag (Russia was forbidden to trade there). O'Cain would then provide all the Russian American Company profit to Baranov in guns, ammunition and other equipment needed for his conquest of the Tlingit homeland. By September 1804 Baranov had amassed his corporate invasion force and began sailing south in a great fleet that consisted of two sloops, two schooners and three hundred smaller boats. By good fortune, a 450-ton Russian frigate, the *Neva,* commanded by Captain Lieutenant Urey Lisianski, was in the region and agreed to aid Baranov's assault.

When the imposing force entered Sitka Sound, Baranov sent a messenger demanding that the Tlingit surrender and leave the region: he would build his next fort and settlement on the very beach where the Tlingit village now stood, he vowed. But the Tlingit remained defiant. There was a bloody battle as Baranov's forces assaulted the Tlingit village, but the Russians were repulsed. Baranov was blasted in the arm before he called on the mighty *Neva* to bombard the Tlingit town with its cannons. They fired on the village for days before the Tlingit surrendered and fled. Later that fall, during formal peace negotiations with the Tlingit, Baranov gained the right to a new location for a Russian American Company settlement, exactly where he had vowed to put it. The Tlingit would remain an independent people from the company and retain their own laws and customs, but they were to be brought increasingly within the economic orbit of the company's operations.

Intermarriage became more common, and the Russian Orthodox Church became more influential. At the new company
base, which Baranov called New Archangel and established as
his head office, he built a shipyard and announced that it would
be open as an international port. For many years, New Archangel was the only free port in Pacific America for shipbuilding,
repairs and reprovisioning. The town, which became known as
Sitka, was to serve as the capital of Russian America until 1867.
A thousand or more people lived there, and dozens of ships
might be at anchor in the bay at any given time. Baranov commissioned a great library and government hall for the colony
there, and formalized the town centre with wooden boardwalks.
The surrounding land became farmland as well as a site for light
industry to service the port.

But the farther Baranov expanded his commercial enterprise
to the south and east, the farther he was from Okhotsk, and the
greater became his logistical problems. All his supplies had to
travel by ship the enormous distance from the Asian mainland,
following the Aleutian Islands thousands of kilometres round
the rim of the Gulf of Alaska in dangerous and uncertain sailing
conditions. All of Baranov's thousands of fur pelts then had to
be shipped back along this same treacherous route to Okhotsk,
before being carted overland into the heart of Asia to be traded
to Chinese merchants at Kiakhta, still the only location where
the Chinese government would permit Russian goods to enter
China. This arrangement was ludicrously inefficient and expensive, eroding the company's profits and saddling Baranov with
unending aggravation. American traders were able to pay native
hunters much more for their furs, and still be profitable because
they were closer to their home market.

But Baranov was a crafty man, not easily thwarted. His solution was to enter into deals with American merchant captains,
who were allowed to trade directly with Canton, to supply the

southern portion of his commercial empire with goods as well as to ship company furs directly to Canton and secretly avoid the Chinese embargo. As a result, by the early nineteenth century, the Boston-Sitka-Canton-Boston trade network, with stops in Hawaii, was well established. Baranov was joining Russian America to the web of Pacific commerce that was then evolving. He wanted a company base on Hawaii and also had his eyes set farther south, on Spanish California. It was certainly good business, but business was only half the guiding principle of the great trading monopolies. Was Baranov's scheme in accordance with the policy of the Russian government?

Not long after taking Sitka Sound and founding New Archangel, Baranov learned that he should expect an official visit from Imperial Chamberlain Nikolai Rezanov, the son-in-law of Baranov's original patron, Shelikhov, and his superior. No company official that outranked Baranov had ever made the crossing to his realm before. Rezanov was now in Japan, and would soon be crossing the Pacific to tour the corporate domain over which he had held titular authority in St. Petersburg for years without ever seeing it.

· 6 ·

AT THE TIME OF HIS VISIT, REZANOV WAS DISTRACTED and irritable, being overcome with grief. His beloved wife, Anna, had died in childbirth the previous year, and he was not his usual clear-thinking self. His diplomatic tour to Alaska on behalf of the Russian government, as well as on behalf of the Russian American Company, was his attempt to distract himself from the depression that had consumed him in St. Petersburg. His entourage included two Russian navy ships flying Russian flags and of course commanded by navy officers, but they had been outfitted and supplied with cargo by the Russian

American Company. Rezanov's official tour highlighted the ambiguous blending of authority and responsibility between corporate interests and state interests. Rezanov and the state were taking a greater interest in Russian America now that Baranov had increased the endeavour's scope and size.

After cruising along the Aleutian chain and stopping at the major company outposts en route, Rezanov arrived in Sitka in the summer of 1805. Rezanov's expectations of Russian America had come solely from the exaggerated stories of his late father-in-law, Shelikhov, and he was ill-prepared for its primitive state. With great ceremony he disembarked from his ships and marched through the new town of Sitka, accompanied by the diminutive, arthritic Baranov, prematurely aged at the age of fifty-eight from his travails on the frontier and his struggle to place the company on a sound financial and political footing. Rezanov found the town to be dirty, cramped and noisy. Mud was everywhere, construction was ongoing and Sitka afforded none of the luxuries to which Rezanov was accustomed. He did acknowledge, however, that it was ideally suited for defence from the Tlingit and for the Russian command of the entire coast. The town's hill was dominated by a solid wooden bastion mounted with twenty guns, while the remainder of the settlement, including the cabins, bunkhouses, a smithy and barns for the small herd of pigs, cows and goats, was enclosed by a rough stockade. Wrinkling his nose in distaste, Rezanov was shown to his private cabin by Baranov and settled down for the winter, during which he would drive Baranov and the others mad. Towards Baranov he was cool, accusing him of drinking too much and being too lenient, and used his authority to end the profitable agreements that Baranov had cultivated with the American traders.

Rezanov also quarrelled with his Russian naval officers and expounded with great distaste about what he saw of Russian

America. He meddled in areas where he knew nothing, insulted people and rudely imposed his authority on them. His official correspondence to St. Petersburg included his suggestions for improving the company colony: banning marriage between Russians and natives, giving Baranov the powers of a provincial governor to punish people, bringing to heel the clergy and increasing the Russian settlement of the region by transporting unwanted drunkards, serfs and bankrupts there, as well as "criminals and men of bad morals" from Russia. In Russian America, they would provide cheap labour and presumably reform their wayward ways. "The dread that this law would produce," Rezanov claimed, hinting at his impression of the company's holdings, "would keep people from dishonouring themselves and would promote confidence and trust toward trade." Rezanov also advocated using bases in Russian America to invade Japan and to attack and destroy all American traders along the coast. Fortunately, all his recommendations were ignored by both the government and the company's board of directors.

After three weeks in Sitka, Rezanov provided the long-suffering Baranov with his list of things to reorganize in order to eliminate what Rezanov believed to be anarchy and poor management. Baranov had been running the enterprise for thirteen years without much institutional support, and had just completed a small war and founded a new settlement that was still under construction. Tlingit warriors still threatened the settlement and were attacking other company outposts along the coast. Nevertheless, Rezanov announced that Baranov should proceed with the rapid development of self-sustaining industries and agriculture—activities that Baranov knew from years of experience to be completely unsuited to either the company's finances or to conditions in Alaska. He must have thought Rezanov either deluded or deranged when the now unwelcome visitor proposed bringing in Japanese settlers and supplying the company's outposts from Japan, to avoid dealing with the Americans. Rezanov was nonetheless horrified when Baranov tendered his resignation: "I tell you, gentlemen," Rezanov wrote the board of directors, apparently changing his tune, "he is truly an extraordinary person and a most original character. His name is famed the length of the Pacific... and yet, though overwhelmed with praise by foreign nations, here he has to drink the bitter cup of disappointment. The directors should approach the Throne in a body and ask new honors for him. Something has to be done to shield him from further insults." Rezanov was referring to the fact that Baranov still had no direct authority to punish the naval officers and navigators who ran all the ships in his domain, many of whom deliberately flouted his authority. However, Rezanov never seemed to consider the fact that one of the greatest insults was his own meddling. He also noted that "had Baranov given up New Archangel as lost after its destruction and not returned here, the value of the Company's stock would not be where it is." Eventually he departed, but not before claiming credit for Baranov's plans to expand south into Spanish California. Still erratic and bewildered, Rezanov ordered some ill-advised raids on the Japanese coast before disembarking in Okhotsk. On the long journey back to Europe, he died of fever while riding his horse, leaving a wake of ridiculous directives that were all ignored.

Although he had tendered his resignation, Baranov quickly returned to the job of running the company, formalizing trade agreements with King Kamehameha of Hawaii, sending hunters as far south as Spanish California in search of sea otters and resuming the use of American traders to conduct company business. Nevertheless he was waiting upon the directors to acccpt his resignation and send out a replacement. Meanwhile, his wife back in Russia had died, and he married Anna, his mistress of many years and the mother of his two Alaskan children. He petitioned to have them recognized as legitimate in Russia so that he could move there with them and enjoy the respect that his wealth and status would command there. To his great pleasure, the government declared his children to be nobles because he had described Anna as "the daughter of the Prince of Kenai"—the Lord of Alaska's native wife's descent from a chieftain under his dominion had secured for him entrance into the Russian nobility! And, by 1808, Baranov had his response from the company's board of directors: do not retire, they pleaded. They could not decide upon a successor. Napoleon was still waging war in Europe; all was in turmoil. The war was distracting the other powers from exploiting Pacific America. Expand south, they urged Baranov, while we have the chance.

So, glowing under the praise of his directors, none of whom he had ever met, and buoyed by his feelings of indispensability, Baranov threw himself with renewed vigour into the task of expansion. Sitka was by now a thriving international port, receiving over fifty ships a year. Many traders sailed directly there to buy their furs from the company and avoid the dangers of dealing with the Tlingit. A prominent feature of the town was its kremlin: an imposing, rough-hewn two-storey timber building where Baranov lived and that also housed the company's administration centre. It was surrounded by a parade ground that proudly displayed the company flag, and boasted a large feast hall, library, piano and European artwork. The people called the building Baranov's Castle.

Baranov loved music and singing and was fond of hosting great celebrations. He provided ceremonial welcomes to all visitors to his capital, giving salutes to all incoming vessels. Of his love for partying, one English captain complained, "They all drink an astonishing quantity, Baranov not excepted . . . It is no small tax on the health of a person trying to do business with them." After years of hardship and struggle, Baranov had at last become the merchant king of his domain: his word was law along thousands of kilometres of coastline, his directives were instantly obeyed. His name was celebrated throughout the Pacific American trading world, and he was loved by many of his men, particularly the old hands who had been with him for years and had shared the struggles and now the success. Others, however, viewed him as a tyrant and wished him dead.

· 7 ·

BARANOV INITIALLY DISMISSED THE RUMOURS AS ridiculous: who would want to kill him and his children? But someone had warned him in the fall of 1809, and the mounting evidence compelled him to be more aggressive in dealing with malcontents in the Sitka garrison. His loyal men raided a secret meeting of nine plotters and recovered documents from a burning woodstove. They were still legible, and the contents chilled Baranov to the bone. Inspired by the revolutionary movements in Europe, the plotters planned to assassinate Baranov and his family, capture a ship in the harbour, kidnap the colony's women and cruise off to found a paradise on Easter Island, in the South Pacific. They had been seeking further converts when their plot was uncovered.

Now Baranov was shaken. He rushed his family to safety on Kodiak Island and dashed off a furious letter to the company's directors demanding that his replacement be sent immediately, and threatening to leave if they did not move quickly enough. Although he had threatened to resign many times in the past nineteen years, this time he truly meant it. He also quickly wrote out his will: "Since my life is in constant danger not only from the hostility of wild tribes but from men often unwilling to submit to discipline, since my strength is exhausted and my health dissipated battling the hardships I have had to endure, I feel that that natural time, the hour of my death, is for me more uncertain than for most men, and therefore I make my will." Considering the risks he had taken and the dangers he had overcome, it was unusual for Baranov to suddenly be gripped by fear. Perhaps it was the inevitable feeling of physical decline natural in a man over the age of sixty, after a hard life. Perhaps he feared for his ability to defend his Alaskan children, who were not yet grown. But apart from this foiled secret plot, Baranov was more secure and powerful than he had ever been in his entire life.

For years no replacement arrived, and Baranov continued to rule from his castle on the hill. The first man sent from St. Petersburg had died in Siberia, after many months of hard travel. It took many more months for the news to reach St. Petersburg and for the company to arrange a second replacement. The second replacement, Baranov was informed, was on the way and was due to arrive in early 1813. During this time, Baranov had not been vigorous in pursuing expansion, claiming it should wait for his successor. He was now sixty-five years old; his eyesight was failing him, his clerk had to read important documents to him. His arthritis was crippling and painful, alleviated only by ever-greater quantities of rum. Baranov had, however, allowed one of his ambitious and energetic officers, Ivan Kuskov, to lead an expedition of twenty-six Russians and about a hundred Aleuts south to California, where Kuskov founded *Krepost Ross,* or Fort Ross, just north of San Francisco, in June 1812. The outpost was soon growing fruit and vegetables and raising domestic animals for the Russian American Company.

In early 1813, while awaiting the arrival of his second replacement, Baranov was exasperated to learn that this man, too, had died on the way, in a shipwreck not far from Sitka. Baranov became thoughtful. He became pious. Perhaps it was his destiny to remain forever in Russian America. After all, an almost ludicrously improbable series of events had conspired to keep him here for most of his adult life despite all his efforts to leave. Indeed, it must be providence. Energized again, he reinstalled his family in his castle, ordered a church to be built at Sitka and arranged for a priest to oversee it, and hired a German governess for his daughter, Irina. An American tutor prepared his eager son, Antipatr, now sixteen, for entrance into the naval academy at St. Petersburg. With his newfound vigour and enthusiasm, Baranov was making the greatest profits yet for the company. A real schemer, he constantly spied opportunities and took advantage of them, even though this often involved dealing with American naval captains to circumvent Chinese restrictions on Russian trade.

When Europe's Napoleonic war ended, however, events transpired to hasten the end of Baranov's reign as the merchant king of Pacific America. When the Russian American Company was officially founded in 1799 it had, like other famous monopolies, been granted a twenty-year licence, the renewal of which was considered a mere formality. After the war, however, the officers of the Russian navy were casting about for reasons to justify their continued employment during peacetime. Naturally they looked to Russian America, where many of them had served and where, they had always felt, government by a mere merchant company was undignified since it was the rightful provenance of noble officers rather than of common traders. Baranov's elevation in rank notwithstanding, these officers still considered him their inferior. For years they had been hired as captains and navigators on company ships and had chafed at the indignity of taking orders from Baranov. Now that the company's licence was nearing its time of renewal, they increased their agitation for "reform."

For years, the Russian American Company had been making enormous profits and paying enormous dividends to shareholders. Its head office was a magnificent, even opulent, former mansion in St. Petersburg that employed dozens of highly paid accountants, agents, secretaries, translators and clerks, in addition to executive managers such as Mikhail Buldakov, the well-connected man who had married Grigorii Shelikhov's eldest daughter and who had been chairman of the board since the company was founded. None of its directors or urbane executives had ever been to Russian America, and none of the great fount of money that Baranov had consistently sent gushing from Pacific America to St. Petersburg had ever found its way back to the colony that the company was semi-officially managing on behalf of the government. There were no real schools in the colony, other than the underfunded, rudimentary ones that Baranov provided. There was no formal legal system, other than Baranov's word. Neither were there physicians or hospitals. When questioned about why the directors had never sent out a physician during the twenty years of their rule, Baranov once admitted, "I do not know whether they trouble themselves even to think about it. We doctor ourselves as best we can, and if a man is so wounded as to need an operation he must die."

It was difficult for the directors to mount an argument as to why the company should be allowed to continue to plunder this valuable Russian colony. Left out of the argument was the question of why arrogant, swaggering naval officers would be more suited to the task of running what was still essentially a commercial enterprise. The navy, through its spokesman, Captain Vasilii Golovnin, without any evidence accused Baranov of negligence and corruption. On one occasion, Baranov had fired Sitka's guns on a Russian ship commanded by a naval officer who had rebelled against his authority and tried to flee. More recently, Baranov had bungled negotiations for a base in Hawaii. So perhaps he was losing his touch and it was time for him to go. On the other hand, the directors, particularly Buldakov, recognized Baranov's seemingly magical abilities to generate profit. They had fought to keep Baranov in power since the beginning, despite the opposition of the church and the navy.

In the end, a compromise was reached between the two opposing entities: the navy agreed to let the company retain its charter, but the colony would be headed by a senior naval officer and his assistants, who would naturally be given company stock and high salaries. Baranov would have to go. Because of the navy's hatred of Baranov and their belief in his corruption, the company's board of directors did not even vote their representative, now aged seventy, a pension or an official letter of recognition. Indeed, one of his bitter enemies, Captain Lieutenant Leontii Hagemeister, was sent out with secret orders to investigate Baranov's activities and depose him.

Baranov ought to have been rich from his years on the frontier. His shares had paid dividends, and his salary was significant. But he harboured a deep secret: he had spent most of his money. Baranov had paid for the education of his employees' children by sending them to Russia; he had bought and imported cattle as gifts to the Aleuts; he had always sent money to his first wife and children in Russia; he had set aside a trust fund for his second wife in Kodiak; he had given away his own shares to dedicated managers he wanted to keep in the colony, when the company was paying them only a meagre wage. He deeply cared about the colony and the people he had worked and lived with for years. Caught in a conflict of interest between his duty to his company and what he imagined to be his duty to his country and his fellow colonists, he had dutifully sent all the colony's profits back to St. Petersburg and supplied the colony from his own earnings. As a result, he had little money left— barely enough to live on without a pension.

Upon his arrival in the colony Hagemeister was rude and belligerent, demanding that Baranov hand over the company's books within twelve hours. It was hard on Baranov; he was humiliated and saddened. As he descended into a bout of drinking, pondering his future and fearing that he had failed to provide for his Alaskan children, hope emerged during what threatened to be an abrupt and ignominious end to his career. On board one of the Russian naval frigates that had put into port in Sitka four months ahead of Hagemeister was a senior lieutenant named Semion Yanovskii. A handsome young man, well read and thoughtful, Yanovskii was impressed with Irina Baranov's beauty and vitality. She was a wonderful piano player with a lively sense of humour and a zest for life. He courted her for months while a bemused Baranov looked on approvingly. Eventually, Yanovskii asked for her hand in marriage and Baranov agreed—it was a good match.

The young man's senior officer, Hagemeister, agreed despite his dislike of Baranov because the marriage would solve one of Hagemeister's greatest problems. A lifetime's habit fades slowly, and most of the citizens of Sitka still deferred to Baranov, as if he were still in charge, as if the navy had no authority to replace him. Owing to many years of bad relations with naval officers, perhaps a third of the employees, both native and Russian, threatened to leave the company's service if the navy took command. So Hagemeister hatched a scheme that would allow for a smooth transition from company rule to navy rule: he named Yanovskii, now Baranov's son-in-law, to the position of governor, replacing the old man. In this way, the colonists' hatred of the navy would be tempered with their respect for Baranov's daughter, providing some continuity during the transition to naval control. After the marriage the happy couple set off on a tour of the colony, while Baranov remained in Sitka moping. He was confused about what he should do: visit his brother in Irkutsk, go to Hawaii, stay near Sitka, return to Kodiak Island? His judgement had been slipping in the past few years, and now the decline became more pronounced. His memory was failing along with his eyesight.

Hagemeister's accountant, in scouring the company's accounts, found no evidence of corruption or plundering. Indeed, he discovered that Baranov was a master of profit-making: net profits on goods shipped from Russia were 90 per cent, with everything accounted for. But Hagemeister still wanted Baranov to leave Russian America, so that he could never again influence events in the colony. With his personal fortune depleted, Baranov could not afford to live in Russia. He planned to go to Hawaii, but the navy was concerned that the presence of one so well known and respected, but living on limited means, would raise eyebrows. Another of the visiting naval officers, the outspoken Captain Vasilii Golovnin, offered Baranov a small company job in St. Petersburg and agreed to sponsor his son in the naval academy. Indeed, he would take Antipatr aboard his warship immediately. With both his children suddenly and unexpectedly looked after, and his wife, whom he had not seen in years, living on Kodiak Island and financially secure, Baranov agreed. He was, however, apprehensive about returning to a homeland he had not seen in over three decades and requested one final voyage north to Kodiak Island, where he had spent so much time in his early years in Russian America. Hagemeister claimed there was no time; he must prepare to leave without delay.

A month later, after many tearful farewells, Baranov boarded a ship for the long voyage round the world to St. Petersburg. Kiril Khlebnikov, the government accountant who had inspected Baranov's books and found them perfectly in order, and who became Baranov's first biographer after hearing the old man's stories while they worked on the accounts, described the scene: "Old, grey-haired men, his comrades in glorious voyages and deeds, sobbed like children at parting with their beloved leader. Many in his entourage grew up during his tenure, others were born while he was boss. He was godfather to one and almost all of the young ones were trained under him. Even the Tlingit who trembled before him, but who respected his brave and decisive spirit, took leave of him with ambivalent feelings in which fear and joy were mingled." He was now an old and tired man of seventy-two, and his years of hard living had caught up with him. On the ship, he grew weary. He caught a fever in Batavia, and died soon after his ship put to sea again on April 12, 1819. His body was dropped into the Indian Ocean.

Corporate rule in Alaska ended with Aleksandr Baranov, just as it had begun with him, although the Russian American Company remained the monopoly commercial entity there and Alaska's Russian settlements continued to fly the company flag alongside the state flag of the Russian Empire. Lydia Black writes in her book *Russians in Alaska: 1732–1867,* "Forthwith, until the end of Russian America in 1867, the colony would be governed by a high-ranking officer of the navy, accountable first of all to the government and concerned primarily with matters of state."

The Russian American Company's fortunes waned as the nineteenth century progressed. The inevitable decline in the quality of sea otter pelts, due to overhunting, a failure to diversify and the lack of interest from distant St. Petersburg were certainly key reasons. The company, however, was also no longer a merchant enterprise, but rather a branch of government; and Russian America had atrophied, overshadowed by Russia's greater interest in events closer at hand in Europe. Under naval rule, the colony lacked the freedom and initiative to adapt to changing times. Another man like Baranov might have staved off the decline, seeing opportunity where others saw only the end; but none was forthcoming, particularly not from the ranks of the navy. On October 18, 1867, all of Russian America was purchased by the United States for $7.2 million, and the company ceased to exist.

Chapter 5

"I consider it quite unnecessary to indent for
Sauces & Pickles on public account . . . I never use fish sauce
in the country, and never saw anyone use it or pickles either.
From the quantity of Mustard indented for, one would suppose
it is now issued as an article of trade with the Indians!"

SIR GEORGE SIMPSON, c. 1843

Empíre of the Beaver

· 1 ·

HE WAS CHAUFFEURED ABOUT THE WILDS OF NORTH-
ern North America in a giant canoe, perched in its centre under
a faintly ludicrous black beaver top hat, exhorting his long-
suffering voyageurs to paddle harder so that he could set speed
records. Seeking to make an impressive arrival, he had a bagpiper in Highland regalia begin braying whenever he neared a
Hudson's Bay Company fort. A respected member of the elite in
Montreal and London, "the Little Emperor" earned a legendary
reputation for stinginess that bordered on cruelty to his employees and customers. Over the decades he fathered at least ten,
and perhaps seventy, children with a number of women in his
vast fur domain, a domain that covered a good chunk of northern and western North America, and that at its height spanned
nearly a twelfth of the world's total land mass. Haughty, impatient and self-important, he was the managerial genius who
steered the Hudson's Bay Company to its greatest financial

success and greatest expansion in the mid-nineteenth century. A balding, chubby and short man with an iron will and an unfashionable admiration for Napoleon Bonaparte, he was as hated by his employees and customers as he was loved by his shareholders and investors.

The story of Sir George Simpson and his empire of the beaver is inextricably intertwined with the founding of the nation of Canada. If not acknowledged as a national hero—he was far too complex, too selfish and, by modern standards, too unsavoury for that—then he is at least known as one of the founding historical figures whose actions laid some of the framework upon which the modern nation was built. The story begins centuries before Simpson was born and is rooted as much in North America as in Europe; as much with the denizens of Restoration London's fashionable drawing rooms as with the North American wilderness and the theatrical antics of two French Canadian fur traders from Quebec.

IN THE fall of 1665 two buckskin-clad coureurs de bois sailed up the Thames River through plague-ravaged London. The scene was a strange contrast to the wild forests, rivers and lakes to which they were accustomed. As they scanned the banks they spied burned-out buildings, deserted streets, looted houses and clusters of ragged refugees. The plague would slay nearly eighty thousand of the city's approximately half a million inhabitants. The stench of death permeated the air, and carts laden with corpses trundled down detritus-strewn roads to dump their loads into putrid plague pits. Clutching perfume-doused handkerchiefs to their faces, the shocked woodsmen continued upriver, past London to the city of Oxford, where the English court had fled to escape the pestilence. They were ushered into an audience with the king, Charles II, the same flamboyant king who had recently declared war on the Netherlands to start the Second Anglo-Dutch War, and who had a year previously authorized his brother James, the Duke of York, to seize the colony of New Netherland from the Dutch West India Company. But it was business, not war, that these French Canadian fur traders wanted to discuss with the king, and Charles 11 had a keen interest in mercantile concerns.

The two men, Médard Chouart, Sieur des Groseilliers (later known in England as "Mr. Gooseberry") and Pierre-Esprit Radisson, were long-time citizens of New France and long-time traders with the native peoples. They had ranged far and wide in North America, meeting a number of tribes—Huron, Sioux and Cree—in the headwaters region of the Mississippi and Missouri rivers and in the forests of the north. The historian Douglas MacKay writes in *The Honourable Company* that "a more daring pair of intentional promoters cannot be found in the history of commerce . . . Glib, plausible, ambitious, supported by unquestionable physical courage, they were the completely equipped fortune hunters." In the spring of 1659 the two brothers-in-law—Groseilliers, the solid veteran, twenty-two years older than the insouciant twenty-year-old Radisson—had ventured farther than usual and had traded for the glossiest and largest beaver pelts they had ever seen. During their two-year expedition into the interior they had heard tales of the Cree who lived in the distant northwest, and of great rivers that flowed north to a frozen inland sea.

When they paddled their canoes back to the St. Lawrence River and Quebec with a great mountain of furs, they were celebrated as heroes. They soon set off on a second expedition, but when they returned the governor of the colony of New France seized a good portion of their furs on the grounds that they had been trading without a licence. He then forbade them to venture west again, fearful that their exploits might shift the focus of the fur trade away from the St. Lawrence and weaken the struggling colony. The governor wanted to promote farming and settlement and to discourage the colony's men from fleeing to the hinterland in search of furs. Refusing to be cowed, the spirited and adventurous duo cast about for suitable allies and settled on New England as it was the nearest. But after a few years of vigorous persuasion that resulted in a failed expedition, they decided to cross the Atlantic and present their case to the English king.

Their plan was sure to interest the king: use English ships to enter Hudson Bay and exploit the vast beaver reserves surrounding the bay, thus bypassing New France altogether. Groseilliers and Radisson's intrigues inspired the English courtiers. Smooth-talking Radisson—famous for his boast about his mastery of the wilderness of Canada: "We were Caesars, being nobody to contradict us"—regaled the gentleman of the English court with the tale of his journey down a great river that flowed "North West into the South Seas" and with his plan for a series of forts along the bay. The English East India Company was finally showing good profits with its monopoly. Was not Hudson Bay first explored by an English mariner? And was not Hudson Bay well known to be on the route to Cathay? Radisson's appeals to his listeners eventually had their intended effect. He and Mr. Gooseberry recruited their investors.

The first royal voyage departed a few years later in 1668. With Groseilliers sailing aboard the *Nonsuch* and Radisson aboard the *Eaglet,* the two ships crossed to Hudson Strait, where storms sent the *Nonsuch* packing back to England. The small fifty-ton *Eaglet,* however, cruised south into James Bay and spent the winter establishing relations with a few hundred local Cree. They traded sundry manufactured metal goods, which were rare and useful implements to the residents along the shores of Hudson Bay, for beaver pelts, the natives' most common and abundant trade item, before returning to London the following

October. Radisson had found no passage to the South Seas, but he had vindicated his and Groseilliers' claims that the fur trade from Hudson Bay would be profitable. Indeed, the prospects seemed so bright that on May 2, 1670, the king agreed to grant to his cousin, Prince Rupert of the Rhine, and seventeen courtier-adventurers a charter giving them the "sole trade and commerce of Hudson's Bay" as "true lords and proprietors" with rights to all the surrounding territory as well, including fisheries and minerals.

Although no one knew it at the time, the region that comprises Hudson Bay's drainage basin constitutes nearly four million square kilometres, over 40 per cent of the later territory of Canada, including all of northern Ontario and Quebec, all of Manitoba, southern Saskatchewan and southern Alberta and a good portion of the U.S. states of North Dakota and Minnesota. Rupert became the first governor of "the Company of Adventurers of England Trading into Hudson's Bay." The new company possessed powers similar to those granted the other great monopolies of the era—a monopoly being necessary, Rupert believed, to succeed in such a risky venture, with a long payback time on investment. Rupert and his cronies put up the capital to finance the venture, but they had obligations that went beyond the requirement to make a profit: they were to continue to search for the route to Cathay and to establish settlements "by meanes whereof there may probably arise very great advantage to us and our kingdome." Certainly the king had in mind the promotion of strategic English trade to counter the expansion of New France.

Soon, flotillas of ships were crossing the Atlantic from England every year, loaded with knives, saws, kettles, utensils, mirrors, muskets, pots, axes, sewing needles, gunshot, powder, wool cloth, beads, tobacco and brandy. When Hudson Bay froze over, they wintered at pre-selected spots along the shore of the bay to trade for mink, fox, ermine, otter, wolverine, lynx and, of course, beaver pelts, the primary object of their trade. The furs were pulled from the hinterlands by native trappers and transported to the bay, where the English traders waited for them to arrive. The company built primitive palisade forts at the mouths of the key rivers flowing into the bay so that they could maintain constant contact with the local people. In that way, it was hoped, each year ever more trappers could be persuaded to make the arduous journey to trade at the forts.

True to Groseilliers and Radisson's predictions, beavers were available in great abundance. Their lustrous pelts were of superior quality, and beaver fur was in particular demand throughout Europe. Numerous seventeenth- and eighteenth-century engravings depict fanciful scenes in which these curious and myopic rodents display their prominent and enormous orange teeth. Sometimes they are shown regal and sphinx-like, posed with their mouths open and their great flat tails splayed out behind, or even walking erect, carrying logs over their shoulders in mighty communal building efforts, like furry anthropomorphized ants going cheerfully about their labours. In these engravings, men with guns line the banks of ponds shooting at the beavers that are gnawing at trees to bring them down and build their dams and houses. These dwellings occasionally appear as multi-storey, apartment-style mounds housing dozens in the centre of a pond. Written accounts of the time had beavers dwelling in giant communal house-villages, speaking to each other and working together to hunt and build. The fur trader and explorer Samuel Hearne, who was very familiar with the more prosaic lives of these furry, flat-tailed rodents, expressed amusement at this attribution of noble traits. In his classic *A Journey to the Northern Ocean,* he wrote: "I cannot refrain from smiling when I read the accounts of different authors who have written on the economy of those animals . . . Little remains to be added beside a vocabulary of their language, a code of their laws, and a sketch of their religion." That such gentle and innocuous creatures should inspire such praise seems unusual. But they were given all the attention not because of their sophisticated and urbane culture, but because of their value: their pelts were then worth, if not their weight in gold, certainly a great deal of money.

Furs have always had value for their warmth, but it was their use in the manufacture of felt that drove the demand in Europe. Felt was primarily used to make hats, an ever-changing fashion accoutrement that was indispensable to gentlemen as well as ladies. Each profession or calling boasted its own hat style, from the distinctive cocked hat of the navy to the tall, imperious Regent or top hat, to the faintly ridiculous-looking "Paris Beau." People wore hats to mark their social position, and the hats carried price tags to reflect that. Some gentlemen's hats were so valuable that even well-off people protected them and dutifully handed them down as inheritances, assuming the fashion had not changed. Although the beaver was virtually extinct in commercial quantities throughout most of Europe, in the seventeenth century the region covered by the Hudson's Bay Company's charter was home to at least ten million beavers. That region, amazingly, contained nearly half the world's supply of fresh water. It was swampy, featuring innumerable lakes and ponds, and was covered with aspen and birch forests, providing prime beaver food. It was one of the greatest beaver habitats in the world.

· 2 ·

AS THE THREE-MASTED SHIP HOVE TO IN A FLOOD TIDE in an estuary off the mouth of the Hayes River at York Factory, it triggered a flurry of frantic activity from the bedraggled onlookers. The Hudson's Bay Company vessel was burdened with supplies and new recruits who were destined for the distant outposts of the company, located on the desolate, pebbly shores of the northern bay where they plied their trade. The small flotilla of which it was a part was the annual convoy that serviced the forts and returned with bales of shiny beaver pelts. These rodent pelts from the wilds of North America had become one of the most valuable commodities in the transatlantic trade.

For much of the eighteenth century the company quietly soldiered on, consolidating its foothold in Hudson Bay and gradually increasing its profitability. There were some attacks from French raiders from Canada during the War of the Spanish Succession and the War of American Independence. Forts had changed hands and trade had been disrupted for years at a time, but for the most part the company posted consistent if unspectacular returns. The Hudson's Bay Company was a small enterprise by the standards of the day, puny even in comparison with the English East India Company, which was still decades away from its glorious rise under Robert Clive. The company retrenched into small-scale trading according to a conservative pattern that saw it devote no efforts to expanding its supply of furs. It peacefully and unobtrusively prospered, dividends flowed and stability reigned.

The company opted for its conservative approach because it was able to take advantage of ancient native trade and travel networks along waterways that wended their way deep into the interior of the continent. The Cree who dwelt closest to the company forts and factories along the bay, and eventually the Assiniboine and Chipewyan, became the middlemen of the trade, operating their own jealously guarded monopoly on trade with the Europeans, and passing on goods at inflated prices to native peoples farther afield. They resisted the movement of European traders into their lands. But nearly a century of contact between these very different cultures had transferred technology both ways: not only did European metal goods bring Stone Age peoples into the Iron Age, in which knives, axes, kettles and guns were the most obviously useful items, but they in turn provided these traders with the means to venture inland, with clothing, snowshoes, bark canoes and toboggans and the knowledge of how to survive in the wilderness. Eventually even the company, with its ossified commercial operations, had to send its employees into the country in quest of more furs. The previously plentiful supply nearer the forts had been exhausted.

In the mid-eighteenth century, the company sent several explorers into the hinterlands to discover what lay beyond the bay. Henry Kelsey canoed and hiked inland to the south and west; James Knight sailed north, along the coast, searching for gold and a northwest passage; Anthony Henday pushed thousands of kilometres west, to within sight of the Rocky Mountains; and Samuel Hearne, led by his "lively and agreeable" Cree guide Matonabbee, ventured north and west searching for copper and the elusive northern waterway to Cathay. In all, the Hudson's Bay Company sponsored nearly sixty inland expeditions at this time to stimulate an increase in the trade—the demand for pelts had increased in Europe and the company feared, accurately, as it turned out, that the rival traders from Montreal were strangling its commerce by meeting the Indian fur trappers inland, along their canoe routes, before they reached the Hudson's Bay Company's forts.

The traders from Montreal, the coureurs de bois, had been pushing west and north throughout the eighteenth century in search of new markets and a "Great Western Sea." One indomitable wanderer, Pierre Gaultier de Varennes, Sieur de La Vérendrye, had wandered as far west as the Black Hills of South Dakota and along the shores of Lake Winnipeg. By the late eighteenth century, the Montreal-based traders were establishing their own trading outposts upstream on rivers leading to

Hudson Bay in an attempt to capture the trade, which was in any case being hindered by the Cree who lived close to the Hudson's Bay Company's forts and who were also aggressively persuading other native trappers to conclude their trade with them and not bother canoeing the remaining distance to the company forts. The company hoped that the defeat of Quebec by British forces in 1759 would rid it once and for all of its pesky competitors, but the opposite proved true. A few years later, the lakes and rivers of the interior—territory granted to the company by its monopoly charter—were packed with canoes dispatched from Montreal. The Montreal traders were now being financed and organized into aggressive partnerships.

The intense competition led the Hudson's Bay Company to reluctantly establish its first permanent inland trading outpost, Cumberland House, in 1773. Six years later, the traders from Montreal were officially organized into the North West Company, which for several years remained a small-scale loose affiliation of Montreal merchants probing the interior with a view to breaking the Hudson's Bay Company monopoly. In 1783 they consolidated into a permanent enterprise with a head office, led by Benjamin and Joseph Frobisher, Simon McTavish and other well-financed investors. Soon they were dominating the fur trade, opening up new regions with forts and outposts further inland. Quick to make decisions and with authority resting with inland field partners, they reacted swiftly to changes and took advantage of opportunities in a way that the entrenched and bureaucratic Hudson's Bay Company, with its rigid command structure and low-paid employees who were powerless to make meaningful decisions, could not. While the employees of the Hudson's Bay Company could be likened to passive branch managers acting for distant shareholders, the partners of the new North West Company were a loose affiliation of individualists who shared in the profits. They were

dynamic and entrepreneurial rather than aristocratic and tra-
dition-bound. The rivalry that quickly developed between the
two enterprises, a rivalry that stemmed from the original battles
between the English company and the French traders along the
bay prior to 1713, was a struggle between two distinct business
models—one imperial, the other colonial. Such different corporate philosophies could not easily blend and were essentially
irreconcilable.

Soon North West Company partners led the trade deep
into unexplored territory, cutting out the native middlemen
and hauling increasing numbers of furs east to Montreal. Their
profits were enormous, their expansion quick, their competition
sleepy and moribund.

WHEN THE buckskin-clad voyageurs of the North West Company launched their huge *canots du maître* into the St. Lawrence
River near Montreal to head for the western trading frontier,
they had a long and unrelenting trip in front of them. Loaded
with up to four tonnes of metal trinkets and tools, kettles and
muskets, bales of blankets and cloth, with pouches of black powder, tobacco and tea packed around kegs of whiskey, the massive
birch bark canoes, holding over twelve oarsmen and passengers,
lumbered west along the Ottawa River, through Georgian Bay
and Lake Huron to Grand Portage on the western end of Lake
Superior. There they transferred the goods into the smaller
canots du nord and struggled up the rapids-riddled rivers from the
Lake of the Woods. They fanned out across the vast prairies as
far west as the Rocky Mountains to supply the increasing number of trading posts in the Athabasca country. And each fall they
remained there, prepared to be frozen in for the long winter.

When the traders hauled their towering bales of pelts back
east the following spring, they followed the same arduous
and unreliable route in a trip that could take many months.

Although they were making enormous profits and had captured the majority of the fur trade from the sleepy factors of the Hudson's Bay Company, for the Nor'Westers running a profitable and stable business was becoming more difficult as each new region became "beavered out." So the fur brigades ventured farther west, and by the early nineteenth century the precarious and inefficient route was almost five thousand kilometres long. And as the fur trade spread west, its shipping costs rose with every mile of travel.

Both of the fur trade companies faced hardships, though. The North West Company had to send its canoes much farther than the Hudson's Bay Company, which could send its ships into the heart of the continent. But the Hudson's Bay Company suffered from a lack of manpower—it maintained only a few hundred employees. The North West Company drew on Quebec's population of sixty thousand, people who were in their homeland, rather than relying on foreigners to board a ship bound for the distant shores of a frozen bay to toil in drudgery and for low wages for several years before returning home to move on to better things. Each business enterprise had its competitive advantages and disadvantages.

The competition between the two companies became so intense that they often built their forts and outposts within sight of each other, each hoping to attract the native fur traders with their unique variation on the standard package of metal trade goods: the Hudson's Bay Company offered good wool blankets and copper pots; the North West Company offered high-quality French brandy and tailored coats. The competition no doubt delighted the native fur trappers, who could bargain hard for their furs, visiting both posts to gain the best deal. But for the companies this commercial conflict was a war of attrition that would slowly exhaust them both.

At some point during the interminable struggle for dominance, the commercial war became an actual war. The companies captured prisoners from each other and then treated their hostages barbarically. They ambushed and shot at each other along the canoe routes. They attacked each other's forts and plundered each other's trade goods and annual fur shipments. They pushed cheap rotgut hard liquor in liberal quantities on the local peoples, which had a demoralizing and destructive impact on the native cultures. The warring companies never outright attacked their customers; they only urged them to violence and trickery against each other and against the other company. With no overall police force to ensure civil conduct or impose civility, no single tribe or nation strong enough to enforce universal customs or laws, the companies, at least in the field, became gangs of unscrupulous hoodlums who roamed northern North America without any restrictions on their behaviour. Soon the traders' ruthlessness began to threaten the very business of trading for furs that justified their existence.

After years of cutthroat competition that was driving both companies to the brink of bankruptcy, the conflict came to a head in 1816, in the Red River Valley, in what is today the Canadian province of Manitoba. It was a conflict in which a young George Simpson emerged as a charismatic and powerful leader.

· 3 ·

GEORGE SIMPSON WAS BORN OUT OF WEDLOCK IN THE small Scottish town of Dingwall in 1792. He was raised by his father's family, particularly by his Aunt Mary. After his aunt married and gave birth to a son in 1807, George set out on his own. Boarding a ship, he sailed from the Scottish north to the city of London to apprentice at his uncle's sugar brokerage firm.

Hardworking, shrewd and charismatic, Simpson quickly gained the confidence of his employers and was particularly liked by the senior partner, Andrew Wedderburn. Simpson was a short but energetic dandy in fine clothes, who frequented the coffee shops as he learned the job of a clerk in the overseas trade. For some reason, he also cultivated an unfashionable fascination for Napoleon Bonaparte, who by then had seized power in France and was at war with Britain.

Simpson's involvement in the sugar trade, which included several trips to the West Indies, introduced him to the slave trade and its prejudices and brutality. This use and abuse of human beings, based on the assumption of the inherent superiority of one's own culture and skin colour, undoubtedly influenced Simpson's attitudes towards First Nations people in Rupert's Land years later. Simpson's most recent biographer, James Raffan, notes in his book *Emperor of the North* that "Simpson would have taken with him into the fur trade and into the rest of his life disturbing notions about the relative power and authority vested in skin colour." The Canadian popular historian Peter C. Newman famously quipped, somewhat less diplomatically, that Simpson was "a bastard by birth and by persuasion."

When Wedderburn's sister married a quixotic gentleman named Thomas Douglas, the fifth Earl of Selkirk, it opened the door for Simpson to try an entirely new career. Extremely wealthy and having a philanthropic disposition, Lord Selkirk took a personal interest in displaced Highland crofters and devised a plan to find them a home in the Canadian territories. At the time, Hudson's Bay Company stock was depressed due to the decreased demand for furs during the Napoleonic Wars and the company's ongoing, commerce-destroying struggle with the North West Company. Selkirk and Wedderburn began buying up Hudson's Bay Company stock and eventually acquired enough shares to give them a controlling interest. As a result, Wedderburn took a position on the board of governors in London, and in May 1811, the company gave Selkirk 300,000 square kilometres of prime land at the forks of the Red and Assiniboine rivers, south of Lake Winnipeg, for his agricultural utopia. The land belonged to the company as part of its original charter. The proposed settlement site, not accidentally, was situated directly on the main transportation route used by the North West Company, between Montreal and the prime fur territory of the northwest.

About one hundred of Selkirk's settlers arrived in the wilds of the Canadian prairies in 1812. They were met with hostility from the North West Company fur traders and their bison-hunting Métis allies, who drove them off their settlement concession, burned their crops and scattered their cattle. Selkirk moved west from Montreal with a hundred mercenaries to help defend the settlement and his crofters. He issued a decree restricting from his territory the export of pemmican, a staple food source for the coureurs de bois consisting of dried bison meat, berries and fat. It was a decree that, if enforced, could destroy the North West Company's operations and endanger the livelihood of the Métis hunters.

The Métis responded by electing a Scots-Cree named Cuthbert Grant as their military leader and preparing for war as they continued to trade with the North West Company. On June 19, 1816, at Seven Oaks, what is now Winnipeg, two hostile bands encountered each other. In the ensuing melee, the governor of the Selkirk colony and nineteen settlers were shot and killed by the Métis. Outraged, Selkirk promptly led his private mercenaries to the North West Company fort at Fort William, on Lake Superior, and arrested most of the trading partners, while throughout the fur country officials from each of the competing companies began attacking and arresting each other on trumped-up charges. As the fighting and reprisals were degenerating into chaos, the Hudson's Bay Company governors made an unorthodox decision, prompted by Wedderburn: they would hire a new backup governor from outside the ranks, and that person would be George Simpson. Simpson was given five days' notice to wrap up his sedate London life. In a letter to a colleague, he related that he was engaged in "important business connected with the affairs of Lord Selkirk, the Hudson's Bay & North West Compys." He would be the acting governor-in-chief of Rupert's Land, ready to assume command if the current governor was arrested or killed by agents of the North West Company.

Simpson sailed for New York, continued overland to Montreal and then proceeded to the interior, ironically following the traditional route of the North West Company rather than that of the Hudson's Bay Company. He travelled by canoe west up the St. Lawrence River and across the Great Lakes to Fort William, where he delivered a letter from Lord Bathurst, British secretary of state for war and the colonies, that called on both companies to immediately cease all hostilities or face the intervention of the British government. Simpson continued on to the Selkirk lands and then pushed through the heart of the fur territory to Fort Wedderburn, on Lake Athabasca. Here, on the lake's frigid, wind-lashed shores, he spent his first North American winter—something he could not have prepared for in terms of harshness or duration, but which he nevertheless seemed to thrive on. For a man who had spent his entire life in Britain, Simpson adapted to the ways of the wilderness unexpectedly well. Primitive conditions, severe weather and isolation from the life he had known seemed not to have perturbed him. Free from the constraints of polite society he could indulge his instinct to impose his authority on the world around him, to reorder it to suit his desires and ambitions. He was in his element.

Simpson proved a tough and stubborn traveller, immediately setting out to learn as much as he could about the land over which he would be in charge. He crammed his head full of knowledge about the geography, the climate, the territory and customs of the various tribes and their politics. He also seemed unconcerned about canoe travel, which he had never done before, or about sleeping in mosquito-infested lowlands or during torrential downpours, claiming in one letter to a friend that his cloak would "answer the purposes of a bed." He was a shrewd observer, quickly taking stock of the situation on the ground. "The N.W. Co. are not to be put down by Prize fighting," he observed, "but by persevering industry, *Oeconomy* in the business arrangements, and a firm maintenance of our rights not by the fist but by more deadly weapons." Discipline and hard work, not violence, would win profits. A stern, stubborn manager with an iron will, Simpson usually prevailed in a dispute and was remarkably adept at banging some semblance of order from the chaos that had overtaken the trading enterprise during the decades of commercial war.

Meanwhile, the financial situation of both companies was dire, particularly that of the North West Company. Bankruptcy loomed. The Hudson's Bay Company was much better financed and could afford to forgo dividends. It also enjoyed the support of the political and financial elite of London, whereas the North West Company had no access to long-term capital and its partners depended on hefty annual dividends; it was less prepared to weather a prolonged commercial war. Under pressure from the British government, it agreed to merge with its archrival. On paper at least, the Hudson's Bay Company amalgamated with the North West Company in the spring of 1821, while Simpson was still in the field. The new enterprise's monopoly over Rupert's Land was not only affirmed but extended all the way west to the Pacific Ocean, as the British government wanted a financially secure British company to counter American expansionism. This new entity would retain the name of the Hudson's Bay Company, yet it was a complex intermingling of style and structure inherited from both parent enterprises. The rigid central control and financial backing of the Hudson's Bay Company, in which all people were employees, was retained, as were the flamboyant, profit-driven partnerships of the North West Company. As hoped, stock in the new monopoly soared in value when news of the merger was released.

Although he was a newcomer to North America, Simpson appeared to be the most capable of running one part of the new venture, not least because his lack of connection with any of the previous decades' violence and reprisals made him a palatable choice to both sides. No doubt his influential patron on the governing board, Wedderburn, helped Simpson's case. He was offered a position in charge of one of two new departments, or regional governorships, into which the new company would be divided. Of the two, the southern department was the more sedate and beavered out. It was in its mature phase of development, whereas the northern department held the greatest potential for expansion and increased profits. Simpson therefore was put in charge of the potentially lucrative northern department, where he could set about bringing profits to the business.

· 4 ·

DURING THE SUMMER OF 1821 ALL THE SENIOR OFFIcers of the two companies voyaged in their canoes down the rivers of the interior to a great concourse at York Factory, a collection of several dozen wooden and stone buildings that formed the old Hudson's Bay Company's main depot on the shore of the bay. It was the first meeting of the new management team after the merger, or at least the first meeting that would not involve guns and threats. The new governor of the northern department had invited them to attend and they could not refuse. As they neared the fort they spied bands of Cree and Iroquois camped around the small fortified community, soon to be joined by hundreds of Métis and voyageurs. The gathering had the air of a festival or celebration, and miraculously the tension evaporated and games and storytelling commenced. In the great hall Simpson presided over feasts of wild duck, Arctic char and venison, with conversation lubricated by overflowing glasses of sherry and port. Old hatreds were set aside, new alliances launched and a new identity forged. Charismatic when he needed to be, caustic when it suited him, self-serving nearly always, Simpson coaxed, smoothed and moulded a new corporate fraternity from the quarrelling clans. Then he set to work to make it profitable.

At the time of their merger the two companies had numerous overlapping forts and far too many employees. There were ninety-seven North West Company forts and outposts and seventy-six belonging to the Hudson's Bay Company. Many of these competing forts were within hailing distance of each other and hence unprofitable. Simpson threw himself into his job with zeal. He shut down redundant posts, either reassigning the employees or releasing them from the service if he felt they were lazy or intractable, and transported them out of his domain when necessary. The aged were also in his sights: "I consider it highly injurious to the general interest to have old worn out men in our councils, they are timid, indolent and helpless and would be of no manner of use in cases of difficulty, danger or emergency. Worn out Indian Traders are the most useless, helpless class of men I ever knew and the sooner the Company can get rid of them after their days of activity and labor are over the better." He got rid of over a thousand "worn out" traders within his first few years at the helm.

Renowned for his snap decisions, Simpson instinctively knew whom to keep, whom to promote and whom to pass over or demote, and he did so quickly and without tact. James Raffan writes that Simpson understood "that there were large-scale patterns of fur out, trade goods in, on which HBC commerce with local trappers was based, but that at each of the posts there were smaller patterns as well—unique circumstances and idiosyncratic politics involving the history and sentiments of the local Aboriginal people, the background and temperaments of the officers and men conducting the HBC's business, and distinctive geographic and climatological issues that had to be understood."

Simpson was preoccupied with petty things like changing the men's diets from meat to fish and cutting all "luxury" goods both from their diet and from their lives. He increased the standard size of transport canoes while simultaneously decreasing the number of men assigned to paddle them. He didn't care if he was liked or hated. In his early years, Simpson poked around in every aspect of the company's operations looking for ways to cut costs. In his opinion there were many overpaid and underworked employees, an observation that did not change much over the years. Most of the *oeconomy* measures that he introduced to reduce expenses were borne disproportionately by the junior or less skilled workers in the lowest ranks. Those who were not compulsive workaholics, and those who questioned his authority, had their wages trimmed by as much as a quarter.

Simpson had an intrusive and infuriating tendency to micromanage everything: from the amount of tea a chief factor might consume to the proper deportment of subordinates, from how to conduct compulsory religious services to which utensils should be used at dinners (tin plates) and how tables should be set (no tablecloth or wine glasses). His preoccupation with the minutiae of his men's domestic arrangements suggests an unhealthy need for control. He took this philosophy to heart, as evidenced by his general memorandum from March 1843 under the heading SAUCES: "I consider it quite unnecessary to indent for Sauces & Pickles on public account . . . I never use fish sauce in the country, and never saw anyone use it or pickles either. From the quantity of Mustard indented for, one would suppose it is now issued as an article of trade with the Indians!" The first step in making money, Simpson believed, was not wasting it on frivolous extravagances.

Towards the native peoples he could be unscrupulous, referring to them as a "Savage race" and plying them with liquor to get what he wanted. "A little rum operates like a charm on the Indians," he once wrote. "They cannot resist the temptation, and if the bait is properly managed, every skin may be had from them." After the merger, he sought to "reconcile them to the new order of things . . . I am convinced that they must be ruled with a rod of iron, to bring and keep them in a proper state of subordination, and the most certain way to effect this is by letting them feel their dependence upon us." He later cut out liquor as a trade item in most regions, not because it was not profitable, but because he felt it made the natives lazy and unproductive.

Under Simpson's regime, trading posts were placed on important and well-used travel routes and evolved to become more substantial and permanent. Along with this new permanent infrastructure, Simpson created an equally substantial catalogue of the company's human assets. He kept a detailed written record of his typically blunt assessments of his officers in his famous Character Book. He began these assessments during his first year in Rupert's Land, before the two companies had united. He even related his opinions on Sir John Franklin's ultimately doomed overland expedition of 1819: "[Franklin] Lacks the physical powers required for the labour of moderate Voyaging in this country," he wrote. "He must have three meals per diem, Tea is indispensable, and with the utmost exertion, he cannot walk Eight miles in one day, so that it does not follow if those Gentlemen are unsuccessful that the difficulties are insurmountable."

The Character Book was a clandestine record of more than 150 senior people under Simpson's command. He recorded no names, but used instead a number system to which only he held the key. He described the French-Scottish Dr. John McLoughlin, one of his most powerful lieutenants, as "such a figure as I should not like to meet on a dark night in one of the bye lanes in the neighbourhood of London . . . Dressed in clothes that had once been fashionable, but were now covered with a thousand patches of different colours, his beard would do honour to the chin of a Grizzly Bear, his face and hands evidently show that he had not lost much time at his toilette. He was loaded with Arms, and his own herculean dimensions formed a tout ensemble that would convey a good idea of the highwaymen of former days . . . [He was] ungovernable [with a] violent temper and turbulent disposition."

John Rowand, the legendary governor of Fort Edmonton, was apparently "of fiery disposition and as bold as a lion. An excellent Trader who has the peculiar talent of attracting the fiercest Indians to him while he rules them with a Rod of Iron." Another trader was singled out as "a boasting, ignorant low fellow . . . a disgrace to the fur trade," while yet another was "one of the worst and most dangerous men I ever was acquainted with. My presence alone keeps him sober, but when left to himself he will assuredly become a confirmed Drunkard." Whereas one was "not quite of Sound Mind," another was "a flippant, superficial, trifling creature who lies more frequently than he speaks the truth." One suspects that Simpson's assessments were not far from the mark and reveal the chaotic, turbulent and volatile crew he had to manage. Some were mere thugs, others brilliant traders and diplomats of questionable loyalty; they were a hard group of strong characters, and it took a man of Simpson's temperament, charisma and vision to impose some order on this motley group. More than anything else the company could control, these traders were the backbone of the fur monopoly, the spine upon which it would either flounder or fly. Perhaps if Simpson had turned his mind to a dispassionate self-assessment, he might have been more charitable to his officers. More likely, he believed himself to be above the rules that governed other men; he was a man who set his own standards of behaviour and would be judged by different criteria.

During his first few years on the frontier in the heart of his emerging fur empire, Simpson began the legendary travelling for which he would become famous, crossing the company's vast territory by canoe while his voyageurs toiled to increase the pace and please their new master. Travelling eighteen hours a day in all kinds of weather was not uncommon. On his famous journey to the Pacific in 1824, Simpson's canoes were launched at Grand Portage, on the shores of Lake Superior. The entourage of voyageurs paddled furiously across the prairies, wound their way through the Rocky Mountains, were propelled down foaming canyon streams, clambered up steep, craggy inclines dragging their canoes and supplies behind them, followed winding mule-paths through mountain passes, and portaged over rattlesnake-infested, sage brush—covered hills on their way to the coast. Simpson and his crew crossed the continent in a mere eighty-four days, twenty days less than the previous record.

Smelling the fresh Pacific air and seeing the whitecapped vista before him, Simpson knew he had finally arrived at the western boundary of his expansive commercial empire—an empire that rolled on from the Red River to the mouth of the Columbia, stretching from the barren beaches of Hudson Bay down to the northern boundary of Spanish California. The

Hudson's Bay Company was the largest business enterprise in North America, and the only non-native government in what is now western Canada and the American states of Montana, Idaho, Washington and Oregon. Fort Vancouver, with blue water rushing rapidly by and the familiar cone of Mt. Rainier in the distance, was built on the north side of the Columbia River by Simpson's decree, in anticipation of a possible international boundary along the river, as Britain had proposed in 1818. Simpson, perhaps having a keener perception of world events, favoured moving the company's central depot "North of this place, about Two or Three Degrees, at the mouth of Fraser's River." To him, the more northern river was the logical choice for the principal western depot because it undisputedly was first navigated by a British explorer and was situated north of the 49th parallel—the boundary requested by the Americans in 1818. If American political claims prevailed, as he suspected they would, the Fraser would still be in British territory. After this monumental expedition, Simpson strategized with his regional henchman McLoughlin on how to keep the Columbia District, as he termed the region west of the Rocky Mountains, free from the American trappers who were just beginning to enter the mountains as they pushed west. He then raced back east to the Red River territory and travelled north to York Factory, where he boarded a ship to London to report on his progress.

Simpson had felt the heady flow of intoxicating power. The land was in transition, he sensed, and on the cusp of some major change, where success was readily available to the one bold enough to seize it. In London he might grub and toil to achieve moderate success, but never greatness, particularly given his bastard birth and humble origins; but in Rupert's Land he might leapfrog all the lower and middle rungs of the social ladder and establish himself at the very top. Certainly there were disadvantages to this wilderness life—there was no social company appropriate to one of his rank, no entertainments and amusements of the sort to be found in London, and he would be far from the pulse of the empire and possibly permanently removed from it, should he have to return—but the compensating factors of freedom, power and pre-eminence were beguiling enough to make him forgo London and gamble his career on the wilderness fur empire. He would return to Montreal, the fur forts of the interior and the life of a virtual dictator. The company directors in London were much pleased by his efforts in North America, and they promoted him to be in charge of both the northern and southern departments. After 1826, Simpson was the undisputed master of an enormous commercial, and increasingly political, empire, with untold power over the people who lived there. His capacity to direct the minutiae of their lives was unparalleled, and he enjoyed lording it over others. He would later earn his unofficial title of "the Little Emperor," the head honcho of the only general store for half a continent.

The company's domain was enormous, almost eight million square kilometres, equivalent to most of Europe and about one-twelfth of the earth's surface, and by the mid-nineteenth century the company had grown so powerful that it dominated the lives of tens of thousands of natives as well as the lives of its employees. Simpson simply viewed indigenous peoples as he did anyone else in his realm: not as independent masters of their own destiny, but as somehow tied to the company as cogs in the wheels of its profit-generating machinery. During Simpson's reign the First Nations increasingly fell under the company's control, their lives shaped and patterned to improve the company's trade efficiency. It was the beginning of the end of their autonomy.

The company had posts as far away as Hawaii; its warehouses in London were the clearing house of most of the fur

traded throughout Europe. But the governor, the deputy governor and the seven directors, or committeemen, who oversaw the
company's operations from their headquarters in London, never
crossed the Atlantic to York Factory, let alone ventured inland
to see the company's immense territories. Like other directors of
the great companies in the Age of Heroic Commerce, these men
had little direct knowledge of what went on in their realm. They
were essentially absentee landlords who never saw the lands
they governed and profited from, leaving ruthless and charismatic men like Simpson to rule with an iron hand. So long as
the profits remained steady, they were left alone, and the greater
the profit the more their putative superiors looked away and
the more powerful was their overlordship. Simpson kept profits high, an accomplishment that ensured his authority would
be unchecked by the board of directors in London. Disgruntled
employee John McLean wrote in *Notes of a Twenty-Five Years' Service
in the Hudson's Bay Territory* that "in no colony subject to the British Crown is there to be found an authority so despotic as is at
this day exercised in the mercantile Colony of Rupert's Land;
an authority combining the despotism of military rule with the
strict surveillance and mean parsimony of the avaricious trade.
From Labrador to Nootka Sound the unchecked, uncontrolled
will of a single individual gives law to the land . . . Clothed with
a power so unlimited, it is not to be wondered at that a man who
rose from a humble situation should in the end forget what he
was and play the tyrant."

Simpson understood that to improve profits, he could either
improve revenue or reduce expenses, or both. He could see well
enough the end of the fur trade's golden era before he had even
ushered it into existence. Regions close to where forts had been
erected had long been "beavered out"—the largest and easiest-
to-obtain animals had already been trapped by the indigenous
hunters. The region where the company made its greatest profits

had been steadily moving west for decades, and would eventually run out altogether. Hence, since the mid-1820s, Simpson had his eye on the greatest unplundered beaver preserve yet remaining on the continent: the little-exploited territory west of the Rocky Mountains.

· 5 ·

IN 1826, SIMPSON ESTABLISHED HIS HEADQUARTERS AT Lachine, near Montreal, where he ensconced himself firmly at the pinnacle of Montreal society and in the Anglo-Scottish business community. He used his home, whenever he was back that way, for lavish dinners and parties for the political and business elite—he was certainly not afraid to mix business and pleasure, and probably saw no distinction between the two, for these social forays were as much for his amusement as for securing and consolidating the company's position. Here he could lobby against decisions that might negatively impact the fur trade, such as higher taxes and the colonial government's desire for an increasingly interventionist role in the lives of the First Nations.

But though Simpson's headquarters were in Montreal, Simpson himself was rarely to be found there. His great passion was for near-continuous overland adventure, touring the far-flung regions of his domain. He was always on the move, showing his presence, issuing decrees and keeping a tight control over outposts across the continent. In 1828 he boarded his giant touring canoe and embarked on another of his famous epic cross-continental voyages, over 11,000 kilometres from York Factory to Fort Vancouver via Fort Chipewyan on Lake Athabasca, across the Rocky Mountains, down the Fraser River to the coast, south into Puget Sound and then finally overland to the Columbia River. He issued hundreds of decrees, chastised lenient traders, caught chief factors off guard and generally absorbed the adulation and subservience that he demanded; one of the surest ways to ingratiate oneself with Simpson and secure a promotion was to show humility and deference—near-grovelling coupled with incredibly long work hours. In the spring he returned east, meeting his councils and then reaching Lachine by the fall of 1829. After this tour, Simpson crossed the Atlantic to London, ostensibly to recuperate from his taxing journeys in the northwest: "Exertions which were formerly but exercise for me," wrote the aging emperor, "are now fatiguing, indeed my snow shoe walk across the Mountains and overland journey from Saskatchawaine have wrought me a good deal."

The following spring, he was not recuperating but rather searching for a bride. He settled on his cousin, Frances Simpson. The daughter of the uncle that gave George his start in life in London, Frances was, at eighteen years old, less than half his age. While wife-hunting he had abandoned one of his North American mistresses, who was then pregnant with one of his many unofficial offspring. Simpson already had plenty of children to his credit, including two in Scotland and five or more in Rupert's Land. He procreated so often that some Canadian writers have referred to him as "the father of the fur trade." Many of his mistresses were the daughters of his chief factors and their native wives at forts throughout his territory. His pattern was to discard his mistresses when he had had enough of the liaison; on one occasion, he informed a subordinate to cast off his "unnecessary and expensive appendage." Historian of the fur trade Irene Spry finds Simpson's womanizing not at all humorous, observing: "His sex-object attitude to women was largely responsible for the breakdown of marriage *à la façon du pays*, which was a humanly decent type of relationship. He created a total dislocation in what had been a perfectly valid type of society." Intermarriage between the native peoples and the white fur traders was one of the social structures that had smoothed relations between people in the trade for decades; Simpson took advantage of this "smoothing" while declining to assume responsibility for his liaisons.

He considered his native and mixed-race mistresses to be beneath consideration as marriage partners. To bolster his social standing, he wanted a white English wife who would be accepted in the salons of London and Montreal, not a hardy native woman from the fur frontier. After his own marriage to Frances, Simpson began to discourage marriage *à la façon du pays* between his officers and native women, preferring that they engage in unattached sexual liaisons. He and his wife refused to host the native wives of his officers as guests in their home. When Frances first crossed the Atlantic with him in 1830, he took her on a grand tour of the fur regions in a giant canoe. She had never before left England and was not prepared either for the Canadian wilderness or for the imperious and kingly role her husband assumed when touring his domain. Never of strong constitution, she did not thrive in this new environment. Despite Simpson commissioning a substantial stone fort at Red River in 1830—the expense of which he tried to delay and conceal from his governing council in London—after three years she returned to England, ostensibly to regain her health, and did not return to North America until 1838. Simpson promptly relocated his headquarters to Lachine from Red River and continued his restless roving about his territories. Meanwhile, political events beyond Simpson's control were conspiring to carve off a large chunk of his hard-won domain.

During Simpson's tenure, the Columbia District, on the Pacific coast, although theoretically jointly occupied by the United States and Britain since the Convention of 1818, remained the sole preserve of the Hudson's Bay Company in practice. There simply was no competition between traders west of the Rocky Mountains. The strategy that Simpson and McLoughlin devised to keep it that way in Old Oregon revolved around the seemingly simple objective of keeping the territory in a perfect state for beaver hunting: preventing American trappers from entering, and restricting agricultural development by sending all the company's voyageurs back east after their contracts were up, rather than letting them settle in the country, despite the promising agricultural potential of the area surrounding Fort Vancouver on the Columbia River. Simpson realized that settlement and agriculture were directly at odds with the commercial objective of the company, which was to extract furs from a sparsely populated wilderness using primarily native labourers and Métis and French coureurs de bois, with the only infrastructure being a loose network of primitive trading posts.

Throughout the 1820s and 1830s, McLoughlin had the difficult task of ensuring that American trappers and settlers stayed east of the Snake River. Left to govern the Columbia District on his own, he took on a legendary stature with both the natives and the Europeans. He became the "White-Headed Eagle" to the natives and the "King of Oregon" to the five hundred company employees and the settlers who eventually trickled into his domain. He had turned Fort Vancouver into a small community, complete with a school, a library, a blacksmith, flour mills and sawmills, and a thriving twelve-square-kilometre farm.

For almost twenty years, McLoughlin ruled like an old-time robber baron—he was shrewd, cunning, paternalistic and sometimes ruthless. He held court in the shadowy depths of a great timber hall behind the palisade of Fort Vancouver and dispensed justice throughout the region according to the dictates of his own conscience—alternately with vengeful wrath or surprising leniency, as the mood was upon him. McLoughlin's justice could be quick. On one occasion, he flew into a murderous rage and publicly caned Herbert Beaver, a visiting British missionary who suggested that his native wife of twenty-five years, Marguerite, was "a female of notoriously loose character." The terrified and bloody Beaver escaped with his life only by the intervention of onlookers. McLoughlin's justice was equally meted out against natives who he felt had transgressed his rigid code. Although the common punishment was to be flogged while strapped to a brass cannon, on one occasion McLoughlin ordered armed company squads to level two encampments of the Clallam tribe on the coast, killing twenty-three natives in retribution for the death of five of his traders. He was known not for leniency, but for even-handed severity—an unusual sense of justice that earned him the respect of many of the tribes in his commercial domain, if not that of the non-natives.

McLoughlin opened the gates of Fort Vancouver to all manner of travellers and wanderers, both native and white, so long as they did not undermine his authority or overtly threaten the fur trade. The nightly feasting of the officers and visiting dignitaries was legendary, and during ceremonial occasions the white-maned despot was flanked by bagpipers braying out the ancient songs of his father's homeland in Scotland, while he pronounced volubly on politics, religion and the fur trade.

During McLoughlin's two-decade reign, he balanced the interests of the company against his own inclinations to generosity, lavish living and piety, and his sympathy for the slowly arriving settlers. He also attempted to counteract the ascetic Simpson, whose visits every few years were marked by quarrelling and acrimonious disagreements about company policy, particularly about what to do with retiring voyageurs. Simpson worked to prevent as many of his employees as possible from remaining in the region after their service with the company had expired, shipping them back to Montreal instead. Going even further, he dismantled the coastal trading forts that McLoughlin had built, in favour of a fleet of roving ships. It was in the best short-term interest of the company, he believed, to keep the territory as wild as possible for as long as possible—a situation that, if he ever chose to think of it, placed him as the unofficial representative of his country, the mercantile arm of his government, in a conflict of interest between the interests of his nation and the interests of his company.

McLoughlin and Simpson constituted the de facto government of the vast territory, dispensing justice not according to the legal code of Britain or various native societies but in accordance with company business interests. On the one hand, Simpson was the head of the only legal commercial enterprise in the land; on the other hand, he was the sole source of civil authority as delegated by the British government, and McLoughlin reported directly to him. Together they were charged with maintaining law and order over all people of European descent within the territory of the company's monopoly charter. Simpson also worked to keep settlers out of other parts of the company's domain. Peter C. Newman writes in his popular history of the company, *Caesars of the Wilderness,* that "except for the traffic in and out of the Red River Settlement, during Simpson's long reign few outsiders were allowed to visit his magic kingdom. Those who did receive permission were mostly artists bent on glorifying the Governor's deeds, members of the British aristocracy engaging in a spot of buffalo hunting, botanists and other natural scientists sent out on behalf of the Royal Society, or land surveyors confirming the full extent of the HBC's impressive holdings."

Simpson and McLoughlin, however, had no control over the American settlers who began to enter the territory in the 1830s to settle along the Columbia River and the Willamette Valley. The flood of settlers increased dramatically after the Panic of 1837, when farm produce prices and land values plummeted in the eastern United States, leaving many farmers and land speculators without homes. The increasing numbers of American settlers arriving at Fort Vancouver, many of them suspicious and anglophobic after years of disharmony between Britain and the United States, began to erode the unchallenged authority of the Hudson's Bay Company. McLoughlin was faced with a dilemma: the settlers heralded the end of his rule in Old Oregon and the end of fur trading (the land south of the Columbia was showing declining fur returns by the early 1840s), but to drive them off the land was not something he would do, even if it was in the best interests of the company. Nor did a policy of peaceful non-interference sit well with the aging McLoughlin, who began to view the Willamette settlements as the beginnings of a new society, of which he was a part, rather than pests who were ruining the fur trade.

By the 1840s more than a thousand settlers a year were arriving at Fort Vancouver. They were often destitute, on the verge of starvation and ill-prepared for the winter. It was a great dilemma for McLoughlin: it was not company policy to extend credit, particularly not to settlers who undermined its livelihood, yet he felt a growing sympathy towards the hopeful, ragged bands of settlers. Resolving his inner conflict, he generously extended aid to all incoming pioneers and restrained natives and settlers alike from attacking each other. Company policy notwithstanding, McLoughlin had doled out over thirty thousand dollars in credit at the company store by 1845, thereby in no small part ensuring the survival of many of the settlers and their budding communities—and provoking the wrath of Simpson, who was taking an increasingly dark view of McLoughlin's support of the foreign settlers who heralded the end of the company's monopoly in Old Oregon.

There was nothing the Hudson's Bay Company could do to thwart the incoming settlers—politically, the entire region was under the joint occupancy of Britain and the United States and open to the commercial development of both nations.

Undoubtedly Old Oregon would be divided, but where it would be divided was a question without an easy answer. McLoughlin still hoped to hold the Columbia River as the border, while Simpson, a more astute observer of the trends sweeping the continent, set his eyes on the Fraser River, just north of the 49th parallel. Simpson made his final visit to Fort Vancouver in 1841, with plans to relocate the company's central depot from Fort Vancouver to a new site farther north. Incidentally, Simpson also visited the Russian American Company headquarters in Sitka, Alaska, as part of this tour and was unimpressed: "Of all the dirty and wretched places that I have ever seen, Sitka is pre-eminently the most wretched and the most dirty."

Simpson and McLoughlin masked their mutual animosity and agreed to send James Douglas, a massive Scottish mulatto of mysterious origin and McLoughlin's right-hand man for almost fifteen years, on an expedition north to Vancouver Island "for the purpose of selecting a convenient situation for an Establishment on a large scale, possessing all the requisites for farming, rearing of Cattle, together with a good harbour and abundance of timber." Douglas departed in 1843 and founded Fort Camosun, soon to be renamed Fort Victoria, on the southern extremity of "this sterile Rock bound Coast." The new headquarters had a commanding view of the Juan de Fuca Strait (in case of future border disputes) and was situated in a deep, safe harbour surrounded by agricultural and pasture land to supply the new outpost.

The political crisis of Old Oregon could no longer be ignored. The death, in 1841, of one of the original American settlers intensified the need for some form of political authority. The man died without a will, leaving a homestead and a herd of six hundred cattle in the Willamette Valley, and the distribution of his estate required a set of laws. When McLoughlin informed Simpson and other officials in London of his inability to govern thousands of American citizens, he received no constructive reply and no instructions. He knew, however, that a private company could not long remain the only official authority in the region. Soon the unruly pioneers, most of them American citizens, would demand a more accountable government. McLoughlin knew that particularly without military help from London or the company, holding Old Oregon would be nearly impossible.

In 1843 settlers along the Willamette united to form a provisional government (based on the legal code of the state of Iowa) that would recognize their land claims and stabilize their communities. Soon the provisional government was passing laws, levying taxes and vociferously pronouncing its affiliation with the United States. Initially, the Canadian settlers, most of them retired fur traders and former employees of the company, held aloof, but with an additional 1,400 American pioneers arriving in 1844 and then 3,000 in 1845, they were being swamped by the rising human tide. In 1845 the settlers elected George Abernethy as governor of a new provisional state and sent delegates to Washington to request entry into the American Union. McLoughlin, left on his own, agreed on August 15, 1845, to "support the Organic Laws of the Provisional Government of Oregon" and to co-operate with the new entity in order to, as he explained to London, "prevent disorders and maintain peace, until the settlement of the Boundary Question leaves that duty to the parent states."

The governing joint occupancy agreement between Britain and the United States had never been satisfactorily or fully resolved. In 1826 the British had proposed to hold all of Old Oregon but allow the Americans a port in Puget Sound, while the Americans countered with the offer of free British navigation of the Columbia River but a boundary at the 49th parallel. In 1828 the joint occupancy agreement was extended indefinitely, but by the mid-1840s the point was almost moot—American citizens were the primary inhabitants of the region (other than the natives, who, in the nineteenth century, were always overlooked), and they had made their wishes known. The weight of historical precedent, favouring Britain's claim, was diminished by the great influx of American citizens entering the territory by way of the Oregon Trail. Partly owing to Simpson's company policy, the number of British settlers in the territory never amounted to more than a few hundred, and they were greatly outnumbered as early as 1843.

American political interest in Oregon reached a peak in 1844 with the election of the ardently expansionist president James Knox Polk, who used the Democratic campaign slogans "Fifty-four Forty or Fight" and "The Re-annexation of Texas and the Re-occupation of Oregon"—phrases that boded ill for the company and for British sovereignty in the Oregon Territory. British diplomats were confused—the suggestion seemed preposterous, but could Polk really be demanding the entire Pacific coast for the United States? Polk persuaded Congress to end the joint occupancy accord in December 1845 and made rumblings of war, while a British Navy ship patrolled the Juan de Fuca Strait.

British officials knew that a war over Oregon would not be limited to the distant Pacific, but would likely be fought as an invasion of Canada, and decided that the disputed territory—a partially depleted fur preserve already occupied by unruly American citizens—was not worth the risk. On the other side, facing an impending war with Mexico over Texas, Polk and his advisers were not eager to antagonize Britain any further. The international border would bisect North America along the 49th parallel to the coast, with the exception of Vancouver Island, all of which would remain British, as Simpson had foreseen. One final concession demanded by the British (to preserve national pride and to placate the company) was that all company property be recognized by the American government and that the Columbia River remain open to company ships as long as they were engaged in the fur trade.

· 6 ·

SIMPSON'S MEDDLING IN INTERNATIONAL POLITICS was not, however, limited to his interest in Old Oregon. He was also a strong advocate for Hawaiian independence. He provided substantial company funds to promote this cause, and actively worked against the islands being recognized as a British protectorate because he believed the best interests of the company, which conducted substantial business with the islands, lay with an independent Hawaiian kingdom rather than with a branch of the British Empire. Ironically, in spite of Simpson's long-standing policy of non-settlement that contributed to the loss of the Oregon Territory to the United States, and his funding and advocacy for the recognition of an independent Hawaiian kingdom against the interests of his own nation, he was knighted by Queen Victoria in 1846 for his, and the company's, support and encouragement of exploration in the Arctic.

After being honoured in Britain, the aging merchant king set off on a grand, nearly two-year adventure around the world. He crossed North America, moved on to Siberia and proceeded west overland back to London. He then commissioned a ghost writer to prepare his lively travel account of the excursion. When he returned to Lachine after his globe-girdling romp, he settled into his role as the patriarch and pillar of Montreal's upper class. Simpson shied away from any mention of his humble beginnings; he was now a man of power, respectability and influence. He was also getting on in years. Now in his sixties, he had considerably less energy to spare for legendary tours of his fur domain. "The journeys to the interior & the duties I have there discharged for upwards of thirty years," he wrote, "are becoming increasingly irksome, & unless circumstances may arise which appear to render my presence desirable I shall not in all probability recross the height of land." His wife died in 1853, and his own declining health limited his physical activities. One of his old field colleagues wrote that "our old Chief, Sir George . . . tottering under the infirmities of age, has seen his best days. His light canoe, with choice of men, and of women too! can no longer administer to his gratification." After the loss of Old Oregon, Simpson was no longer the undisputed master of the company's formidable holdings. Its monopoly and Simpson's power began to erode in other ways too.

The idea of monopoly had fallen out of favour. Free traders were cropping up throughout Simpson's domain, just as they had appeared around Fort Vancouver before it became American territory. In 1849 a free trader in the Red River colony, Pierre-Guillaume Sayer, was captured by the company and charged with the crime. But instead of receiving a prison sentence or banishment, he was merely released by the magistrate. This mild response effectively ended the company's government-sanctioned monopoly. The Métis community would no longer tolerate the authoritarian dictates of Simpson or the company. As the nineteenth century progressed and scattered communities and settlements sprang up, other commercial activity unrelated to the dwindling fur trade evolved. The people who founded these communities were not prepared to accept that the Hudson's Bay Company store must be their only source of goods and provisions. There were complaints about the company's high-handed tactics, which included searches and damage to property, threats and general harassment. One report describes how "company clerks, with an armed police, have entered into settlers' houses in quest of furs, and confiscated all they found. One poor settler, after having his goods seized, had his house burnt to the ground, and afterwards was conveyed prisoner to York Factory... On our annual commercial journeys into Minnesota we have been pursued like felons by armed constables, who searched our property, even by breaking open our trunks; all furs found were confiscated." The land was no longer an uncharted wilderness, and the company could no longer continue as its only government. Indeed, the company had become an embarrassing anachronism.

In 1849 the company lost some of its power on Vancouver Island with the creation of the Crown Colony of Vancouver Island and the appointment of a governor for the new colony. When he resigned two years later, however, his job was assumed by James Douglas, the head of the company's Pacific District, and for a while Douglas acted as both the governor of the colony and head of the company while negotiating punitive treaties with the thirty thousand native residents of the region. In 1858, after a gold rush and an influx of American prospectors from California, the company's control over its territory on the mainland Pacific coast was ended with the creation of the Crown Colony of British Columbia. Pieces of the empire were falling away.

Simpson wrote a letter to the London Committee in 1856, presciently pointing out their "very critical position, the authorities being overawed by the numerical strength of the Halfbreed race; so that, at any moment an unpopular measure of accidental collision might lead to a general rising against the Company and the destruction of their establishments. In the meantime, by tact and forbearance, we contrive to maintain the peace and are making large returns—a state of things which may continue one, two or more years, although at all times liable to be interrupted suddenly." Racist condescension aside, the note reveals that Simpson's intelligence was still keen, even if his body was failing, and that he had not lost his legendary understanding of the way of things on the ground. When the company was founded, it had held absolute power over its employees. Later, it became so powerful that it could impose its authority on an increasing number of its customers, the First Nations. But when the company's territories, despite Simpson's efforts, attracted settlements of English-speaking peoples of European descent— including the "halfbreeds" or Métis he sneered at (though most of his children were Métis)—the company's dictatorial monopoly powers had to end. Improved methods of travel and communication meant that the company could no longer control the reports of activities from within its domain.

Word was getting out denouncing the company's heavy-handed defence of its profits for the absentee lords who owned and controlled it. Simpson might delay the process, but the inevitable end was in sight. An editorial by George Brown in the Toronto *Globe* concluded that "there can be no question that the injurious and demoralizing sway of that Company over a region of four millions of square miles, will, ere long, be brought to an end, and that the destinies of this immense country will be united with our own. It is unpardonable that civilization should be excluded from half a continent, on at best but a doubtful right of ownership, for the benefit of two hundred and thirty-two shareholders." Others echoed the sentiment, both in Canada and, more importantly, in London.

In the 1850s Simpson still sallied forth for an annual inspection of the company's forts, but his personal business interests had shifted more to activity in Montreal than in Red River or the Athabasca country. While he continued to lobby officials on behalf of the company, he broadened his involvement in other business ventures, particularly railways, mining concerns and steamship operations. He was not above manipulating high-placed political and financial figures to meet his goals. On one occasion, he famously offered "10,000 golden reasons" to a prominent official to secure government contracts for one of his steamship lines.

The Hudson's Bay Company's licence was up for renewal in 1859, coinciding with the rising public antipathy to its practices. In 1857 Simpson was called to provide testimony to a British House of Commons select committee investigating the activities of the ancient monopoly. Then sixty-five years old, Sir George Simpson strategically coughed, paused and delayed under repeated questioning. He still managed to proclaim that Rupert's Land was unsuitable for settlement, despite the success of several agricultural communities such as the Red River colony and the thriving company farms on the Pacific coast, despite even his own countering opinions in his 1843 book, in which he lauded the great agricultural potential of the very lands he now described as only suitable for beaver trapping. Not surprisingly, Simpson's opinion, once virtually unchallenged, was now considered not to be credible, if not directly misleading. The select committee recommended that all of Rupert's Land be annexed by the Province of Canada and that the company and its several hundred wealthy British shareholders should lose all their vaunted powers and privileges.

In 1870 the entire remaining territory of the Hudson's Bay Company became part of a new nation, the Dominion of Canada. The company's despotic days had ended; it would now have to live or die as a regular business, albeit one with vast landholdings in western Canada and with entrenched supply lines and depots spanning half a continent. Tragically but not surprisingly, the hundreds of thousands of indigenous peoples were not consulted in this monumental business transaction between the British company and its colonial government. But Simpson did not live to see it. He died in Lachine in 1860, before his company was stripped of all its special powers.

Even the loss of a monopoly could be turned to profit. The venerable company set about selling its land to the incoming settlers who were pushing west as the century progressed. When they could no longer defend their monopoly—whose value, in any case, had declined—the company supplied the settlers with goods from the company store, fought for exclusive rights to transportation along key waterways and generally prospered. Several company fur trade forts later became provincial capital cities in the country of Canada: Fort Garry became Winnipeg, Manitoba; Fort Edmonton became Edmonton, Alberta; and Fort Victoria became Victoria, British Columbia.

Simpson, "the Little Emperor," charted the course for one of the most unusual business enterprises in history, the empire of the beaver. Propelling it to meteoric success, he arguably contributed to a great territorial loss for his nation in Old Oregon by pursuing policies of short-term benefit to his employer, yet his expansive, profit-driven vision ultimately laid the foundation for the British political dominance of northern North America. Like many of his contemporaries, but perhaps even more so, Simpson was a sexist, racist, domineering braggart who manipulated politicians and business associates to gain what he wanted: more power and money for himself and the Hudson's Bay Company. The narrow focus of his interests in life, his use and abuse of others, his role in suppressing indigenous culture and autonomy, do not leave much to be admired by our modern sensibilities. He left nothing of his vast estate, estimated to be in excess of 100,000 pounds, to any of his numerous children who had indigenous mothers, and he instructed his executor to withhold the substantial stipends to his "official" daughters if they chose to marry an inappropriate suitor.

Personal foibles aside, Simpson was undeniably one of the most successful global merchant kings of all time. He directly altered the course of North America's history with his commercial acumen, iron determination and arrogant self-assurance, coupled with his seemingly unfathomable devotion to make ever more money for his company, even at the expense of all other facets of his life. A year before his death, he wrote his titular bosses on the London Committee, in a fitting epitaph to his life, warning them of his impending resignation after forty years of service: "During that very long period I have never been off duty for a week at a time, nor have I ever allowed Family ties and personal convenience to come in competition with the claims I considered the Company to have on me."

At the end of his life, he had been preceded in death by nearly everyone who had been a part of his life, from his wife to his business comrades and numerous enemies. But Sir George Simpson was not one of those men who outlive their era, diminishing in fear and confusion as the world changes around them. Simpson was such a dominant and powerful force for four decades, an unchallenged autocrat ruling half a continent, that his era ended only with his passing and with the loosening of the reins of power he had firmly grasped for himself four decades earlier.

An early nineteenth-century sketch of Aleksandr Baranov drawn in Sitka near the end of his life, the only known portrait of the famous Russian merchant king.

This nineteenth-century print shows Baranov's Castle atop a commanding hill in New Archangel, or Sitka, Baranov's residence and the main port for Russian America.

The imperious Sir George Simpson, or "the Little Emperor" as he was sometimes known, is shown with clenched fist and determined visage in this famous nineteenth-century portrait.

Regally perched in the middle of his canoe, top hat firmly in place, Sir George Simpson arrived at his wilderness fur trade forts to the braying of his personal bagpiper, Colin Fraser, as depicted in this 1923 Hudson's Bay Company calendar.

The Hudson's Bay Company coat of arms. For nearly two centuries the company held titular sway, a grant from the English King Charles II, as "true lords and proprietors" over millions of kilometres of North America.

A troop of industrious anthropomorphised beavers communally labour in this fanciful seventeenth-century scene from Hermann Moll's *The World Described*.

Cecil John Rhodes was the founder of the diamond conglomerate
De Beers and the monopoly British South Africa Company, which
used a private army to invade central eastern Africa. He allowed
the new territory taken by his company troops to be called Rhodesia
in his honour.

Resembling ants on a giant hill, miners toil amidst the dust and heat in this early 1870s photograph of the Kimberley diamond mine in southern Africa.

The African king Lobengula is surrounded by supplicants and retainers in his inner compound at Gubulawayo, in this print from the 1880s.

In this drawing from *Punch* magazine in 1892, a stylized and heroic-looking Cecil Rhodes bestrides Africa like a colossus boldly holding aloft a telegraph wire that stretches from the Cape in the south to Cairo in the north.

· Chapter 6 ·

"Great Britain is a very small island. Great Britain's
position depends on her trade, and if we do not open up the
dependencies of the world which are at present devoted to
barbarism, we shall shut out the world's trade. It must be
brought home to you that your trade is the world, and your life
is the world, not England. That is why you must deal with these
questions of expansion and retention of the world."

CECIL JOHN RHODES, c. 1895

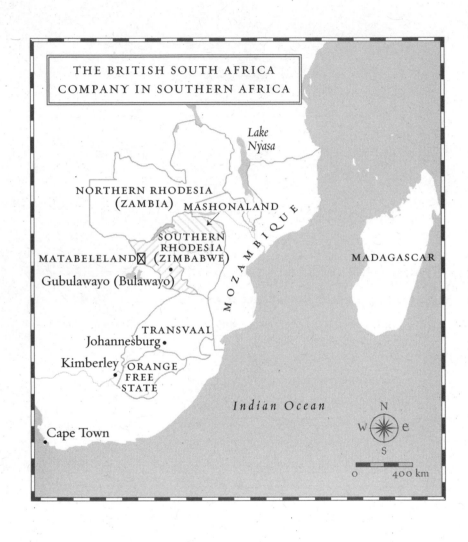

THE BRITISH SOUTH AFRICA
COMPANY IN SOUTHERN AFRICA

Lake
Nyasa

NORTHERN RHODESIA
(ZAMBIA)   MASHONALAND

MOZAMBIQUE

SOUTHERN
RHODESIA
MATABELELAND   (ZIMBABWE)

MADAGASCAR

Gubulawayo (Bulawayo)

TRANSVAAL
Johannesburg

Kimberley   ORANGE
FREE
STATE

Indian Ocean

Cape Town

N
W   e
S

0   400 km

Diamonds and Deceit

CECIL JOHN RHODES AND THE
BRITISH SOUTH AFRICA COMPANY

· 1 ·

THE OPEN-PIT DIAMOND MINE THAT THE YOUNG CECIL John Rhodes beheld in 1871 was to some observers a marvel of modern industrial know-how; to others it was a horrid blemish, a gash in the landscape. The mine was a 35,000-square-metre, irregular, 70-metre-deep hole gouged into the earth in South Africa. The soil, light brown near the surface, shaded towards a darker blue near the bottom, where it was harder to work. The hard blue soil was to be the young man's destiny. Thousands of black Africans hacked at the earth with picks and shovels haul-ing the potentially valuable earth to the surface in horse-drawn carts. When the sun had settled later in the day and the heat had subsided a little, the workers emerged from the pit "as flies come up a wall, only capering as flies never caper—and shout-ing as they come," in the words of contemporary traveller Anthony Trollope. In the early 1870s hundreds of independ-ent mining claims had been staked in the pit, each one owned by lone, mostly white, miners who employed a handful of black African labourers to tease the diamonds from the soil. By the end of 1871 more than fifty thousand stake-owners and workers crowded the pits and nearby communities. The work sites may not have looked impressive at first sight, but fortunes were being made here in short order. Rhodes, accompanied by two Zulu labourers and an ox cart full of tools and supplies, set off towards the makeshift city of canvas tents that dotted the horizon, through the throngs of rough and dirty fortune seekers to find his brother. He was going to stake a claim and hunt for diamonds.

Rhodes had arrived in southern Africa for the first time at the tender age of sixteen, joining his older brother Herbert, who had established himself as a cotton farmer in the Cape Colony. While his father was urging Rhodes towards a career in the clergy, he preferred a career as a barrister, a choice opposed by both his parents. Deferring his education and joining his brother was a family compromise that temporarily preserved the peace. At the time, no one could have known that he would spend the rest of his life in southern Africa, returning only periodically to Britain, nor that he would have an enormous impact on southern Africa's future and die there after a distinguished though tarnished career.

He had not been born or raised to expect such things. Born in Bishop's Stortford, Hertfordshire, on July 5, 1853, Rhodes was the fifth son in a large family. His parents were devoutly religious; his father was a vicar in the Church of England, and young Cecil, whose interest was in history and classics, was an upstanding member of the congregation, a teacher of Sunday school and Bible classes. As Cecil was a sickly, asthmatic boy, his parents hoped his trip to Africa, with its hot, dry climate, would prove beneficial for his weak constitution.

At that time southern Africa was a patchwork of nationalities and political jurisdictions, dominated but not firmly controlled by the British. Although Portuguese mariners had originally pioneered a sea route around the Cape of Good Hope in the late fifteenth century, it was the English mariners of the English East India Company and the Dutch mariners of the Dutch East India Company who were frequent visitors to Table Bay en route to and from the spiceries in the early seventeenth century. In 1650 the Dutch monopoly company sent Jan van Riebeeck to establish a fort and small settlement at the Cape to resupply ships. He was also given the task of locating and befriending the Khoikhoi people, the local inhabitants, hiring them as hunters and buying cattle from them so that the community of around eighty settlers would be mostly self-sufficient. Initially the settlement grew extra vegetables and fruits that served as provisions for the scurvy-ridden mariners of the company as they passed through on their way to and from the East Indies.

Eventually, however, the colonists grew weary of the Dutch company's monopoly powers and moved farther inland, driving the indigenous cattle herders out of their territory. In order to retain its jurisdiction over the migrating colonists, the company continuously expanded its borders, which in turn pushed the settlers even farther inland. In 1714 the company outlawed further migration to the colony in an attempt to keep the independent-minded colonists from migrating beyond its control. Many Khoikhoi had retreated with their herds far inland in the sparsely populated region, while those who remained perished from a smallpox epidemic. The deaths of so many of the herders upon whom it relied for food made the company decide to import West African slaves as labourers.

In 1815, as a result of the Napoleonic War with France, Britain gained control over the Cape Colony. At that time the colony hosted about sixteen thousand Europeans, mostly Boers (descended from the Dutch), and about the same number of imported West African slaves, as well as several thousand Khoi-khoi and San people. In addition to taking over the resources of the colony, Britain inherited its social problems, particularly the simmering conflict between the Boers and Bantu cattle herders in the east, a problem made worse as the century progressed and Zulu raiders drove the Bantu ever farther south, which increased the competition for scarce land and evolved into a complex and continuous struggle between rival peoples. The ongoing con-flict resulted in the British Cape Colony expanding its borders in an attempt to bring peace and stability to the region. The con-tinuing migration of the Boer cattle herders culminated in the Great Trek of 1837, in which thousands of them fled the Brit-ish territory and its laws and regulations. In particular, they sought to escape laws prohibiting the enslavement of imported West Africans and local Khoikhoi. Slave trading within British territories had been outlawed in 1807, and slave owning was out-lawed about twenty-five years later. Without this cheap labour, the Boers faced labour shortages and discipline problems among their workers. The Great Trek led to further violence, as the Boers clashed with the various peoples whose lands they were entering. After much conflict and bloodshed between the British, Boers, Zulu and Bantu, there were three independent republics— the Cape Colony, the Orange Free State and the Transvaal—as well as the powerful Zulu kingdom, with a population of around 250,000, ruled by Shaka.

In 1852–53 Great Britain recognized the independence of the Boer republics: the Orange Free State and its population of around twelve thousand, and the Transvaal, with a popula-tion of about fifteen thousand. Britain also moved towards limited self-government for the much larger English-speaking Cape Colony, and a very tenuous and fragile peace took hold among the groups of quarrelling peoples. By the 1860s, before the region's valuable minerals had been discovered, the republics' economies were pastoral, and small railways had begun to be constructed in the western Cape and Natal. All travel to and from the interior was still done on foot or by ox cart or horse. The economic products of the region included wool, wine, cereal grains, cattle and sheep.

The political situation, and the fragile peace, became more complicated after diamonds were discovered in 1867. Suddenly there was heightened interest from Belgium in the Congo, and Germany in South-West Africa and East Africa. Then as now, diamonds had enormous potential value, and the rush to find them greatly exacerbated the quarrels over land and the colonies' ill-defined borders. The main discoveries occurred in regions not clearly within the jurisdiction of either the Cape Colony or the two Boer republics and, not surprisingly, were quickly claimed by all three governments. (The original diamond hunters proclaimed yet another local republic, which was soon annexed to the Cape Colony.) The imperialist "race for Africa" was beginning—a volatile and changing period, ideally suited to opportunists, and a time for crafty, canny and unscrupulous entrepreneurs to thrive. Luck, heady success and the intoxicating creed of imperialism fuelled the fervour and provided the justification for activities that in other times might have led to self-doubt.

· 2 ·

IN 1870, THE YEAR IN WHICH THE HUDSON'S BAY COMpany ceded its territory to the new nation of Canada, Cecil Rhodes spent seventy-two days aboard a creaking and aging sailing ship cruising south from England, past the equator and to the Cape Colony. The young man disembarked in Durban to find that his unreliable older brother, Herbert, was off adventuring in the interior with a band of diamond seekers. Left on his own, Rhodes set off for his brother's farm in the Umkomaas Valley and began to learn about farming before Herbert returned. He built a small cabin and readied the fields for plowing, using Zulu day labourers. When Herbert returned, he and Cecil worked together for a few months, but Herbert departed again the following spring and left Cecil to take care of the fall harvest in 1871.

An astute observer of trends, Cecil, still only seventeen years old, realized that the cotton boom was drawing to a close and decided to join Herbert on his diamond claim in Colesberg Kopje, a region later renamed Kimberley, after the British secretary of state for the colonies. He set off on the 650-kilometre trek in October with high hopes, which were soon dashed. His pony died during the journey, and Cecil struggled on foot for the entire gruelling distance, plodding from dawn to dusk for about twenty kilometres a day under the crushing weight of his supplies. He arrived in November at the squalid sprawl of the new mining community, then on its way to becoming the second-largest settlement in southern Africa. For a youth used to the middle-class amenities of England, it must have been an eye-opening experience.

Thousands of recent arrivals dwelt in the blasting heat without running water or sanitation. One traveller described "dust so thick that the sufferer fears to remove it lest the raising of it may aggravate the evil, and of flies so numerous that one hardly dares to slaughter them by ordinary means lest their dead bodies should be noisome." Hot winds swirled the dust into great clouds that covered everything so "that it would seem that the solid surface of the earth had risen diluted into the air... In Kimberley and its surrounding nothing was pretty." The inhabitants, more than half of them black Africans, toiled in appalling conditions and were housed in corrugated iron sheds or dirty canvas tents that were crammed together in makeshift rows. The workers sustained themselves on rancid meat and butter and wilted vegetables. "It is like an immense number of ant-heaps covered with black ants, as thick as can be," Rhodes wrote in a letter to his mother; "the latter represented by human beings; when you understand that there are about 600 claims on the kopje [small hill], and each claim is generally split into four, and on each bit there are about six blacks and whites working, it gives a total of about ten thousand working every day on a piece of ground 180 yards by 220."

Prospectors from a multitude of nations crowded the pit. They were tough customers, certainly not the genteel, educated middle-class individuals that Rhodes was accustomed to. (Rhodes was a "gentleman," in the terminology of the day, though he did not yet possess a gentleman's education.) Many of the assorted hangers-on were veterans of mining booms from around the world: tradesmen, vagabonds, shady merchants, cattle dealers, thieves, whores and gamblers. Meanwhile, most of the physical labour was done by thousands of transient Bantu labourers who were earning money to buy cattle or wives or guns before returning to their homelands. Drunkenness and gambling were the chief pastimes in the rowdy community, but apparently it suited Rhodes. He settled in, assumed responsibility for one of his brother's three claims and got to work. Soon his ne'er-do-well brother was off again, back to the cotton farm, apparently uninterested in the tedium and drudgery of life at the mines, leaving the now eighteen-year-old Cecil in charge. The younger brother prospered, digging his pit ever deeper and sifting though the dirt to gain about a hundred pounds of diamonds each week. When Herbert returned some months later, with another brother in tow, he informed Cecil that he had sold the cotton farm. He was astounded at Cecil's progress and at his force of will. Even when he was in a violent dispute with a much older prospector whose claim encroached on his a little, Cecil showed no signs of backing down. He had learned how to hire and fire workers, grade the diamonds, haul the "pay dirt," fend off interlopers and deal with unscrupulous diamond brokers. "Cecil seems to have done wonderfully well as regards the diamonds," Herbert reported home. Around this time, Cecil also suffered his first heart attack, and he spent some weeks recovering.

One of the many legends about Cecil Rhodes's life before his rise to the pinnacle of riches and fame (or infamy, as some would have it) has the young Rhodes gazing down into the cavernous pit of the Kimberley diamond mine. His companion, seeing his far-off, distracted look, reputedly asks: "What do you see here?" Without taking his eyes off the scene, "with a slow sweep of his hand, Rhodes answers with the single word: 'Power.'"

Portraits and photographs of Africa's greatest merchant king do not dwell on the sickly teenager who arrived to hustle a living from the diamond fields. They focus instead on the staid, heavy and ponderous mask of authority and respectability that he assumed not many years later. In his most famous formal photograph, he looks tired, world-weary. His flaccid face sags, and with the bags under his eyes he does not at all resemble the strong-featured adventurer apparent in the statues. Overall, this portrait gives the appearance of a benign uncle: chubby, bland and unnoteworthy, like any number of anonymous middle managers, functionaries or agents of the era. But the unremarkable appearance concealed an inflexible core of political and social orthodoxy, one that is considered repugnant today. Rhodes was a great believer in the supremacy of the

Anglo-Saxon race and fervently hoped for a global government founded on that supremacy. One of his old comrades, Dr. Leander Jameson, recalled that Rhodes "was deeply impressed with a belief in the ultimate destiny of the Anglo-Saxon race. He dwelt repeatedly on the fact that their great want was new territory fit for the overflow population to settle in permanently, and thus provide markets for the wares of the old country—the workshop of the world." Rhodes himself declared, "We must find new lands from which we can easily obtain raw materials and at the same time exploit the cheap slave labour that is available from the natives of the colonies."

Arrogant, racist and insufferably smug, Rhodes embodied many of the less attractive characteristics of the expanding British Empire. Following many decades of commercial prosperity and increasing free trade in the mid-nineteenth century, when Britain truly was the master of the seas, unchallenged in military supremacy and commercial success after its defeat of Napoleon, chartered monopolies were out of fashion. There was no immediate need for commercial enterprises to be linked to national political and diplomatic interests, and indeed most of these monopolies had disappeared or lost their exalted status by the late nineteenth century. But this era, in which Rhodes grew to manhood, also saw the emergence of an imperialism and nationalism that once again created a fertile environment for the re-establishment of chartered companies as a tool to achieve diplomatic, political and strategic goals by tapping private capital. But now, for the first time, the concept of a racial hierarchy, derived from the philosophy known as social Darwinism, provided the justification for Europe's subjugation of non-European peoples.

Rhodes had been inundated with this potent cocktail of nationalism, racism and imperialism from an early age. He firmly believed that the extension of British rule throughout the world would be in "the best interests of humanity." While recovering from his first heart attack in Kimberley in 1872, Rhodes read Winwood Reade's *The Martyrdom of Man,* a perversion and extrapolation of Darwin's theory of natural selection, wherein Reade espoused the concept of racial superiority: certain races were innately superior to others, and through survival of the fittest they would come to dominate. Repulsive, anachronistic and foolish as these notions now seem, Rhodes was inspired by these and similar ideas that flowed freely in his time, and he in turn was an inspiration for others with his speeches. Although these views were not accepted by everyone, they were certainly part of mainstream thought and public discourse.

Britain's trade and economy were linked through colonies around the world, went the argument, and they needed common goals and objectives to strengthen their ties. Nationalism and racism were linked with imperialism to justify the continued expansion and the governance of non-English-speaking peoples. Efforts to strengthen the relationship between the mother country and the British-dominated colonies became popular. In *Cecil Rhodes: The Anatomy of Empire,* John Marlowe writes: "The ideological concept of race, which was the basis of unity between the 'white' colonies and the mother country, was easily up-graded into the concept of racial superiority in order to provide justification for Anglo-Saxon rule over 'backward' peoples." The political notions of "painting the map red"—after the colour commonly used on maps to show territories under the sway of the British Empire—and assuming the "white man's burden" with respect to subject peoples became wildly popular among the British. The trajectory of Rhodes's career more or less matches the three decades during which this doctrine of imperialism was ascendant. Rhodes himself came to be one of the popular faces of this movement.

· 3 ·

CECIL RHODES WAS ALREADY BECOMING QUITE
wealthy by mid-1872. He worked constantly and pursued very
few other interests, apart from a weekly dinner and gathering with some of the more educated citizens of Kimberley. He
felt keenly his lack of formal education, viewing it as a sort of
character flaw that needed to be rectified. In the meantime, he
worked and saved. He made one trip away from the diamond
mine, an extensive tour of the surrounding land by ox cart, since
there were no real roads at the time. But even this jaunt was
not exclusively for pleasure: Rhodes was always searching for
new business opportunities and, perhaps without knowing it at
the time, laying the foundation of a grand vision for the entire
territory. He purchased a farm in the nearby Republic of the
Transvaal, hired some black African labourers to work it and
entered into a partnership with a friend named Charles Rudd,
whom he had met in Kimberley. They pooled their resources to
buy out Rhodes's brother Herbert and gain his diamond claims
for themselves. Herbert lacked the dedication to do the hard,
monotonous work necessary to succeed at diamond mining and
headed north for adventure. Cecil, however, plodded on with his
new partner. They bought claims in Kimberley, improved them
and sold them at a profit, and then invested all their profits in
less expensive claims at the nearby De Beers mine, named after
the Dutch farmer on whose land the mine was located. The duo
was shrewd and hard-working, starting numerous businesses
and then selling them when they had become profitable.

In mid-1873 Cecil left his business operations in Rudd's
hands and sailed back to England to enroll at Oriel College,
Oxford, to gain the education he coveted and complete the
acquisition of his credentials as a gentleman. While studying, he
hoped to keep abreast of developments at the mines, but during
his first term, his mother died unexpectedly. Devastated by the

loss, and suffering another illness of the lungs, Rhodes returned to Kimberley in the spring of 1874 to regain his health and resume making money. Education could wait. He was still only twenty years old. By this time he already dreamed of owning as much of the diamond industry as he could, by buying claims and consolidating them.

Rhodes returned to Oxford in 1876 and stayed for two years, spending his vacations at Kimberley. Between 1878 and 1881 he was mostly at Kimberley, returning to Oxford for a final term to collect his degree at the age of twenty-eight. Although he was not a scholar but rather a very practical man, at Oxford he learned to dream big, to see life as an enormous canvas, with the possibility to make history. He was also exposed to the beginnings of the populist imperialist fervour that was then sweeping the land, particularly the dream of a Cape-to-Cairo corridor of British influence, an idea that would later become his passion. This dream motivated him to make even more money as a means of realizing his goal. Rhodes's Oxford education also gave him confidence in his decision making and secured his status as a gentleman rather than as just another money grubber, if a successful one. He learned to socialize with gentlemen and perhaps to use or dominate gentlemen, to understand their motivations and their foibles. Rhodes also observed the power that his money brought him. "The Oxford system," he wrote, "in its most finished form looks very unpractical, yet, wherever you turn your eye, except in science, an Oxford man is at the top of the tree." His love of Oxford University, and the life purpose he believed he had gained from that institution, remained with him his entire life.

Around this time Rhodes wrote a paper expressing his budding ideas, which were similar to those gaining popularity in Britain. "I contend," he wrote, "that we are the first race in the world, and that the more of the world we inhabit, the better it is for the human race. I contend that every acre added to our territory provides for the birth of more of the English race, who otherwise would not be brought into existence. Added to which, the absorption of the greater part of the world under our rule simply means the end of all wars." By the time he had graduated, many of his philosophical ideas about the world and its relation to the British Empire had crystallized: one should, he thought, work for "the furtherance of the British Empire, the bringing of the whole uncivilized world under British rule, the recovery of the United States of America, the making of the Anglo-Saxon race into but one Empire." It was the first written expression of what historian John Marlowe called Rhodes's "queer mixture of intellectual immaturity and practical genius," a sort of nationalism with pseudo-scientific race theories as its foundation. His ever-increasing wealth, Rhodes believed, would be the means of acting on these philosophies and dreams.

During these years, the settlement of Kimberley changed. The streets were paved, the ramshackle tent city was replaced with more permanent structures, and law and order were smoothing the rough edges of the chaotic settlement. Some miners and citizens even had families. After years of sinking all of their profits into buying up claims on the De Beers mine, which at first seemed to be less profitable than the Kimberley mine, Rhodes and Rudd now owned a substantial portion of the mine. The easy top soil was dug down, revealing the harder blue earth underneath, and the days of small claims worked by hand were ending. Large amounts of capital were needed to purchase the expensive machinery that would be capable of digging into the harder earth. The two partners decided to take on other partners and to continue buying as many claims as they could. They formed a limited company and were searching and scheming for a means of acquiring the entire De Beers mine site. In 1879 Rhodes met Alfred Beit, a German Jewish diamond dealer with global financial connections who had arrived in Kimberley a few years earlier. Rhodes reputedly spied Beit working late in his office one night, wandered over to see what he was up to and eventually asked him what he planned to accomplish by working so hard. Beit replied that he planned on controlling Kimberley's entire diamond production. Rhodes replied: "That's funny. I have made up my mind to do the same. We had better join hands." The company they formed in 1880 was called De Beers. That same year Rhodes, now one of the leading citizens of the town, was elected to the Cape Parliament. Although he now had a budding political career, he kept a firm focus on the De Beers diamond company which in 1883 had already quadrupled its initial capital of 200,000 pounds.

Rhodes was too busy to officially move to Cape Town, the seat of the parliament, so he spent the next seven years travelling back and forth between Cape Town and Kimberley, where he lived with a couple of business associates, Neville Pickering and Dr. Leander Jameson. He attended alternately to his business and his political interests, which, not surprisingly, occasionally overlapped. Rhodes was, in fact, attracted to schemes that blended business with politics. His efforts to push a railroad through to Kimberley amply illustrate how he directed his political efforts to improve his business prospects. Stability and increased settlement, he argued, would justify a railroad, which would in turn increase profits for businesses throughout the region. To this end, the already politically astute young man set out to better relations between the English and Dutch in the Cape Colony as a way of encouraging British southern Africa to adopt a single government. As part of his overriding objective of expanding British culture around the globe, Rhodes envisioned a grand union of all the peoples of southern Africa under the government of the Cape Colony, which would then expand north into central Africa, into territory yet to fall under the control of any European power.

But other European powers—Belgium, France, Portugal and Germany—harboured ambitions of expanding into central Africa. Very much aware of this, Rhodes vowed to gain the territory for Great Britain, where also, coincidentally, his own commercial interests lay. "Give me the centre," he claimed, "and let who will have the swamps which skirt the coast." He set his eyes on the narrow stretch of land running north from Kimberley, west of the Transvaal and east of the Kalahari Desert. This land corridor, known as the Missionary Road because David Livingstone and dozens of other missionaries had travelled north into the interior along it, could provide easy access to the high plateau of central Africa. However, a conflict between the Republic of the Transvaal and the Cape Colony over control of the "road to the north" dragged on for years. Rhodes rightly saw the corridor as the key to dominating the region and wanted to ensure that it was controlled by British interests, preferably his own. Fearing that the Transvaal might block British expansion along the corridor and seize the area's resources for itself, he strategically projected that expanding the Cape Colony around the Transvaal republic would cut the Transvaal's communication and supply lines, compelling it to join the Cape Colony under British rule.

Still only in his early to mid-thirties, Rhodes was an astute observer of the geopolitical situation, foreseeing the possible future moves of the many players who would seek to expand their claim to southern Africa's geography. It was like a giant game board to him: he already knew what to do, but he still lacked the power to be taken seriously. "He was no more a conventional politician than he was a conventional businessman," John S. Galbraith writes in *Crown and Charter: The Early Years of the British*

South Africa Company. "The limitations imposed on government by the representative process were repugnant to his being. Governments responsible to the parliamentary process he saw as inherently weak, unworthy of the greatness of the people whom they were elected to lead. The destiny of the Anglo-Saxons could not be realized by the agency of governments; the necessary force and fire must be provided by men eager to devote their lives, their energy, and their money to the mission." And Rhodes knew that political power would never be enough; he would need vast sums of money to make his vision a reality.

· 4 ·

BY THE MID-1880S RHODES WAS A RICH MAN, WELL known as one of Kimberley's leading citizens and already earning a reputation in Cape Town as a promising politician. His dreams for De Beers were as ambitious as his vision for a British-dominated southern Africa, but they were progressing more quickly. Under the tutelage of Rhodes, Beit and Rudd, the De Beers Company was thriving and was proving to be ever more profitable, thus providing the partners with a handsome income. But although Rhodes was rich, he was not yet all-powerful. There remained seven other claim holders at the mine site. For years the De Beers corporate strategy was to plod profitably along, buying more claims as financing became available, incrementally expanding the company's hold on the mine and the industry. In 1887 Rhodes bought all the remaining mine concessions in the DeBeers mine, and immediately consolidated its operations and cut expenses by moving the living quarters of the African labourers, who formed the vast bulk of the workforce, into an isolated, company-run shantytown, where they were housed, fed and each day searched for illicit diamonds. With these economy measures, profits began to soar—as did dividends paid to shareholders, which rose from 3 per cent before 1887 to 25 per cent by 1888, even while the global price of diamonds declined slightly. Rhodes instinctively knew that the global demand for diamonds would remain constant, so increased production would eventually be met with a concomitant decrease in price. Thus, to squeeze more profit from De Beers, he would need to control nearly the entire world supply of diamonds or arrange some form of cartel to restrict supply and thereby keep prices high. Although he had not yet told De Beers's shareholders about his patriotic ambitions, dominating the southern African diamond industry would allow Rhodes to finance his imperial dreams.

By 1887 two companies controlled most of southern Africa's diamond trade: the De Beers Company at the De Beers mine, and the Kimberley Central Company at the nearby and larger Kimberley mine. Barney Isaacs, a young Londoner who went by the name of Barney Barnato, had grown Kimberley Central in the same way that Rhodes and his partners had developed De Beers: by slowly buying up mining concessions over the years. Barnato was reputedly as rich as Rhodes, and perhaps even richer. The two companies would either have to fight or come to some agreement regarding production if the market was not to be flooded. Rhodes chose to fight. First, he arranged through European agents to purchase the outstanding shares of the French company that owned the remaining concessions at the Kimberley mine. Rhodes made a special trip to London and met with Lord Rothschild, through contacts arranged by Beit, and borrowed 750,000 pounds for this purpose. He then borrowed another 750,000 pounds from a Hamburg financier and contacted the head of the French company, offering 1,400,000 pounds for the entire operation, a fair price. But Rhodes always worked on more than one level. He had arranged to pay the interest on this massive loan with De Beers Company shares, but with a twist: if the De Beers shares rose in value and were higher at the end of a stipulated time period, any profit from this increase would be shared equally between De Beers and the lenders. Rhodes suspected that the shares would rise in the near future and wanted to make sure that he and his company benefited from the increase.

Before Rhodes's offer had been accepted by the French company's shareholders, Barnato got wind of the deal and quickly put together a counter-offer, proposing to pay them even more for their shares. (The new telegraph lines running from Cape Town to Kimberley made all these rapid offers and counter-offers possible.) Rhodes, unperturbed, approached Barnato and persuaded him to retract his offer to the French company. As compensation, Rhodes promised to sell Barnato and Kimberley Central the French company for the same price that De Beers had paid; that is, he agreed to pass on the shares at no profit. Rhodes's one requirement, however, was that Barnato pay him not in cash but in Kimberley Central stock. Barnato agreed. When the deal was completed, De Beers was the owner of about 20 per cent of Kimberley Central's stock, and Kimberley Central controlled the entirety of the Kimberley diamond field. Only two companies now owned both of the major diamond mines in the world. Now Rhodes made his big gamble. With the help of Beit, he raised even more capital and began buying as many shares as he could of Kimberley Central. Barnato urged his shareholders not to sell and then counter-offered with higher prices. Share prices in both companies spiked (earning Rhodes and De Beers a tidy sum, as they split the difference of the share increase with their European financial backers). As the market rose, many of the investors sold their shares in both companies and took their profits. Rhodes's backers, however, who were mostly in Europe, had a vested interest in the success of his gambit and held firm. (Most of the shareholders in

Kimberley Central lived in Kimberley.) After a short period of hectic buying, Rhodes and De Beers held a controlling stake in Kimberley Central.

Rhodes then convinced the shareholders of the two companies to amalgamate, the investors exchanging their shares for shares in a new holding corporation called De Beers Consolidated Mines. The only stumbling block was the trust deed of De Beers Consolidated, which would define the parameters of the new company's operations. Barnato and others wanted the trust deed to state that the activities of the company would be restricted to the diamond industry. Rhodes wanted no such restrictions and eventually prevailed, ensuring that the new company could engage in other businesses. The list of powers available to the new company were extraordinary and unusual. They included the right, should the need ever arise, to annex territory not already legally held by European powers; the ability to raise a private army to accomplish this goal; and provisions to engage in banking and other financial sponsorship of suitable enterprises yet to be determined. Rhodes and his cronies, including Barnato—who some biographers suspect was a willing participant in the scheme from the start, colluding with Rhodes to drive up the value of shares and make them both an emperor's fortune—were made life governors of De Beers Consolidated Mines. They were guaranteed an enormous income, hundreds of millions of dollars each, so long as the company remained profitable.

Rhodes was now in control of a company that held a virtual monopoly on diamonds, about 90 per cent of the world's supply. But he was only getting started. In a speech to the shareholders of the new amalgamated enterprise, he clarified his immediate goal. "Our ambition," he stated, "is to make it the richest, the greatest, and the most powerful company the world has ever seen." At this time the impoverished workers, mostly black Africans who toiled in the heat and dust extracting the diamonds from the earth, lived in abysmal conditions. They were virtual prisoners in company-run compounds, forced to spend their hard-earned wages at the company store. One commentator, John Merriman, observed that it was "a scandal and a disgrace to everyone whose moral sense is not blunted by the habit of looking at them as mere working animals." When the amalgamation was complete, about a half of the black workers were fired, as were a quarter of the white workers. The company's shares rose in value, profits soared and working conditions deteriorated as competition dwindled.

But Rhodes's money-making schemes were not limited to diamonds and De Beers. In 1886 gold was discovered in a region south of Pretoria called the Witwatersrand. The region, which became known as the Rand, evolved to become the richest gold mine in the world. A city called Johannesburg grew up nearby. Overcoming his initial reluctance, Rhodes became involved in a big way by forming alliances with wealthy and connected partners, none more connected than himself. Although he never dominated or understood the gold mining industry as he did the diamond industry, Rhodes made an immense amount of money from his initial speculation and, later, an enormous annual income from his ownership position and appointment as a managing director and chairman of the holding company Consolidated Gold Fields of South Africa. This move, too, opened the prospect of the company investing in a wide variety of enterprises, the same way De Beers Consolidated had done.

Although Rhodes was preoccupied with commercial activities during these years, his evolving empire-building political views meshed nicely with this commercial foundation. In 1890 he became the prime minister of Cape Colony, and his views now carried new weight. He was by far the wealthiest and most powerful person in southern Africa. Anticipating that "occupied land"—land occupied by indigenous peoples—would be an impediment to commercial development, Rhodes spoke out against the right of Africans to vote. (They were already prohibited from voting in the Boer republics of the Transvaal and the Orange Free State.) Since he believed the world would be improved by unrestrained and unregulated industrial development, he didn't want native Africans to obstinately cling to their land and stand in the way of "progress," particularly industrial development and mining. Rhodes also introduced laws beneficial to mining and industrial interests as he looked north to south-central Africa. He had great plans and dreams for this "empty" land. He had access to the capital and the political clout needed to develop the land, if he so chose, and it was to this end that he devoted an ever increasing amount of his energy.

· 5 ·

SINCE THE DISCOVERY OF GOLD ON THE RAND, PROS-pectors had cast their eyes northward beyond the fringes of the European-style colonies of the Cape and the Boer republics. Why should the sources of diamonds and gold be limited to the mines already discovered? In the 1880s numerous explorers and prospectors were trickling north into Matabeleland, the territory of Lobengula, the king of the Matabele. The Matabele were an offshoot of the Zulu tribe, who occupied the prime grazing lands of the Limpopo River, southwest of the Great Lakes of Central Africa. In the 1880s they were the most feared tribe in southern Africa, numbering around sixty thousand. Raiders and slavers, the Matabele frequently forayed deep into surrounding lands from their central settlement at Gubulawayo. Antony Thomas, author of *Rhodes: The Race for Africa,* likens the Matabele to the warriors of ancient Sparta, and Gubulawayo to a "huge military encampment, roughly circular in shape and half a mile in diameter, surrounded by a strong stockade of Mopani poles and thorn bushes. Immediately inside this outer ring was a circle of tightly packed grass huts, six rows thick and built in the traditional beehive shape," where the king's attendants and warriors dwelt. The king's inner sanctum was surrounded by yet another stockade enclosing two large brick houses. "The inhabitants lived an ant-heap sort of life," wrote the traveller A.T. Bryant. "There was no such thing as privacy; their souls were not their own; they were oppressed by a great fear of offending the elephantine King or his witch-doctors, and everybody moved like a puppet twitched by his will."

Lobengula himself was a powerfully built and regal figure of meticulous grooming. He was sensitive to protocol and appearances. "Like all the Matabele warriors who despise a stooping gait in a man," wrote one impressed visitor, "Lo Bengula walks quite erect, with his head thrown back and his broad chest expanded, and as he marches along at a slow pace with his long staff in his right hand, while all the men round him shout his praises, he looks the part to perfection." Lobengula's many appellations included "Eater of Men!" and "Stabber of Heaven." His "great bulging, blood-shot eyes" could induce terror when he "look[ed] you up and down, in his lordly way." The few European traders who were permitted to settle near Gubulawayo, squatted around the outer palisade. Lobengula called them his "white dogs," and none had ever been given permission to mine in his territories. If new sources of valuable minerals or gems were to be found, Rhodes believed they would be here, in Lobengula's kingdom. "The Matabele King . . . is the only block to Central Africa," Rhodes claimed. "Once we have his territory, the rest is easy."

The race for Africa was on, and the European powers were searching for territories to conquer and exploit, while preventing others from doing the same. Most people in Britain, indeed Europe, were increasingly of the belief that they had the right to occupy, develop or exploit any territory in Africa that was not already occupied or fully utilized by African peoples. One speaker and writer of the time, Joseph Chamberlain, clearly expressed this view: "So far as unoccupied territories between our present colonial possessions and the Zambezi are concerned, they are hardly practically to be said to be in the possession of any nation. The tribes and chiefs that exercise dominion in them cannot possibly occupy the land or develop its capacity, and it is as certain as destiny that, sooner or later, these countries will afford an outlet for European enterprise and European colonization."

Lobengula's court thronged with people seeking concessions for mineral claims, though the king remained independent and disdainful of the overtures of mining companies and European governments alike. The Portuguese, however, had claimed part of his territory, and the German government sent an envoy. British missionaries sought to operate in his lands as well, while mining company representatives, sometimes affiliated with European governments, angled for permission to operate in Lobengula's realm and with his blessing. The Europeans assumed that the recognition of a claim over African territory was determined by effective occupation. Rhodes feared that if Britain did not quickly expand northward, his dreams of a British corridor of political control from the Cape to Cairo would be dashed by the prior claims of some other European power. His greatest fear was that the Boer trekkers of the Transvaal would attempt to seize control. In 1887 they tried this very tactic by tricking Lobengula into placing his royal mark on a document that gave them exclusive trading rights to, and forbidding anyone else from entering, the territory.

Rhodes, even while he was preoccupied with his machinations to control the diamond industry, was furious at being pre-empted in 1887, though the sham document was repudiated by Lobengula and never gained wide acceptance. Always working on more than one facet of his grand scheme at any one time, he began laying the plans for his future expansion into Lobengula's domain. In August 1888 he sent six emissaries from Kimberley in ox carts heavily laden with gold and gifts for the king. Travelling for weeks across the plains, they arrived in Gubulawayo and sought an audience with the king. They persuaded him to affix his seal to a document titled the Rudd Concession, whereby Lobengula was to receive many gifts including one hundred breech-loading rifles and shot and an armed steamboat, to be delivered by sailing it up the Zambezi River. Lobengula in turn granted to Rhodes and his cronies "the complete and exclusive charge over all metals and minerals situated and contained in my kingdoms, principalities and domains, together with the power to do all the things that they deem necessary to win and procure the same ... And whereas I have been much molested of late by divers persons seeking and desiring to obtain grants and concessions of land and mining rights in my territories, I do hereby authorize the said grantees ... to take all necessary and lawful steps to exclude from my kingdom all persons seeking land, metals, minerals or mining rights therein." It is unlikely that Lobengula, a shrewd and calculating ruler who maintained his pre-eminent position by manipulating and terrifying others, was given an accurate translation of the document. He later claimed that he was told the concession provided for a maximum of ten miners to operate within his kingdom at any one time. Nevertheless, as soon as the document was signed, Rhodes's emissaries rushed south to make it public and Rhodes himself quickly boarded a ship to London on a related mission.

Rhodes wanted to secure a British government monopoly for a company to exploit the fantastic mineral resources he imagined lay within Lobengula's kingdom. He had created a new company and called it the Rudd Concession Syndicate, whose sole asset was the dubious concession itself, and approached the British Colonial Office to obtain a charter for a company to expand telegraph and railroad lines, establish banks and exploit mineral resources in the territory. With its own capital, the syndicate would not only stimulate the commercial development of the territory but forestall other European advancement. Rhodes began the behind-the-scenes work necessary for the founding of the British South Africa Company, which would eventually raise its own police force, rule everyone within the territory and make treaties with neighbouring peoples from the Limpopo River to the Great Lakes region. He set to work talking, using his considerable charm, political acumen, money and connections to overcome the diplomatic hurdles to such an audacious request.

No accurate records exist detailing how he managed to convince so many high-placed government officials to back his plan, but Rhodes observed cynically on more than one occasion that "every man has his price." The charismatic force of his personality and his visionary conviction probably won over just as many adversaries as his chequebook; he persuaded them that his cause was their cause, that it was all for the good of the empire and the nation.

Rhodes also used other tactics that were more subtle, such as appointments to the board of directors, selling shares at a discount to influential people and donating money to cherished political causes. A monopoly company with a government charter would not only benefit the downtrodden African people, he argued, it would advance British interests in central Africa against the encroachment of other European powers. Best of all, it would be done at no cost to the government. Soon, influential people had bought into his scheme; opposition melted as he widened the circle of those who would benefit from the company's monopoly charter. The territory "is rich," declared the London *Times,* "fabulously rich, we are told, in precious metals and half a dozen others besides, as well as being only in need of scratching to smile with corn and all kinds of agricultural wealth." Through the shifting of shares in various holding companies before the British South Africa Company was opened up to public investment, Rhodes and his principal backers also secured a hefty profit.

The company's charter gave it "all powers necessary for the purpose of government . . . the right to establish banking and other companies and associations; to make and maintain railways, telegraphs and lines of steamships; to carry on mining operations and license mining companies; to settle, cultivate and improve the lands; to preserve peace and order . . . and for that object obtain a force of police and have its own flag." It was also mandated to eliminate the slave trade and restrict the sale of spirits. All the powers normally vested in a crown colony were given to the company for an initial period of twenty-five years. The board was to have seventeen directors, but Rhodes from the very start was a virtual dictator; the directors rubber-stamped his decisions, which often had been made without even consulting them.

The full value of Rhodes's new chartered company could not be realized, however, until Lobengula gave up his obstinate insistence on preserving his authority. The company's charter was based on the questionable legality of its fraudulently obtained concession and Rhodes's promises to engage in noble activities such as freeing the African people from the cruel despotism of Lobengula and other kings. The flimsy concession upon which the charter was based would never survive careful scrutiny. Since war with the Matabele was inevitable, Rhodes reasoned, the sooner the better. By December 1889 he had issued orders to "break the power of the Matebele" and depose Lobengula, and he hired a young military officer, Frank Johnson, to lead the secret expedition. The plot was uncovered, however, when someone reported it to colonial authorities, but Rhodes of course denied all knowledge of and responsibility for the affair. A different plan was soon hatched, again with Johnson as its leader. Hundreds of "good fighting men" enlisted. Known as "Rhodes's angels," they were drawn "as far as possible from the sons of the leading families in each district of the Cape." Rhodes's backup plan was that if his men got into trouble and were "surrounded and cut off," their families would demand their rescue. "And who shall rescue you, do you think?" he asked Johnson. "I will tell you—the Imperial Factor . . . And who do you think will bring pressure to bear on the Imperial Factor and stir them to save you? The Influential fathers of your young men!"

In the summer of 1890 a heavily armed advance force of nearly two hundred, followed by five hundred officers and men of Rhodes's British South Africa Police and over a thousand other troops, mostly black Africans, set off for the north. The column marched around the edge of Lobengula's territory, hoping to provoke him. Meanwhile Rhodes was busy with his duties as prime minister of Cape Colony. In his book *Rhodes: The Race for Africa,* Antony Thomas remarks, "It must surely have occurred to someone to question how Mr. Rhodes, the prime minister, could possibly deal with matters affecting Mr. Rhodes, the diamond monopolist, or enter into contracts with Mr. Rhodes, the Chairman of Gold Fields, or Mr. Rhodes, the railway contractor, or Mr. Rhodes of the Chartered Company." Yet there were no objections at the time to these enormous, obvious and blatant conflicts of interest.

The British South Africa Company troops, along with miners and settlers, wound their way into Lobengula's territory, building forts along the route and marking land for future colonization. Trade and mining were perhaps negotiable, but Lobengula had never agreed to colonization. The troops did not directly attack Lobengula; that would have been illegal. So they remained on the fringe of his kingdom, in a territory known as Mashonaland that was dominated by Lobengula but not directly under his control, and began scouring the land for evidence of mineral wealth. After one year of searching, they had not uncovered any of its much-lauded mineral resources. One report by a British mining expert was non-committal: "It cannot be denied that the high hopes which were entertained... as to the great mineral or agricultural wealth of Mashonaland have not been justified or nearly justified... Mashonaland so far as is known, and much is known, is neither an Arcadia nor an El Dorado."

Disgruntled, the miners and prospectors turned to land speculation and farming. Rhodes's settlers advanced on Mashonaland's villages and demanded at gunpoint that the people provide unpaid labour for their farms. The indigenous people were killed, their cattle were stolen and their villages torched. Vigilante justice prevailed. In October 1891 Rhodes travelled north and entered "his" country for the first time, a territory now being called Rhodesia by the settlers. He had already begun a telegraph line into the region, and by the end of 1891 it was almost completed. Rhodes visited his new capital, Salisbury, a ramshackle cluster of rudimentary houses and stores near the ruins of Great Zimbabwe, the evidence of an ancient empire that was protected by great granite walls and supported by legendary gold mines. Rhodes credited the ancient ruins to the ancient Phoenicians rather than to the local Shona people. Undoubtedly, admitting that the structure had been built by local peoples would have undermined his conviction that they were in need of civilization.

The gold of ancient Great Zimbabwe proved elusive, however, and soon the settlers of the shabby little outpost were eyeing the territory closer to Lobengula's fort—perhaps the gold and diamonds were there. But Rhodes was faced with the same problem that had stalled his advance earlier: declaring war and invading Matabeleland was illegal and would endanger the company's charter. The company had spent a great deal, including money it had borrowed from De Beers Consolidated and Consolidated Gold Fields, but it had not yet discovered anything of value to justify either its initial investment or the ongoing expense of maintaining the expeditionary force. And the labour problems for Rhodes's settlers persisted because of Lobengula's raiding forays against the Shona. The Shona were afraid to work, even when their villages were threatened, for fear of Matabele reprisal. How could company settlers improve the land without cheap and plentiful labour? The relations between them were becoming more strained, and violence was more common. Something had to be done, but the British South Africa Company would remain stalled in its advance so long as Lobengula united the Matabele.

Perhaps sensing this drift in Rhodes's strategy, Lobengula consistently refused to be provoked into an outright attack. He resisted the urgings of his warriors to retaliate even when he was publicly insulted. Around this time, Rhodes received a missive from one of his agents suggesting a way of solving the problem: "Rhodes might consider the advisability of completing the thing... We have the excuse for a row over murdered women and children now and the getting of Matabeleland open would give us a tremendous lift in shares and everything else." The company would use a perhaps fictional raid on women and children by a band of Lobengula's warriors as an excuse to invade his territory. So the company army advanced, a ragged band of irregulars, prospectors and prospective settlers who would be guaranteed their pay in the form of loot from the sacking of Lobengula's stronghold. Half of the plunder would go to the company, while the remaining half was to be divided among the officers and men, according to their rank. Lobengula reputedly had a vast trove of gold, guns and diamonds, as well as over 300,000 head of cattle. Rhodes also promised land to the company's army.

Rhodes's propaganda campaign for this major offensive included the use of his own newspapers in the Cape Colony, particularly the *Cape Argus,* to spread false rumours of Matabele warriors massing for an attack on the English settlers, in defiance of the Rudd Concession. One of Rhodes's long-time lieutenants, Leander Jameson, readied 1,400 men in October and, using rumours of the Matabele attacks on white settlers as his justification, marched on Gubulawayo. When the two forces converged, the 5,000 Matabele warriors were devastated by the modern cannons and machine guns. Over 3,000 Matabele perished in this short battle while only a handful of company men died. Jameson then marched on Lobengula's now-burning capital and planted the company flag in the smouldering ruins. Rhodes, who had been standing by, entered Gubulawayo soon after the battle to celebrate his victory. As the prime minister of Cape Colony he was far to the north of any territories that he officially governed, but as the managing director of the British South Africa Company he was right in the heart of his new, ill-gotten domain. He proceeded to build himself a house on top of the ruined foundations of Lobengula's royal compound and then spent several days overseeing the staking out of the business district for the new capital, which was to be called "the new township of Bulawayo."

Faced with public criticism and attempts by a small contingent of British troops to halt the settler army's plundering and pillaging of Lobengula's realm, Rhodes immediately launched another press campaign. This one warned Great Britain not to interfere in the company's activities, lest it have to face "a new Republic, which would cause more blood... than the whole Matabele nation is worth." On July 18, 1894, Britain acknowledged the British South Africa Company's jurisdiction over the newly conquered territory. The founding of Rhodesia was complete, and the company's stock skyrocketed to eight times the value it had before the battle. Rhodes, now a hero to the savage band of Rhodesian "pioneers" as well as to the company's shareholders, exulted that the company "possessed a very large piece of the world . . . everything within it and everything upon it except the air." He and the company had dispossessed the Matabele from their lands and succeeded in reducing them to an industrial and agricultural proletariat. Together they ruled a land comprising more than a million square kilometres. And they had convinced themselves that their aggression had been carried out in the name of progress.

· 6 ·

AS THE PRIME MINISTER OF CAPE COLONY AND "CHAIRman" of Rhodesia, Cecil Rhodes had achieved the pinnacle of power, authority and respect. In the Cape Colony he continued to manage his commercial interests and to work towards bridging the widening gap between the Cape's Boer and English colonists. Stability would not only be good for business, it would be absolutely necessary for the company to fully exploit Rhodesia. In order to advance this agenda, Rhodes needed the support of both Boer and English parliamentarians and made some odious concessions to secure that support. In Parliament, he made many deals with the Boers to secure his business interests, such as railroads where he wanted them, particularly railroads heading north into Rhodesia. He also stilled opposition to De Beers's abusive treatment of workers and deferred plans for a tax on diamonds. In exchange, he supported laws and regulations that discriminated against black Africans and that were advocated by the Boers. Antony Thomas writes that there were "two important considerations that moved Rhodes towards a racist position—a politician's need for votes and an industrialist's need for a controlled labour force."

A third consideration was Rhodes's belief in the need for a common "native" policy among all the republics. In the Boer republics of the Transvaal and the Orange Free State, black Africans had no voting rights, and Rhodes supported the proposals to limit the black vote in the Cape Colony as well. He began by implementing policies that denied the vote to those who owned land communally, a move that gained him political favour with many of his Boer constituents. "We have to govern the natives as a subject race," he announced. "By the last census [perhaps around 1890] there are 1,250,000 natives in the Colony and 250,000 Europeans. Under the present franchise, if they were to exercise it, the natives would have a majority of votes." He went on: "Treat the natives as a subject people as long as they continue in a state of barbarism."

Rhodes was continually working towards a union of the southern African republics, and he knew that the Cape Colony's relatively liberal policies regarding black Africans would always be a major stumbling block to any unification with the Boer republics. So he set about working to change the laws in the Cape Colony, supporting legislation to legalize the flogging of disrespectful (black) servants; voting to raise, again, the property-ownership requirements for voting; introducing an education test, an action that disenfranchised yet thousands more black voters; and annexing more native lands by force and moving thousands of black Africans onto reserves. "My idea is that the natives should be kept in these native reserves and not mixed with white men at all," he pronounced. He passed laws that made farms undividable, which meant that farmers' younger sons and unmarried daughters were forced to leave the land, conveniently providing a stream of cheap labour. Not yet satisfied, Rhodes eliminated missionary schools so that black Africans would not gain an education. "When I see the labour troubles that are occurring in the United States," he observed, "and when I see the troubles that are going to occur with the English people in their own country... I feel rather glad that the labour question here is connected with the native question... If the whites maintain their position as the supreme race, the day will come when we shall all be thankful that we have the natives with us in their proper position." He imposed curfews on black Africans and racial segregation in public institutions. All these changes were supported by Rhodes's newspapers, particularly the *Cape Argus*. By 1895 he had essentially established all the key foundations of an apartheid regime that would come into full force half a century later. And, in Rhodesia, Rhodes's Land Commission removed natives from their land and placed them in poorly situated reserves so that their territories could be opened to white settlers.

Even Cecil Rhodes, though, was not invincible. His downfall was swift and of his own making. His health was deteriorating. He suffered from heart problems, exacerbated by smoking, drinking and a substantial gain in weight. He was only in his early forties, but he looked and acted much older. He began to feel like he was running out of time to fulfill one of his greatest ambitions: the consolidation of all the independent republics of southern Africa under one banner. So far, the mineral prospects in Rhodesia had not shaped up as he had hoped. After an extensive tour of the region, one of his mining engineers reported, "I urge the investing public to exercise due discrimination." It appeared that the great gold deposits in the Transvaal, around Johannesburg, did not extend north, as many had assumed they would. Not only were Rhodesia and the British South Africa Company failing to meet the earlier optimistic predictions of incredible mineral wealth, but the great gold fields of the Transvaal were propelling the Boer republic to become the richest state in southern Africa—a situation that would forever prevent its unification with the Cape Colony. In addition, Rhodes had a personal hatred of Paul Kruger, the president of the Transvaal, and became involved in a scheme to invade the Boer republic, overthrow its president and forcibly annex it to the Cape Colony.

Rhodes's plan was similar to the one that had succeeded in his seizure of Lobengula's kingdom: a staged uprising calling for intervention. His main henchman in this instance was the same Leander Jameson who had led the charge in Rhodesia, and who would again lead a private force to the rescue in the Transvaal; it all would be done simply and cleanly. The British government had considered a similar scheme, but had abandoned it for various reasons, so Rhodes had reason to believe that Britain would not be averse to the operation, once it was complete. However, the raid, an elaborate plot involving journalists, industrialists and government officials, was a complete disaster. Jameson and eight hundred raiders charged into the Transvaal expecting an uprising in their support, but the revolt never materialized and the invaders were surrounded, captured and taken into custody for questioning by Transvaal forces. Though he protested his innocence, Rhodes was forced to resign as prime minister. The charter for his company was nearly revoked, and he paid massive fines. But he was never directly linked to the invasion; all his men remained silent and even went to prison without uttering a word of his direct involvement. Two years later, Rhodes tried for a political comeback but lost by one seat, despite his enormous expenditures and his ownership of much of Cape Town's "free" press. He then set his eyes on Rhodesia—"his" north, he called it—and spent a lot of time getting railways and telegraphs built and locating and developing mines and other resources.

The Boer War, when it started in 1899, was more or less inevitable given the glaring and increasing differences between the Boer republics and the Cape Colony, and their struggles for pre-eminence. Rhodes took an active part in the defence of Kimberley and his diamond mine during the conflict that engulfed the entire region. After suffering tens of thousands of deaths, British forces defeated the Boer republics, and eventually the Orange Free State and the Transvaal were amalgamated with Cape Colony into the Union of South Africa.

Cecil Rhodes spent the remaining few years of his life preoccupied with rebellions in Rhodesia and with his deteriorating health. He was hounded, and probably blackmailed, by a Polish princess named Catherine Radziwill, who forged promissory notes in his name, spread rumours that they were engaged, proposed marriage to him and generally harassed him by following him back and forth from London to Cape Town several times. Eventually, when all her overtures were rebuffed, she accused him of criminal fraud. She apparently possessed documents that Rhodes did not want released to the public, and so managed to obtain large sums of money from him. Radziwill continued to haunt him until his death on March 2, 1902, at the age of forty-nine. He died in Cape Town and was buried in Rhodesia.

The British South Africa Company, however, lived on, although Rhodes's charismatic optimism had concealed the fact that the company was not profitable. The wars to subjugate the natives and reparations paid to settlers for damaged property consumed vast amounts of its wealth. And, although Rhodesia did contain mineral wealth, it never proved to be the great bonanza that Rhodes and the company's initial shareholders imagined. Land proved to be the company's most valuable asset, but controlling it entailed keeping the Africans permanently off of it. For years the company continued to lose money, and for the shareholders it must have been painful to learn that invading and running a country is not an inherently profitable business endeavour. There was, as well, the moral disadvantage of being implicated in human rights abuses on the grossest scale against a subjugated people.

Nevertheless, the company organized campaigns to encourage the settlement and the sale of its land, and by the First World War the white population—the people who owned all the land in Rhodesia—had reached 31,000. Agricultural production increased dramatically, as did mining production. But the shareholders saw little profit during this time; the costs of running Rhodesia were too high, and maintaining a strong military force to keep native Africans from reclaiming their territory was a very expensive undertaking. The company's rule in Rhodesia ended in 1923, when the settlers demanded responsible government and were granted their request by the British government. Britain also decided that the ownership of all unclaimed land did not reside with the company, as it was no longer the agent of the Crown. The shareholders were, however, paid several million pounds as compensation for the loss of this land.

· 7 ·

BY THE TIME OF RHODES'S DEATH, BRITONS REGARDED his accomplishments with a mixture of distaste and admiration. The *Times* recorded, "He has done more than any single contemporary to place before the imagination of his countrymen a clear conception of the Imperial destinies of our race, but we wish we could forget the other matters associated with his name." He and other imperialists like him, the newspaper concluded, "provoke a degree of repugnance, sometimes hatred, in exact proportion to the size of their achievements." To some admirers he was a great visionary, a prophet of imperial expansion and destiny, working tirelessly to expand the British Empire for the benefit of less civilized peoples and achieve his noble dream of a global English-speaking empire, centred in Great Britain, that would bring peace and prosperity to the world. He was "the great white man." Others, not quite so enamoured, saw his actions in a different light: the man used his considerable wealth and influence to acquire the veneer of legitimacy from a chartered company in order to mount a private invasion of territories in southern and eastern Africa, controlling the media through his ownership of newspapers and his bribery of officials, while his corporate mercenaries toppled governments and paved the way for land to be unlawfully seized from local peoples in order to expand his mining interests and warped neo-colonial dreams.

Rhodes schemed and behaved like a politician, not a merchant. He acted with the ruthlessness and calculated brutality of a mediaeval warlord. He was a brilliant manipulator and, some would argue, swindler, his actions made noteworthy by his audacity. The legends and myths surrounding him are legion. He bought newspaper companies, both secretly and openly, because of his conviction that "the press rules the minds of men." He has been accused of pressuring doctors to suppress information concerning a smallpox epidemic among the African labour force of his diamond mines, believing that this information would disrupt production because labourers would steer clear of the region; and it would, of course, cost money to pay for inoculations—money he did not want to spend. As a result, 751 people died before the disease was finally brought under control. Rhodes used his power and authority in government to support legislation that strengthened mine-owners' rights and weakened native Africans' voting and land rights. In the House of Assembly in Cape Town, he made a speech claiming that "the native is to be treated as a child and denied the franchise. We

278 · Merchant Kings

must adopt a system of despotism in our relations with the barbarians of South Africa."

Antony Thomas has characterized Rhodes's life as a tragic tale of idealistic youth corrupted by the pursuit of power, and it is hard to disagree. Having no family, no wife and few close friends, Rhodes devoted himself to continuous work and scheming, despite having amassed enough wealth to provide for several decades of indulgent living. He seemed to live for the chance to exercise power, never tired of it and consumed large portions of his vast fortune in promoting what he considered to be the greatest cause: the advancement of the British Empire. His life, like that of other larger-than-life men, is replete with myths and fantastic stories, and many of his early biographies—Cecil John Rhodes inspired dozens of them—contain variations of his rags-to-riches rise to become one of the wealthiest men in the world by virtue of his hard work and talent. For Rhodes, money was power: the ability to use it to command other men to do his bidding, to fulfill his dreams and ambitions. But he was not a philosopher; he was a man of action, a planner and a doer rather than a thinker, an actor on the ideas of others that he applied to his situation.

Rhodes's repulsive beliefs and actions, unlike the near-psychopathic legacy of Jan Coen two centuries earlier, were the product of his era, his upbringing and his sudden and early wealth. Certainly he believed in his personal greatness and destiny, in his superiority within his race and his race's superiority within the human family—a meteoric rise in wealth and power can produce such impressions in a young man—but he also believed he was doing good in the world and a good turn for the people with whom he clashed. Although he did monstrous things, dispossessing people of their land by unscrupulous and sometimes violent means, he believed his cause would result in their eventual betterment. Deluded, and not a particularly deep thinker, he did not believe he was doing evil. Coen, on the other hand, knew he was sowing mischief and doing harm to others, but he did not care, so long as it benefited him, his company and his country—in that order. Rhodes was an arrogant, smug know-it-all who believed the ends justified the means. He had gambled early in life and won big, and was then propelled to greater success by both good timing and the gambles made possible by his impressive initial jackpot. Having always won when he made decisions, he grew to believe that others would be better off if their decisions were also made by him. To those who were killed or displaced by the corporate policies of merchant kings like Rhodes and Coen, their motivations mattered little, but their motivations speak to their character. Rhodes was like a missionary, convinced of the truth of his divine mission; Coen was a bandit and a thug, however fine his clothing and grooming.

Rhodes was lauded as a hero by many, not only by his company's colonists in Rhodesia, but also throughout the British Empire. Oxford University bestowed an honorary doctorate on him. When he returned to Cape Town, banners lined the streets proclaiming "Welcome Home Empire Maker," while newspapers—some of them owned by Rhodes himself—lavished praise on his accomplishments. Rhodes added a great deal of territory to the British Empire through his British South Africa Company, and he made many people a lot of money. During one of his meetings with Queen Victoria, he proudly, perhaps smugly, responded with mock humility to her query about what he had been doing since their previous meeting: "I have added two new provinces to your possessions, Madam, since we last met." He would no doubt have continued his bloody expansion in Africa, consolidating his gains and pushing farther north, had he not died at the age of forty-nine. Continuous expansion was something he dwelt on. "To think of these stars that you see overhead," he observed, "these vast worlds which we can never reach. I would annex other planets if I could; I often think about that. It makes me sad to see them so clear and yet so far."

But Rhodes was also despised by many during his lifetime. Mark Twain thought that he ought to be hanged. "I admire him," he quipped. "I frankly confess it; and when his time comes I shall buy a piece of the rope for a keepsake." Rhodes was accused publicly of bribery, corruption, neglect of duty and "harshness to the natives," as well as of being "utterly unscrupulous." Some of his racial ideas, which were popular during his lifetime and politically championed by him during his tenure as prime minister, later found their outlet in the ideologies of the Nazis and of South Africa's apartheid regime. Rhodes has had a lasting and continuing negative impact on South Africa as well as Zimbabwe and Zambia, the countries of the former Rhodesia, stemming from his early support for the racist policies that tore those countries apart.

Rhodes's most enduring positive legacy, perhaps his only positive legacy, was his donation to Oxford University of an enormous sum of money to fund the scholarships known as the Rhodes Scholarships. Rhodes had been meticulously planning his legacy for decades. "What is life worth with no object, no aim?" he wondered as an Oxford student in the 1870s. Like another nineteenth-century titan of industry, Alfred Nobel, who left his vast estate resulting from the invention of dynamite to fund enormously prestigious prizes in physics, chemistry, medicine, literature and peace, Rhodes had been thinking of sponsoring scholarships for many years. He wrote seven different wills during his lifetime, each one refining the details of the distribution of his vast and ever-expanding estate. He provided annual funding for three years to a select number of students from the British colonies of Rhodesia, the Cape Colony, Natal, New South Wales, Tasmania, New Zealand, Newfoundland, Bermuda and Jamaica as well as the Canadian provinces of

Ontario and Quebec. He also included among the beneficiaries students from the United States, perhaps to further his avowed hope that the nation would eventually be rejoined with Great Britain. And he added as an addendum the inclusion of five German students per year: "The object is that an understanding between the three great Powers will render war impossible and educational relations make the strongest tie."

Rhodes had specific criteria regarding the eligibility for his prizes, and academic achievement was not foremost. He did not want the beneficiaries to be "merely bookworms." Rather, he stressed athletic ability as well as nebulous traits such as "fondness for and success in manly outdoor sports such as cricket, football and the like; his qualities of manhood, truth, courage, devotion to duty, sympathy for and protection of the weak, kindliness, unselfishness and fellowship, and his exhibition during school days of moral force of character and instincts to lead and to take an interest in his schoolmates, for these latter attributes will be likely in after life to guide him to esteem the performance of public duties as his highest aim." Many of the altruistic and perhaps even chivalrous characteristics that Rhodes deemed necessary for receipt of one of his scholarships were traits that he did not possess himself. His criteria seem out of line for someone whose own career can be summed up in one word, "unscrupulous"; he would never have qualified for one of his own awards and certainly was aware of it. Was he trying to protect the world from the depredations of others like himself? Or was he so compelled to win at all costs that during his own life his competitiveness negated or dominated his other, moral traits?

Interestingly, Rhodes also specified that "no student shall be qualified or disqualified for election to a Scholarship on account of his race or religious opinions." He only stipulated that the scholarships go to men. Considering his prominently racist views, indeed his introduction and support of racist policies during his tenure as prime minister of the Cape Colony, this qualification seems unusual. There is evidence that Rhodes's views had begun to change as he grew older, and perhaps, with no further need for the political support of the Boers in Parliament to further his unification agenda, he abandoned those views that were most dear to the Boers: racial hierarchy and segregation based on skin colour. Near the end of his life, Rhodes described to a journalist his views on human rights. "My motto," he claimed, "is equal rights for every civilized man south of the Zambezi. What is a civilized man? A man whether white or black, who has sufficient education to write his name, has some property or work, in fact is not a loafer." Unfortunately, his earlier political support for racist policies had set the entire region on the disastrous path towards the institutionalization of racial hierarchy. Perhaps Rhodes died before he could work towards undoing his earlier policies, if indeed he ever would have done anything about them.

A conflicted and complicated colossus, Rhodes cast a huge shadow on the history of the era. His varied commercial interests and near-monopoly of the diamond industry made him one of the richest men on earth. He lived a sober and quiet life, never marrying or having flashy affairs, yet he had the pride and arrogance to name a medium-sized country after himself when his company conquered it. Variously lauded and loathed for his ambition, ruthless tactics, belligerence and abuses of other people and cultures, he and his companies brought chaos and upheaval to southern and eastern Africa in ways that have not been resolved today. Through the British South Africa Company, he ruled conquered lands as virtual fiefdoms. He was alternately a charming and charismatic host and orator, and a domineering bully. He inspired great numbers of people into action in his interests, and in what he believed to be the interests of the British Empire. Even his harshest critics conceded that he wasn't motivated by money for the sake of conspicuous consumption or display. It was this widespread belief in his higher, more noble motives that caused the actions of his company to be condemned while Rhodes himself seemed to float above the dirty dealings done in his name or at his command.

As John S. Galbraith has written, "In an age when doubts had begun to intrude as to the permanence of British supremacy, the exploits of Rhodes were a reassurance that the great days were not yet over. He asserted the superiority of Britons, and he extended the empire at no cost to the British taxpayer." Although the assessment of his accomplishments was mixed during his lifetime, he was elevated to near-demigod status by the mid-twentieth century as a tamer of savages and promulgator of "white" culture. Now, however, he is regarded as faintly embarrassing, one of those men whose actions and views are so out of step with contemporary thought that they are best forgotten. But his actions and legacy, and those of the British South Africa Company, can hardly be forgotten in the place where his impact was the greatest: southern Africa.

The great tragedy of Rhodes is that a man of such intelligence, charisma, power and wealth should have squandered his talents and fortune on an ever-spiralling series of acquisitions and expansions, making more and more money, far beyond the point of needing it, and doing this by restricting the rights of workers, pursuing a policy of violent annexation of vast territories and subjugating their peoples, all to gain access to more mineral deposits and expand his own commercial empire and the British political empire. In the end, his business consumed his life, narrowing it to the adrenaline rush of scheming and victory over rivals. Although Rhodes put himself forward as the great champion of empire, in the end his policies served only to eliminate the possibility of a bright future for southern Africa for generations, heaping enormous moral debts and a tarnished legacy on the generations to come. Like many merchant kings, Rhodes was consumed by the contest and forgot that there could be—indeed, should be—a purpose to his life other than the continued struggle to conquer and expand.

Epilogue

WHEN COMPANIES RULED THE WORLD

"Monopoly . . . is a great enemy to good management."

ADAM SMITH, *The Wealth of Nations*, 1776

"OF COURSE, THE WHOLE ENTERPRISE WAS IN THE LONG run a scheme to enrich a few on the blood and guts of a subject people," Hector Chevigny wrote of the Russian American Company. The same could be said about any of the mighty commercial monopolies of the Age of Heroic Commerce. But all corporate behaviour does not lead to this; indeed, the desire to barter and exchange products is as old as humanity itself. The merchant kings and their monopoly corporations epitomize the nightmare of unscrutinized and unchallenged power combined with ideology—in this case, controlling whole civilizations and societies for the maximum gain of distant shareholders. These monolithic corporate entities were less the product of free-market capitalism than the commercial extension of European national wars and struggles for cultural and economic supremacy. They occupied the muddy grey zone that exists between government and enterprise.

Initially, granting monopoly trading rights was a convenient way for European governments to bankroll the astronomical costs of colonial expansion and commercial wars by tapping private capital. The policy failed, however, when home governments allowed the companies to become the only local civil authority as the trading outposts grew in population. By offloading the responsibility for their own citizens and by claiming power over the indigenous residents of the territories absorbed by their enterprises, European governments created the conditions that had often horrific consequences. In other cases, the use by monopoly corporations of their home nation's goodwill for their own personal gain resulted in substantial losses for the mother country, such as the Netherlands' loss of control over Manhattan and New Netherland and Britain's loss of control over Old Oregon, or the use of national revenues to fund the military defence of the companies' territories and privileges.

The monopolies provided great benefits to their host nations for a limited time, but like all institutions they outlived their usefulness and caused great damage when their powers were not curtailed. The fact that many of these entities ended up relying on government bailouts has relevance to modern times. As with the giant multinational financial institutions and manufacturers during our current area, many of the great historical monopolies became so large and complex, and employed so many people— overshadowing economies and occasionally being wielded as a tool of foreign policy—that to allow their failure or collapse would have been devastating to the national morale as well as the national economy. They became too big and important to be allowed to collapse. The profits were enjoyed disproportionately by a few individuals for decades, but the cost of failure was borne equally by the whole society through taxes.

The merchant kings led their enterprises away from their purely commercial origins and towards the social exploitation and political subjugation of entire societies. The incredible distance between their home countries and the arena of their commercial activity enabled the merchant kings to pursue their grand overriding visions: once their sailing ships left port for voyages lasting up to a year or more, they and their officers were not subject to the laws of their home nations. Yet neither were they subject to the rules governing foreign societies because of their technological prowess and the incapacity of those local governments to police them. Once they were far from home, in a world without reliable communication or even trustworthy charts of the regions being exploited by their enterprises, the merchant kings could do business as they pleased, with free rein to indulge their impulses, impose dictatorial power and plunder rapaciously. They were able to do so because they were free of the moral and legal strictures that would have bound or at least tempered their behaviour and business activities at home. Most Europeans, apart from a select few insiders, had no idea how abusive some of these companies were in their overseas practices or that they routinely flouted the laws and customs that bound society in Europe.

The merchant kings and their monopoly corporations show us the potential danger of our current trends of globalization: the greater the distance between the product and the consumer, the less opportunity for consumers to oversee production, to ensure that in the producing countries the producers adhere to the laws and recognize the same rights enjoyed by the citizens of the nations where their products are sold. This is equally applicable to the spice trade in the seventeenth century, and the fur trade in the nineteenth century, as it is to footwear or electronics manufacturing in the twenty-first century.

The great theorist of free markets, Adam Smith, was very aware of the drawbacks of monopolies, of the dangers they presented both to their customers and to the societies in which they operated. A company will always act in what it believes are the best interests, sometimes only short-term, of itself and its shareholders; that is its purpose. A monopoly can operate without checks and balances—without a second set of eyes, those of the competition, in the same field and region. The merchant kings went even further by seizing political power in addition to possessing their commercial monopoly; we have seen the Dutch East India Company's dominance throughout Indonesia, the Dutch West India Company's control over New Netherland, the English East India Company's rule of Bengal, the Russian American Company's hold on Alaska, the Hudson's Bay Company's governance of much of North America, and the British South Africa Company's power in southern Africa. In the Western world we have reached a point, however, where nothing like those great monopolies could exist in the same manner any more. There are at present no completely unregulated enterprises that can engage in cultural and environmental annihilation with impunity.

Western societies strive for a separation of religion and the state, but what ought to be the relationship between commercial enterprise and the state? It seems clear from studying these merchant kings and their monopoly companies that the conjoining of commerce and the state during the Age of Heroic Commerce produced a series of "bad marriages," which can be seen as cautionary tales about how such relationships can go drastically wrong. These historical examples demonstrate that corporate enterprise as political authority eventually runs counter to the interests of the people and the state, even though they may seem compatible for a time. Ultimately, commerce and responsible government are working towards different goals, and for the benefit of different people. Commercial enterprise is vital to the prosperity of peoples and thus is a primary facet of society, but it must operate under the auspices and political control of the governing society, rather than compelling that society to act subserviently, as the merchant kings sought to do. The monopoly corporations described in this book failed their host nations when they resisted the transition to true government: people cannot be kept indefinitely as employees, customers or competitors without being granted personal freedoms and civil rights. In any event, the great monopolies that imposed political control on subject peoples were eventually faced with the reality that governing people responsibly was not an inherently profitable field of enterprise. In the short run, exploitation certainly could be profitable, but eventually it tainted the exploiters morally. Even when they were good companies, they made for bad governments; the ultimate objectives of government and commerce were shown to be inherently incompatible.

The leaders of these successful companies shared a variety of characteristics: they could be extremely competitive and ruthlessly determined to get their way, to impose their will on others in order to increase their power. None of them were born into wealth, social status or power, but the struggle to win the contest, as they perceived it, was of paramount concern. The merchant kings were also tactically brilliant and possessed an expansive vision that directed the activities of millions. These traits, however, led them to make unsavoury decisions. Was it a corrupt personality, however brilliant and decisive, that led these merchant kings to the pinnacle of their success, or did their meteoric success give rise to the less flattering aspects of their personalities? Should we overlook their moral failings because they effected revolutionary changes in the course of world history? Many of them were celebrated as heroes during their lifetimes but are viewed much less favourably today. Even certain brutal kings, emperors and generals have the word "great" appended to their names, yet the merchant kings as a group fail to elicit this kind of historical respect.

The merchant kings of the Age of Heroic Commerce were a rogue's gallery of larger-than-life merchant-adventurers who, during a period of three hundred years, expanded their far-flung commercial enterprises over a good portion of the world for no other purpose than to generate revenue for their shareholders, feather their own nests and satisfy their vanity. Heroes or scoundrels; patriots or thieves; sagacious administrators or greedy plunderers—these are often flip sides of the same coin. Squint your eyes or shed light elsewhere to shift the shadows, and one can become the other. Contemplating the merchant kings of those earlier times is like looking in a rear-view mirror: remove the cultural veneer, and the same sorts of people, mixing business and politics, are making our world even today.

Sources

I APPROACHED THIS PROJECT AS AN INTERESTED GEN-
eralist with a background in history. The book is written for
other interested generalists, as a history of individual merchant
kings and their monopoly companies rather than as a technical
history of global trade or colonial expansion. I stick to generally
established chronologies and facts, and the key sources are ref-
erenced in the text. My focus is on the people and personalities
that drove these commercial enterprises to seize political power,
rather than on the minutiae of trade statistics, profit margins
and so forth. I wanted to tell the stories of the merchant kings'
lives, the stories of what motivated them, what gave them pleasure or drove them into a fury, why they pushed themselves and
their companies to dominate others and then to crush all competition. Was it merely money that motivated these actions? I
think not, and the stories show that something more unfath-
omably intangible, yet human, drove these complicated and
intriguing individuals.

With the exception of Coen, and to a lesser extent Baranov, the merchant kings whose stories appear here have been profiled in numerous biographies over the decades, although they have never been considered together as a group. The companies they headed are also well documented and studied. Whole books have been written on each of these individuals, and whole books on each of these mighty monopoly corporations. Because I cover six of them in one volume, much detail, technical and personal, has been omitted. The complex interactions of generations of company men, whether in Indonesia, Africa, India or North America, could easily fill an entire book. In preparing the selected bibliography I have only listed those resources that I found useful and relied upon as authoritative, insightful or both. Most of the contemporary quotes of the merchant kings come from collected volumes of their correspondence, speeches and memoirs or have been reproduced in the appendices of scholarly works.

For further reading on Coen and the Dutch East India Company, consult Femme S. Gaastra's *The Dutch East India Company: Expansion and Decline*. Giles Milton's *Nathaniel's Nutmeg: How One Man's Courage Changed the Course of History* is a colourful narrative of the struggle between the Dutch and English companies to control the Indonesian spice trade. The best book to further an interest in Stuyvesant and corporate Dutch Manhattan is Russell Shorto's fascinating work *The Island at the Center of the World: The Epic Story of Dutch Manhattan and the Forgotten Colony that Shaped America*.

Regarding Clive and the English East India Company, a veritable mountain of literature has been written. Start with Michael Edwardes's *Clive: The Heaven-Born General* or Robert Harvey's *Clive: The Life and Death of a British Emperor*. John Keay's *The Honourable Company: A History of the English East India Company* is a highly readable, thorough and lucid overview of the company's activities over the centuries. Baranov, and Russian America in general, have been less studied, but a good overview is contained in Lydia Black's *Russians in Alaska, 1732–1867,* whereas Hector Chevigny's *Lord of Alaska: Baranov and the Russian Adventure* is a colourful, if not entirely trustworthy, narrative of Baranov's life. For a thorough and lively account of Simpson's life and the later history of the Hudson's Bay Company, consult James Raffan's *Emperor of the North: Sir George Simpson and the Remarkable Story of the Hudson's Bay Company.* Shelves of books have been written about Cecil Rhodes, many of them scarcely veiled hagiographies from the early twentieth century. I found the most readable and nuanced general account to be Antony Thomas's relatively recent *Rhodes: The Race for Africa.*

Selected Bibliography

Alekseev, Aleksandr Ivanovich. *The Destiny of Russian America, 1741–1867.*
Edited by R.A. Pierce. Translated by Maria Ramsay. Kingston, ON:
Limestone Press, 1990.

Black, Lydia. *Russians in Alaska, 1732–1867.* Fairbanks: University
of Alaska Press, 2004.

Bowen, H.V. The *Business of Empire: The East India Company and Imperial
Britain, 1756–1833.* New York: Cambridge University Press, 2006.

Bown, Stephen R. *A Most Damnable Invention: Dynamite, Nitrates and the
Making of the Modern World.* Toronto: Viking, 2005.

Boxer, C.R. *The Dutch Seaborne Empire, 1600–1800.* New York: Knopf, 1965.

Braudel, Ferdinand. *Civilization and Capitalism, 15th–18th Century.* New York:
Harper & Row, 1984.

Brierly, Joanna Hall. *Spices: The Story of Indonesia's Spice Trade.* Oxford:
Oxford University Press, 1994.

Burrows, Edwin G., and Mike Wallace. *Gotham: A History of New York City
to 1898.* New York: Oxford University Press, 1999.

Cawston, George. *The Early Chartered Companies, A.D. 1296–1858.* London: Edward Arnold, 1896.

Chevigny, Hector. *Lord of Alaska: Baranov and the Russian Adventure.* New York: Viking, 1942.

———. *Russian America: The Great Alaskan Venture, 1741–1867.* New York: Viking Press, 1965.

Clive, Robert. *Lord Clive's Speech, in the House of Commons, 30th March 1772, on the Motion Made for Leave to Bring in a Bill, for the Better Regulation of the Affairs of the East India Company, and of Their Servants in India, and for the Due Administration of Justice in Bengal.* London: J. Walter, 1772.

Condon, Thomas J. *New York Beginnings: The Commercial Origins of New Netherland.* New York: New York University Press, 1968.

Curtin, Philip D. *Cross-Cultural Trade in World History.* Cambridge: Cambridge University Press, 1984. Davies, D.W. *A Primer of Dutch Seventeenth Century Overseas Trade.* The Hague: Martinus Hijhoff, 1961.

Dodwell, Henry. *Dupleix and Clive: The Beginning of Empire.* London: Archon Books, 1968.

Edwardes, Michael. *Clive: The Heaven-Born General.* London: Hart-Davis, MacGibbon, 1977.

Furber, Holden. *Rival Empires of Trade in the Orient, 1600–1800.* Minneapolis: University of Minnesota Press, 1976.

Gaastra, Femme S. *The Dutch East India Company: Expansion and Decline.* Zutphen: Walburg Pers, 2003.

Galbraith, John S. *Crown and Charter: The Early Years of the British South Africa Company.* Berkeley: University of California Press, 1974.

———. *The Hudson's Bay Company as an Imperial Factor.* Toronto: University of Toronto Press, 1957.

———. *The Little Emperor: Governor Simpson of the Hudson's Bay Company.* Toronto: Macmillan of Canada, 1976.

Gehring, Charles, trans. *Laws and Writs of Appeal, 1647–1663.* Syracuse: Syracuse University Press, 1991.

Gibson, James R. *Imperial Russia in Frontier America: The Changing Geography of Supply of Russian America, 1784–1867.* New York: Oxford University Press, 1976.

Griffiths, Sir Percival. *A Licence to Trade: The History of English Chartered Companies.* London: Ernest Benn, 1974.

Hagemeister, Leontii Andreianovich. *The Russian American Company: Correspondence of the Governors, Communications Sent, 1818.* Translated and with an introduction by Richard A. Pierce. Kingston, ON: Limestone Press, 1984.

Hanna, Willard Anderson. *Indonesian Banda: Colonialism and Its Aftermath in the Nutmeg Islands.* Philadelphia: Institute for the Study of Human Issues, 1978.

Hart, Simon. *The Prehistory of the New Netherland Company: Amsterdam Notarial Records of the First Dutch Voyages to the Hudson.* Amsterdam. City of Amsterdam Press, 1959.

Harvey, Robert. *Clive: The Life and Death of a British Emperor.* New York: Thomas Dunne Books, 2000.

Hearne, Samuel. *A Journey to the Northern Ocean: The Adventures of Samuel Hearne.* Surrey, BC: TouchWood, 2007.

Jacobs, Jaap. *New Netherland: A Dutch Colony in Seventeenth-Century America.* Leiden: Brill, 2005.

Jourdain, John. *The Journal of John Jourdain, 1608–1617: Describing His Experiences in Arabia, and the Malay Archipelago.* Edited by William Foster. London: Hakluyt Society, 1905.

Keay, John. *The Honourable Company: A History of the English East India Company.* London: HarperCollins, 1991.

Khlebnikov, K.T. *Baranov, Chief Manager of the Russian Colonies in America.* Edited by Richard A. Pierce. Translated by Colin Bearne. Kingston, ON: Limestone Press, 1973. First published in Russia in 1835.

Lankevich, George J., and Howard B. Furer. *A Brief History of New York City.* New York: Associated Faculty Press, 1984.

Lawford, James P. *Clive: Proconsul of India; A Biography.* London: George Allen & Unwin, 1976.

Lawson, Philip. *The East India Company: A History*. London and New York: Longman Group, 1993.

MacKay, Douglas. *The Honourable Company: A History of the Hudson's Bay Company*. Freeport: Books for Libraries Press, 1970. Reprint of the 1936 original.

Malcolm, John. *The Life of Robert, Lord Clive: Collected from the Family Papers Communicated by the Earl of Powis*. Boston: Elibron Classics, 2002. Reprint of the 1836 original.

Marlowe, John. *Cecil Rhodes: The Anatomy of Empire*. London: Paul Elek, 1972.

McLean, John. *Notes of a Twenty-Five Years' Service in the Hudson's Bay Territory*. London: Richard Bently, 1849.

Meilink-Roelofsz, M.A.P. *Asian Trade and European Influence in the Indonesian Archipelago Between 1500 and About 1630*. The Hague: Nijhoff, 1969 (reprint).

Meredith, Martin. *Diamonds, Gold and War*. New York: Public Affairs, 2007.

Miller, J. Innes. *The Spice Trade of the Roman Empire, 29 BC to AD 641*. Oxford: Clarendon Press, 1969.

Milton, Giles. *Nathaniel's Nutmeg: How One Man's Courage Changed the Course of History*. London: Hodder & Stoughton, 1999.

Morrison, Dorothy Nafus. *The Eagle and the Fort: The Story of John McLoughlin*. Portland: Press of the Oregon Historical Society, Western Imprints, 1984.

Newman, Peter C. *Caesars of the Wilderness*. Toronto: Viking, 1987.

Nicholls, John. *Recollections and Reflections*. London: Longman, Hurst, Rees, Orme and Brown, 1822. Microfilm. New Haven, Conn: Research Publications, 1980.

Orme, Robert. *A History of the Military Transactions of the British Nation in Indostan, from the year MDCCXLV. To which is prefixed A dissertation on the establishments made by Mahomedan conquerors in Indostan. The second edition, corrected, with alterations, additions, and an index. By the author*. London: F. Wingrave, 1803; Madras: Pharoh & Co., 1861.

Parker, John. *The World for a Marketplace: Episodes in the History of European Expansion*. Minneapolis: Associates of the James Ford Bell Library, 1978.

Parsons, Neil. *A New History of Southern Africa.* London: Macmillan, 1993.

Pierce, Richard A. *Russian America: A Biographical Dictionary.* Kingston, ON: Limestone Press, 1990.

Pomeranz, Kenneth. *The World that Trade Created: Society, Culture, and the World Economy, 1400–the Present.* New York: M.E. Sharpe, 1999.

Raesly, Ellis Lawrence. *Portrait of New Netherland.* Port Washington: Ira J. Friedman Inc., 1965 (originally published by Columbia University Press).

Raffan, James. *Emperor of the North: Sir George Simpson and the Remarkable Story of the Hudson's Bay Company.* Toronto: HarperCollins, 2007.

Rhodes, Cecil. *Cecil Rhodes: His Political Life and Speeches.* Edited by Reverend F. Verschoyles. London: Chapman and Hall, 1900.

Rich, E.E. *Hudson's Bay Company, 1670 1870.* 3 vols. Toronto: McClelland & Stewart, 1960.

Rotberg, Robert I. *The Founder: Cecil Rhodes and the Pursuit of Power.* New York: Oxford University Press, 1988.

Sarkar, Jagadish Narayan. "Saltpeter Industry of India." *Indian Historical Quarterly,* 13, 1938.

Shorto, Russell. *The Island at the Center of the World: The Epic Story of Dutch Manhattan and the Forgotten Colony that Shaped America.* New York: Doubleday, 2004.

Simpson, George. *Fur Trade and Empire: George Simpson's Journal Entitled Remarks Connected with the Fur Trade in the Course of a Voyage from York Factory to Fort George and Back to York Factory, 1824–1825.* Edited by Frederick Merk. Cambridge, MA: Harvard University Press, 1968.

———. "Governor George Simpson's Character Book." Edited by Glyndwr Williams. *The Beaver,* Summer 1975.

———. *Narrative of a Journey Around the World, 1841 and 1842.* London: 1847.

Spry, Irene. "The Great Transformation: The Disappearance of the Commons in Western Canada." In *Man and Nature on the Prairies.* Edited by R.A. Allen. Regina: University of Regina, 1976.

Starr, Frederick. *Russia's American Colony.* Durham, NC: Duke University Press, 1987.

Stavorinus, Johan Splinter. *Voyages to the East Indies.* Translated S.H. Wilcocke. London: Dawsons, 1969. Facsimile reprint of the 1798 original.

Stejneger, Leonhard. *Georg Wilhelm Steller: The Pioneer of Alaskan Natural History.* Cambridge, Mass.: Harvard University Press, 1970. Reprint of the 1936 original.

Stent, Vere. *A Personal Record of Some Incidents in the Life of Cecil Rhodes.* Cape Town: M. Miller, 1924.

Stuyvesant, Peter. *Correspondence of Petrus Stuyvesant, 1647–1653.* Translated by Charles Gehring. Syracuse: Syracuse University Press, 2000.

———. *Correspondence of Petrus Stuyvesant, 1654–1658.* Translated by Charles Gehring. Syracuse: Syracuse University Press, 2003.

Thomas, Antony. *Rhodes: The Race for Africa.* London: BBC Books, 1996.

Tracy, James D. *The Rise of Merchant Empires: Long-Distance Trade in the Early Modern World, 1350–1750.* New York: Cambridge University Press, 1990.

Travers, Robert. *Ideology and Empire in Eighteenth Century India: The British in Bengal.* New York: Cambridge University Press, 2007.

van der Donck, Adriaen. *A Description of New Netherland.* Edited by Charles Gehring and William A. Starna. Translated by Diederik Willem Goedhuys. Lincoln: University of Nebraska Press, 2008.

van Goor, Jurrien. *Prelude to Colonialism: The Dutch in Asia.* Hilversum: Uitgeverij Verloren, 2004.

Verschoyles, Reverend F. *Cecil Rhodes: His Political Life and Speeches.* London: Chapman and Hall, 1900.

Vlekke, Bernard Hubertus Maria. *Nusantara: A History of Indonesia.* Chicago: Quadrangle Books, 1960.

———. *The Story of the Dutch East Indies.* Cambridge, MA: Harvard University Press, 1945.

Timeline for the Age of Heroic Commerce

1587 Jan Pieterszoon Coen is born.

1588 Spanish Armada fails to conquer England.

1600 The English East India Company is founded.

1602 The Dutch East India Company is founded;
       the Amsterdam stock exchange is established to deal
       in the company's stock and bonds.

1609 Henry Hudson sails up the Hudson River for the
       Dutch East India Company.

1612 Pieter Stuyvesant is born.

1618 Coen is promoted to head of the Dutch East India
       Company's eastern operations.

1621 The Dutch West India Company is founded to
       trade with North America and to plunder Spanish
       shipping in the Caribbean.

1623   Dutch East India Company employees kill English East India Company employees during the massacre at Ambon.

1629   Coen dies in Batavia.

1647   Stuyvesant arrives in New Amsterdam as the new governor of the Dutch West India Company.

1652   States General orders the Dutch West India Company to establish a responsible municipal government.

1657   Oliver Cromwell gives a new charter to the English East India Company, whose activities are focused on India.

1664   Stuyvesant surrenders New Amsterdam to English forces without a shot being fired.

       La Compagnie des Indes Orientales is founded in France to operate in India.

1670   The Company of Adventurers of England Trading into Hudson's Bay is founded in London to exploit the fur trade in northern North America.

1672   Stuyvesant dies in New York.

1705   The Mughal emperor Aurangzeb dies and central authority begins to decline in India.

1725   Robert Clive is born.

1741   Vitus Bering captains a voyage of discovery from Kamchatka to Alaska, beginning Russian exploration and trade in the region

1747   Aleksandr Baranov is born.

1748   The siege of Arcot establishes Clive as a formidable military leader in the struggle between the English and French companies in India.

1757   At the Battle of Plassey, Clive leads troops of the English East India Company to victory over the French in India; English company rule in India begins.

1763   The Seven Years' War between France and England ends.

1764   The original Dutch West India Company collapses under its debt load.

1768–71   Lieutenant James Cook leads his first voyage of discovery in the Pacific.

1774   Robert Clive dies by suicide.

1775–83   The War of American Independence is fought.

1776   Adam Smith publishes *The Wealth of Nations*.

1782–84   Fourth Anglo-Dutch War

1784   Pitt's India Bill introduces controls on the English East India Company's powers.

1790   Baranov arrives in Alaska.

1792   George Simpson is born.

1799   Czar Paul I founds the Russian American Company monopoly and places Baranov in charge of its operations.

The Dutch East India Company is officially dissolved after bankruptcy.

1807   Slave trading is outlawed within British territories.

1815   Napoleon is defeated at the Battle of Waterloo.

1818   Baranov is deposed from his position as head
of the Russian American Company.

1819   Baranov dies at sea.

1820   Simpson arrives in North America as acting
governor-in-chief of the Hudson's Bay Company.

1826   Simpson becomes governor of both the
northern and southern departments of the
Hudson's Bay Compay, the virtual dictator
of northern North America.

1831–36   The *Beagle* departs England and explores
South America and the Galapagos with
Charles Darwin as naturalist.

1846   The Oregon Boundary Dispute is resolved as
the 49th parallel becomes the border between
Canada and the United States.

Simpson is knighted by Queen Victoria.

1852–53   Britain recognizes the independence of the
Boer republics in South Africa (Orange Free
State and the Transvaal).

1853   Cecil Rhodes is born.

1858   British troops crush an Indian uprising.

1860   Simpson dies near Montreal.

1867   The United States purchases Russian America.

       Alfred Nobel invents dynamite, revolutionizing mining and construction. Canada becomes an independent nation.

1870   Cecil Rhodes arrives in Cape Colony.

       Canada assumes the territories of the Hudson's Bay Company, ending their monopoly.

1874   The East India Stock Redemption Act ends the existence of the English East India Company.

1876   Queen Victoria assumes the title Empress of India.

1880   Rhodes forms the De Beers Company and is elected to the Cape Parliament.

1889   Rhodes secures a royal charter from the British government for the British South Africa Company to colonize and exploit south-central Africa.

1894   Britain acknowledges the authority of the British South Africa Company over the territory of Rhodesia.

1901   The first series of Nobel Prizes is awarded.

1902   Cecil Rhodes dies, leaving a legacy to establish the Rhodes Scholarships.

1918   The First World War ends.

1923   The British government revokes the British South Africa Company's charter and grants self-governing colony status to Southern Rhodesia (Zimbabwe) and protectorate status to Northern Rhodesia (Zambia).

Acknowledgements

TURNING A MANUSCRIPT INTO A BEAUTIFUL BOOK IS not a simple or easy endeavour. It involves the talents and creative efforts of a great number of people. I would like to thank Scott McIntyre and Scott Steedman for their enthusiasm for this project and for reminding me to keep my mind open to the full spectrum of the merchant kings' personalities; these "kings" were each far too complex to be dismissed as mere robber barons.

I was particularly fortunate to again have the insightful and diplomatic John Eerkes-Medrano as my editor. Michael Mundhenk provided a thorough and informed copy edit that saved me from several inconsistencies and smoothed the rough edges of my prose, while Ruth Wilson's eagle eye caught remaining inconsistencies. Designer Naomi MacDougall designed the beautiful cover and matched it so beautifully to the interior. The production, editorial and publicity team at Douglas & McIntyre continue to be a pleasure to work with. Thanks also to Frances and Bill Hanna. Thanks to the Alberta Foundation for the Arts for the support and to the staff at the Canmore Public Library for fulfilling my requests for unusual books and for returning mountains of them even when I had lost the slips. Last but never least, I would like to acknowledge the incredible support of my wife, Nicky Brink, for putting up with my absent-minded distraction and odd, out-of-context dinner-table conversation about long-dead people, and for her perceptive reading of my first draft.

Index